Uncommon Faithfulness

Uncommon Faithfulness

The Black Catholic Experience

M. Shawn Copeland, editor
with LaReine-Marie Mosely, S.N.D.,
and Albert J. Raboteau

ORBIS BOOKS

Maryknoll, New York 10545

Founded in 1970, Orbis Books endeavors to publish works that enlighten the mind, nourish the spirit, and challenge the conscience. The publishing arm of the Maryknoll Fathers and Brothers, Orbis seeks to explore the global dimensions of the Christian faith and mission, to invite dialogue with diverse cultures and religious traditions, and to serve the cause of reconciliation and peace. The books published reflect the views of their authors and do not represent the official position of the Maryknoll Society. To learn more about Maryknoll and Orbis Books, please visit our website at www.maryknollsociety.org.

Library of Congress Cataloging-in-Publication Data

Uncommon faithfulness : the Black Catholic experience / M. Shawn Copeland, editor, with LaReine-Marie Mosely and Albert J. Raboteau.
    p. cm.
    Includes index.
    ISBN 978-1-57075-819-5 (pbk.)
    1. African American Catholics. I. Copeland, M. Shawn (Mary Shawn) II. Mosely, LaReine-Marie. III. Raboteau, Albert J.
    BX1407.N4U53 2009
    282'.7308996073—dc22

                                                          2008046300

With heartfelt gratitude
for the uncommon faithfulness of those
religious orders of women and men
whose historic mission has been
the care of black souls

The Oblate Sisters of Providence
The Sisters of the Holy Family
The Sisters of the Blessed Sacrament
The Franciscan Handmaids of Mary

St. Joseph Society of the Sacred Heart
    (Josephites)
The Society of the Divine Word
Congregation of the Holy Spirit (Holy Ghost
    Fathers, Spiritans)
The Society of St. Edmund

Contents

Foreword

TIMOTHY MATOVINA

I am honored to welcome readers to this volume whose contributors encompass leading and rising scholars of black Catholics in the United States. Their essays enhance previous studies—a number of them by writers in this current work—that made significant strides toward mapping out the long sojourn of African American Catholics in church and society. It is frustrating to note that the process of incorporating their research and insights into course offerings and textbooks of U.S. Catholic history and theology, as well as pastoral planning within U.S. Catholicism, has been painstakingly slow. Nonetheless, thanks to the collective efforts of black Catholic scholars such as these, there is no excuse for us, their colleagues in academia and ecclesial life, to remain ignorant of the contours of the black Catholic experience.

As their scholarship shows, oppression and struggle form the broad context for that experience. Racism and violence are not evident merely in particular events and persons. Rather, for half a millennium they have systemically impinged on day-to-day life throughout the hemisphere. The establishment and development of Catholic communities in the "New World" was a highly conflictive and coercive imperial enterprise involving African, native, European, and mixed-race peoples. It is a story of violence, cultural confrontations, accommodations, faith, endurance, change, and the emergence of new traditions. This historical process often driven by greed, racial and cultural oppression, and exploitation gave birth to new societies that to this day live with the legacy. The immensity of this painful experience should never be underestimated or forgotten, nor should the uncommon faithfulness of those who have endured it with unyielding struggle and gospel hope for a more humane world.

African American Catholics are an integral part of this hemispheric saga. Given the treatment they have received at the hands of their coreligionists, I marvel that three million of them continue to strive to make a home for themselves within Catholicism. One incident that strikes me as among the most tragic is the 1863 draft riots in New York. When

President Abraham Lincoln signed into law a military draft to support the northern Civil War cause, New Yorkers, many of them immigrant Irish Catholics who vied with African Americans for jobs, assaulted black residents in one of the bloodiest riots in the history of the city. M. Shawn Copeland outlines many other such atrocities in her fine introduction to this volume. She touches on every period of U.S. history from the colonial era to the present. The essays that follow relate the struggles and steadfastness of particular black Catholics in greater detail.

Mirroring their subjects, authors in this volume have themselves been uncommonly faithful in their labors to establish black Catholic studies and refashion the general historical narratives, theological agenda, and pastoral priorities of U.S. Catholicism. Through their leadership in initiatives like the Institute for Black Catholic Studies (IBCS) at Xavier University in New Orleans and the Black Catholic Theological Symposium (BCTS), contributors M. Shawn Copeland, Cyprian Davis, Diana L. Hayes, and Jamie T. Phelps are at the core of a small band of collaborators who have shouldered the burden of recovering the black Catholic heritage and articulating theological insights and wisdom from black Catholic faith. Despite scarce resources and often tepid support from their peers, for over three decades they have taught, cajoled, and demanded the need for greater attention to African American Catholics in the church, in the academy, and among African Americans who do not share their Catholic faith. They have also sought to nurture new collaborators for their enterprise, several of whom join them in this present work. All of us who study, teach, and seek to enhance the vitality of American Catholicism are in their debt.

This volume examines the latest scholarship on African American Catholics in theology, history, and pastoral ministry. It conjoins some of the best work currently being done in the field. Collectively, these essays also explore critical issues for the ongoing development of black Catholic studies and its contribution to wider intellectual and ecclesial conversations: the relationship between race and religion, the wider lens of Catholics in the African diaspora, the interrelations between African American Catholics and the growing number of African immigrant Catholics in the United States, the evangelical legacy and witness of black Catholic lives and sacred music, and black Catholic theological investigations on topics such as God-talk, communion ecclesiology, ethics, the blues, and hope. If the heart of Christianity is remaining faithful, both in season and out of season, no one has more to teach their fellow believers than black Catholics, who have remained unwavering in their faith against all odds. Welcome, dear reader, to this book and its journey among the uncommonly faithful.

Acknowledgments

On behalf of the contributors, I express gratitude to Dr. Timothy Matovina and Dr. LaReine-Marie Mosely, S.N.D., for their enthusiasm and commitment in staging the conference that inspired this work. We are grateful as well for the practical generosity of the University of Notre Dame where the conference was held.

I am grateful to the contributors for their cooperation, especially to Dr. Albert J. Raboteau and Dr. LaReine-Marie Mosley, S.N.D., for editorial suggestions.

Special words of thanks are due to Susan Perry of Orbis Books, whose careful eye, wise counsel, and patience have been indispensable.

Introduction

M. SHAWN COPELAND

Uncommon faithfulness: this phrase aptly and poignantly describes the black Catholic experience in the United States. Historians of American religion have unmasked the blemished record of the Catholic Church on slavery. While the church did not split over slavery, it did accommodate slavocracy's prevailing culture and custom. Some clergy, vowed women religious, and laity practiced slaveholding. Few Catholics supported abolition; most simply abstained from any opinion or action. "In the seven provincial councils of Baltimore (1829–49)," writes historian Cyprian Davis, "neither slaves nor African Americans in general were mentioned."[1]

Following the Union victory in the Civil War, the Vatican urged the U.S. bishops to develop a national plan for the evangelization of the newly freed people. No such program or policy emerged from their conversations, but the bishops did agree that those who had blacks in their dioceses would decide for themselves the best course of action. The failure of any coordinated national action remains, in the words of Davis, "one of the tragedies of American church history. . . . Whether many blacks perished spiritually is one question that cannot be answered; that many black Catholics would be turned away from the 'means of salvation' is a fact."[2]

Yet the Spirit would not be quenched! For nearly 450 years on the North American continent, Catholics of African descent nurtured and maintained their faith and took courage and inspiration from it to sustain resistance against the oppression of slavery and create life-giving spaces and opportunities. This was nearly 450 years of uncommon faithfulness. Consider that the oldest Roman Catholic ecclesiastical documents for the United States, dating from the sixteenth century, record the births, baptisms, marriages, and deaths of black Catholics—slave and free.[3] Consider that enslaved Africans in South Carolina, BaKongo in culture and Catholic in faith, led the Stono rebellion, one of the fiercest uprisings against enslavement in the United States.[4] Consider that in the face of racial intransigence Elizabeth Lange and Henriette Delille would not be

1

dissuaded from supporting the call to vowed religious life on the part of black Catholic women. Consider that despite racial arrogance Augustus Tolton would not be deterred from following the call to priesthood, literally crossing the Atlantic for seminary studies and ordination. Consider that despite racial gradualism black Catholic laymen and laywomen initiated the Black Catholic Congresses and the Federated Colored Catholics to evangelize, serve, educate, and minister to the black community. At every turn, black Catholics met rejection and derision, benign neglect, and indifference with uncommon faithfulness.

During the black cultural movement of the 1960s, black Catholics refused to set racial-cultural identity over against religious heritage and created unique spaces—the National Black Catholic Clergy Caucus, the National Black Sisters' Conference, the National Black Lay Catholic Caucus, and the National Office for Black Catholics—for intellectual, religious, cultural, and social growth. When black Protestant theology challenged the racism of white U.S. Christianity, black Catholics took up exploration of the Catholic historical, theological, intellectual, spiritual, and philosophical heritage to critique and enrich it with the gift of blackness. With uncommon faithfulness, black Catholics refused calls for uncritical conformity.

The essays gathered here were written by black Catholic theologians, scholars, and ecclesial leaders who participated in a conference entitled Uncommon Faithfulness: The Witness of African American Catholics, which was conceived and organized by Timothy Matovina, director of the Cushwa Center for the Study of American Catholicism at the University of Notre Dame, in collaboration with LaReine-Marie Mosely, S.N.D., of Loyola University Chicago. With generous funding from the University of Notre Dame, Matovina and Mosely brought together more than three hundred participants of all races and cultures—educators, catechists, pastors, ecclesial lay ministers, and diocesan administrators—for three days of communal worship and extraordinary conversation.

The essays that constitute Uncommon Faithfulness reveal, engage, and celebrate the steadfast fidelity of African American Catholic women and men, alerting us, once again, to the presence of more than three million Catholics who, too frequently, continue to find themselves and their faith praxis marginalized, overlooked, and rendered invisible to both the larger Catholic and African American communities. These theologians, scholars, and ecclesial leaders seek to make African American fidelity, creativity, sorrow, struggle, and joy an intimate part of the ongoing record of American Catholic life.

Uncommon Faithfulness also extends a collaboration among black Catholics begun in four earlier collections: Black and Catholic—The Challenge *and Gift of Black Folk: Contributions of African American Experience and Thought to Catholic Theology*,[5] *Taking Down Our Harps: Black Catholics in the United States*,[6] an issue of the journal *Theological Studies* on the Catholic reception of black theology,[7] and *"Stamped with the Image of God": African Americans as God's Image in Black*.[8] The first three volumes broke ground on theological fundamentals (religious experience, method, and doctrinal interpretation), placed race and racism at the center of Catholic moral reflection, and expanded the ongoing work of womanist and liturgical theologies. The fourth volume exemplifies black Catholic ressourcement, presenting original documents—some more than five hundred years old.

Uncommon Faithfulness presses similar questions and introduces new voices and themes. The first part of the book mines the rich *historical experience* of black Catholics. Albert J. Raboteau's essay argues that slavery is as crucial to understanding American religious history as the prevailing interpretative motifs of Puritanism and pluralism. Diane Batts Morrow and Cyprian Davis provide examples of nineteenth-century black Catholic female agency in treatments of the Oblate Sisters of Providence, the first Catholic religious congregation of black women in the United States, and of Henriette Delille, foundress of the Sisters of the Holy Family. Cecilia A. Moore and Katrina M. Sanders engage twentieth-century black Catholic history, bringing out new findings and insights into the Catholic reaction to desegregation as well as involvement in the civil rights movement.

Works by M. Shawn Copeland, LaReine-Marie Mosely, Jamie T. Phelps, Diana L. Hayes, and Bryan N. Massingale form the second part, on *theology* and *ethics*. Copeland offers a theological meditation on the blues, drawing an analogy between the black Catholic theologian and the blues musician. Mosely examines the work of Daniel Rudd, publisher and editor of the nineteenth-century newspaper the *American Catholic Tribune*, as an instance of educating and transmitting the Catholic tradition. Phelps identifies and unpacks the social, cultural, and theological challenges both to a theology of *communio* and to the realization of authentic ecclesial communion in the United States. Drawing on biblical and contemporary models of women who contributed to building up the community of faith, Hayes advances a womanist theological reading of black Catholic women's experience. Bryan N. Massingale reflects on the cruel protracted pandemic of HIV/AIDS through the spirituals' confidence in resurrection faith.

The third part contains essays on the changing *pastoral situation* of Catholics of African descent in the United States by Archbishop Wilton D. Gregory, Kevin P. Johnson, Paulinus I. Odozor, and Clarence

Williams. Gregory discusses the pastoral situation of African American Catholics since the publication in 1984 of the black Catholic bishops' pastoral letter *What We Have Seen and Heard*. Taking the pioneering compositions of the late Rev. Dr. Clarence R. Rivers as a point of departure, Johnson examines the inclusion of African American sacred music in Catholic worship. A native of Nigeria, Odozor points out some of the difficulties and challenges immigrants too often face in attempting to practice their faith. Williams reports on the work done by African American Catholic clergy both to correct cultural stereotypes and to welcome black immigrants from the Continent, the Caribbean, Latin America, and Europe.

As theological and practical reflection on black Catholic experience, *Uncommon Faithfulness* adverts to issues that influence the present and future of black Catholic life—the aging of Catholic clergy, the paucity of vocations to priesthood and religious life, financial shortfalls in dioceses, the closure of offices of black Catholic ministry, parish mergers, and the closing of Catholic schools in urban areas. The national situation—high rates of black unemployment or disemployment, mortgage foreclosures, poverty, and spiraling violence—spawns intractable disorder. Nearly all the essays not only call for increased ministerial attention and action from the official church, but also urge black Catholics to act—to take up, once again, the tasks of evangelization, religious formation and education, prayer, and study.

In order to shape and sustain an authentic black and Catholic future, black Catholics must take action. For nearly thirty years the Institute for Black Catholic Studies (IBCS) at Xavier University of Louisiana, New Orleans, has provided a rigorous educational setting for theological and religious formation, cultural and practical preparation, and appropriately inculturated transmission of faith. The Institute provides critical and necessary space for prayer and worship, study, and research. Here black Catholic clergy and laity and vowed religious women and men work alongside European American, African, Asian, and Latino clergy and vowed religious who seek to minister effectively among and with black Catholics. Embodying the legacy of uncommon faithfulness, the Institute places black religious experience, history, and culture in humble and serious dialogue with the Roman Catholic mediation of the Christian tradition.

Increasingly, the Institute reflects the cultural diversity and engagement of African, Caribbean, and African American faculty and students. Moreover, the presence in the United States of black Catholic immigrants, including clergy and vowed religious, from the African continent, the Caribbean, and Latin America not only throws light on the global vitality of black Catholicism, but highlights both awkwardness and grace in concretely living out cultural diversity among peoples of African descent. To borrow a phrase of Jamie T. Phelps, "home grown" African Americans must examine their own inner-group dynamics and reactions in relation to this new experience of "black" diversity.

The Institute also has the knowledge, means, and skill to assist immigrants in negotiating race. Thinking about and acting on race in the United States is shaped both by a process of social formation and by ideology. Social formation coaches "home growns" and newcomers in the codes and restrictions concerning relations among and between the races. Racial ideology, which spills into racism, crudely detaches race from culture. Catholic immigrants—whether Yoruba or Haitian or Cuban or Mexican or Brazilian—require effective culturally and spiritually appropriate ministry from the church. Understandably, the first focus is on language, for worship and prayer in one's native tongue is an absolute necessity. But if language is taken as the sole arbiter of culture in a monolingual United States, then multi-linguality signals difference, signals an "other" culture.

Ministry among African American Catholics presents a different case in relation to language and culture. In brief, the line of reasoning runs something like this: The new immigrants have a language other than and different from English; therefore, they have culture. African Americans have no other than or different language from English; therefore, at best, they have no culture, they have race. This crude detachment and degradation of culture violates the rich notion of culture as a set of meanings and values that informs a way of life. Thinking of culture in this latter way means that there are as many cultures as there are ways of formulating and expressing meanings and values. Of course, considering culture in this manner calls for nuance and complexification, and it deemphasizes numbers, thereby, shifting the ministerial economy. When ecclesial and national situations drive institutional thinking in the church, whether unintentionally or intentionally, market values surface and numbers count. In particular, African, African American, and Latino/a Catholics must be wary of techniques and decisions that, even unintentionally, manipulate, divide, and turn racial-ethnic cultural groups against each other.

By a lived witness of uncommon faithfulness, black Catholics have much to offer the millions of European American Catholics in the United States and beyond who are determined to keep the faith but also committed to change the church. Indeed, black Catholics have kept the faith, and in doing so they have changed the church. They have done this by being black Catholics: by prayer and sacrifice, discipline and fasting; by healing and creating in their own circumstances, by making and wading in rivers of music; by striving for excellence in all that they do for the greater honor and glory of God; by teaching and sharing the strengths and weaknesses, lessons and achievements of nearly 450 years of uncommon faithfulness.

NOTES

[1] Cyprian Davis, *The History of Black Catholics in the United States* (New York: Crossroad, 1990), 116–17.

[2] Ibid., 116–20.

[3] Ibid., 30–33.

[4] John K. Thornton, "African Dimensions of the Stono Rebellion," *American Historical Review* 96, no. 4 (October 1991): 1101–13.

[5] Jamie T. Phelps, ed., *Black and Catholic—The Challenge and Gift of Black Folk: Contributions of African American Experience and Thought to Catholic Theology* (Milwaukee, WI: Marquette University Press, 1998).

[6] Diana L. Hayes and Cyprian Davis, O.S.B., eds., *Taking Down Our Harps: Black Catholics in the United States* (Maryknoll, NY: Orbis Books, 1998).

[7] *Theological Studies* 61, no. 4 (December 2000).

[8] Cyprian Davis, O.S.B., and Jamie T. Phelps, O.P., eds., *"Stamped with the Image of God": African Americans as God's Image in Black* (Maryknoll, NY: Orbis Books, 2003).

PART I

HISTORY

Chapter I

Relating Race and Religion

Four Historical Models

ALBERT J. RABOTEAU

In 1441, Portuguese knights of the military Order of Christ returned home from an exploration and raiding expedition off the coast of Africa. Near Arguim in present-day Mauretania they had taken captive over two hundred men, women, and children. Several years later the royal chronicler Gomes Eannes de Zurara composed a description of the arrival and distribution of this first shipment of slaves taken from sub-Saharan Africa to Europe by way of the Atlantic Ocean:

> On the next day, which was the 8th of the month of August, very early in the morning, by reason of the heat, the seamen began to make ready their boats, and to take out those captives and carry them on shore, as they were commanded. And these, placed all together in that field, were a marvelous sight; for amongst them were some white enough, fair to look upon, and well proportioned; others were less white like mulattoes; others again were as black as Ethiops, and so ugly, both in features and in body, as almost to appear (to those who saw them) the images of a lower hemisphere.

Zurara reported that many onlookers were reduced to tears by the cries and prayers of the African captives as they were parceled out to different people, separating in the process husbands from wives, parents from children, kin from kin, friend from friend. But despite the human pathos "their condition was now much better, because before they lived only in bestial sloth without housing or knowledge of wine," now they had the blessings of Christianity and civilization. Zurara's religious justification for enslavement was not new, nor was his singling out of black Africans as pejoratively different, but his restatement of

9

these old themes would prove tragically prescient as the Atlantic slave trade developed into a system of racial slavery based on the inferiority of black Africans designated by nature and Providence for enslavement of body as a means to the salvation of soul.[1]

The interlocking relationships among religion, race, and slavery are arguably as important a narrative theme of American religious history as Puritanism or pluralism, the two traditionally dominant motifs.[2] In my reading, reflection, and teaching over the years I have been interested in the relationship between race and religion within the context of African American communal identity. I have studied the complex ways in which African Americans have interpreted race and religion to narrate their past, understand their present, and predict their future in a society dominated by a Christianity that justified or accommodated their enslavement and oppression. In effect, African American religious narratives have functioned as rhetorical challenges to the conscience of whites, as well as rhetorical strategies for the survival and flourishing of black communities.

It seems to me that four models of relating religion and race can be extrapolated from African American religious narratives. In proposing these four models I do not claim that they are inclusive or mutually exclusive. None of the four wholly contains the unruly detail of historical events that continually escape the tidy margins of any generalized model. I identify the models as (1) redeeming the religion of the master; (2) erasing the color line; (3) identifying religious/racial origins; and (4) searching for community. I have intentionally used action phrases to emphasize the dynamic nature of these models (and because I couldn't come up with single-word captions) for all four.

REDEEMING THE RELIGION OF THE MASTER

In a profound comment Howard Thurman, pastor, university chaplain, ecumenist, poet, and mystic, described the distinctive character of the Christianity adopted and adapted by African Americans: "By some amazing but vastly creative spiritual insight the slaves undertook the redemption of a religion that the master had profaned in his midst."[3] The profanation, of course, consisted in the accommodation of Christianity to slavery—what Frederick Douglass in the appendix to *The Narrative of His Life* (1845) called the hypocritical false religion of American slave-holding Christianity.

American slaves early on observed an egalitarian impulse in Christianity, an impulse the masters labored mightily to hold at bay. Colonial legislation that baptism did not require manumission attempted to restrict this impulse to the spiritual realm. Francis Le Jau's requirement that slaves vow they were not seeking baptism as a route to freedom was designed to disabuse slave catechumens as well as wary masters of the notion. The conscious and unconscious uneasiness of the English over this issue was revealed in the comments by Swedish traveler Peter Kalm relating his observations of master-slave relations between 1748 and 1750:

> It is . . . greatly to be pitied, that the masters of these Negroes in most of the English colonies take little care of their spiritual welfare, and let them live on in their Pagan darkness. There are even some, who would be very ill pleased at, and would by all means hinder their negroes from being instructed in the doctrines of Christianity; to this they are partly led by the conceit of its being shameful, to have a spiritual brother or sister among so despicable a people; partly by thinking that they should not be able to keep their negroes so meanly afterwards; and partly through fear of the negroes growing too proud, on seeing themselves upon a level with their masters in religious matters.[4]

This leveling threatened the distinction between African and English upon which the social order depended. It is clear that Anglo-Americans feared the precise ethos that the slaves quickly recognized and valued in Christianity: the incorporation of Africans into the church community changed the relationship of master and slave into one of brother and sister in Christ, a relationship that corroded the prevalent sense of difference, color, language, origin, religion, which undergirded the slave system. By the 1770s American slaves were publicly proclaiming their belief that slavery violated the fundamental law of Christian community:

> There is a great number of us sencear . . . members of the Church of Christ. . . . Bear ye onenothers Bordens How can the master be said to Beare my Borden when he Beares me down With the Have chanes of slavery and opperson against my will . . . how can the slave perform the duties of a husband to a wife or parent to his child[?][5]

Slave owners were well aware that slaves interpreted Christianity as sanctioning their desire for freedom in this life as well as in the next, forcing missionaries to propagate evangelization as a system of slave control.

By the end of the eighteenth century, two Christianities had emerged in the United States, one white, and one black. Slaves risked severe punishment to practice what they saw as true Christianity, and many suffered for the exercise of a religious freedom that was not guaranteed for them. In 1792, Andrew Bryan and his brother Sampson were arrested and hauled before the city magistrates of Savannah for holding worship services. Together with about fifty of their followers, they were imprisoned twice and were severely whipped. Andrew reportedly told his persecutors "that he rejoiced not only to be whipped, but would freely suffer death for the cause of Jesus Christ." The narratives of former slaves from the antebellum period are studded with references to slave Christians suffering for their faith. Henry Bibb and Eli Johnson, for example, both ignored their master's threats of five hundred lashes for conducting prayer meetings. Johnson claimed he stood up to his master and declared, "In the name of god why is it that, I can't after working hard all the week, have a meeting on Saturday evening? I'll suffer the flesh to be dragged off my bones . . . for the sake of my blessed Redeemer."[6]

In the North, black Christians had more leeway to express their religious freedom. But there too discrimination, the failure to condemn slavery, and the refusal of white clergy to allow black initiative and leadership led to the establishment of institutional autonomy, first among the African Methodists, led by Richard Allen in 1816, congregational separatism among black Baptists and within constraints of denominational polity, other black congregations as well.

Biblical stories and images fed and sustained the separate identity of African American Christians as specially chosen children of God. The biblical accounts of the mighty deeds of a God who miraculously intervenes in human history to cast down the mighty and to lift up the lowly, a God who saves the oppressed and punishes the oppressor, provided the leitmotif of meaning for their experience. They made the biblical stories their story. One story in particular fired their imagination and affirmed their identity. The story of Exodus, as Eddie Glaude has so thoroughly demonstrated in his book of that title, inculcated in African American Christians, slave and free, a sense of being a specially chosen people whose election and destiny were of historic importance in the providence of God. Addressing an audience of free and slave blacks in Philadelphia, some of whom had been born in Africa, Absalom Jones applied Exodus to the abolition of the slave trade to the United States on January 1 of 1808:

The history of the world shows us that the deliverance of the children of Israel from their bondage is not the only instance in which it has pleased God to appear in behalf of oppressed and distressed nations, as the deliverer of the innocent, and of those who call upon his name. . . . He has seen the affliction of our countrymen, with an eye of pity. . . . He has heard the prayers that have ascended from the hearts of his people; and he has, as in the case of his ancient and chosen people the Jews, come down to deliver our suffering countrymen from the hands of their oppressors.[7]

For black Americans the Exodus story took on the force of an archetypal myth, one that inverted the dominant myth of America as the Promised Land. White Christians might claim that America was a new Israel, but blacks knew that it was Egypt, since they, like the children of Israel of old, still toiled in bondage. And unless white America repented and released God's dark Israel from bondage, they too would experience the plagues of Egypt.

Black Christians believed that they belonged to a long line of prophets, apostles, saints, and martyrs, a tradition of spiritual aristocracy made up of those who suffer for the truth of God's elect. James Baldwin spoke eloquently of the matchless authority that came from this suffering in several passages of his first novel, *Go Tell It on the Mountain* (1953) and in his book of essays, *The Fire Next Time* (1963). The articulation of this suffering in the expressive culture of African American Christianity, especially the spirituals, achieved worldwide recognition for the authenticity that comes, that can *only* come from suffering. Thus the relationship between race and religion in this model is one that might be called transposition. The racial degradation of African Americans is transposed or inverted into a racial election, a moral superiority of authentic—and even—heroic Christianity.

A prophetic stance condemning the failure of white American Christianity constituted the hortatory strategy of this rhetoric, expressed powerfully, for example, in David Walker's *Appeal to the Colored Citizens of the World* (1829), a black jeremiad warning the nation to abolish the sin of slavery lest it suffer the fate of ancient Egypt. The changes on this theme were rung at the end of the nineteenth century by black theologians James Theodore Holly in "The Divine Plan of Human Salvation, in Its Ethnological Development," published in the *AME Church Review* in 1884 and Theophilus Gould Steward in *The End of the World* (1888). Here a set of Christian characteristics or virtues was transposed to the darker peoples of the world, depicted as Christlike, peaceful, and blessedly free of materialism, racism, and class-conscious prejudices. Steward claimed that European-American Christianity had turned Christianity into a clan religion, so corrupting its original message that it was incapable of preaching the gospel to the pagan nations. Fratricidal warfare among the so-called Christian nations would end the present age and a new and final age of a race-less and peaceful Christianity would begin in which the darker peoples of the world would hear and accept the pure gospel of Christ, undefiled by Anglo-Saxon prejudice. Holly, in a striking reversal of the legend of Noah's curse of Canaan, described the three dispensations of God's plan of salvation. Sons of Shem (Semites) preserved the word of God; Sons of Japheth (Europeans) preached the word of God; Sons of Ham (Africans) will finally put the word of God into practice.

While the tremendous hortatory power of this model would ensure its repetition through the twentieth century, it generated four main criticisms. First, the ideal of redeeming the religion of the master leads to political quietism and lethargy—too much trusting in the intervention of the biblical God. In answer to this charge, defenders point to the activism of black ministers and churches and argue that Christianity acts as a bulwark against black dehumanization. A second criticism of this model accuses it of fostering a debilitating attitude of racial messianism. Why should black folks be portrayed as, or expected to be, better than other people? Especially when attached to the idea of suffering, it degenerates into a kind of racial masochism (as Malcolm X would trenchantly assert in the 1960s). Third, the historical optimism of the model, particularly its Exodus motif, is naive. "De preachers would exhort us dat us was de chillen o' Israel in de wilderness an' de Lord done sent us to take dis land o' milk and honey. But how us gwine-a take land what's already been took," scoffed former slave Charles Davenport.[8] Or, as Henry Highland Garnet so powerfully stated at the 1840 Negro Convention in Buffalo, "Pharaoh is on both sides of the blood stained water." Fourth, that racial separatism in the institutional form of the black church remained captive to the racial categories of the dominant society. This last accusation was voiced most cogently by the proponents of my second model of relating religion to race.

ERASING THE COLOR LINE

If the first model, which I have called transposition, was represented by the African American evangelical Protestant tradition, the second was most sharply articulated by African American Catholics. For black Catholics, Catholicism offered the centuries-old rituals of the mass, the sacraments, and devotional piety focused on the Virgin and the saints. The experience of Pierre Landry, a slave in Louisiana, illustrates the power of the sacramental tradition to arrest and attract the religious imagination:

> My early religious training was in the Roman Catholic Church at Donaldsonsville. I was prepared for first communion in a large class of both white and colored youths. The sacrament was administered on an Easter Sunday morning, and I shall never forget the impressiveness of the services that day. The august presence of the bishop who confirmed the class was to me typical of extraordinary grandeur and power, and when it came to my turn to kiss the signet ring of His Grace, the jewel appeared to me as a blazing torch in which were reflected the burning candles of the resplendent altar.[9]

Though Landry himself would become a Methodist minister after Emancipation, his memories focused significantly upon the sacramental piety at the center of Catholicism. It was this age-old sacramental ritual opening a window upon a transcendent world impinging on and transforming this world that affected black Catholics' understanding of the relationship between religion and race.

The lack of a black clergy corresponding to the leadership of black Methodist and Baptist clergy, which emerged in the latter third of the eighteenth century, did not prevent black laity from asserting that the true religious home of black people was Roman Catholicism. (Until 1891, when Charles Randolph Uncles was ordained in Baltimore, only four priests of African ancestry served in the United States, three of them brothers of one family, Patrick, James, and Sherwood Healy, and one, born a slave, Augustus Tolton, all ordained abroad.) From 1889 to 1894 delegates from different sections of the country met together in five annual congresses of African American Catholics. They met to discuss common issues, to encourage education of black Catholic youth, and to protest discrimination within the church. The organizer and leading spirit of these congresses was Daniel A. Rudd, a descendant of Catholic slaves from Kentucky. Rudd, a journalist by profession, edited and published a black Catholic newspaper, the *American Catholic Tribune*. In its pages Rudd conducted a running battle with black Protestant editors such as the Episcopalian George Bragg and the Baptist William Simmons. He argued that salvation for African Americans, personally and racially, lay not in Protestant "race churches" but in the inclusiveness of universal Catholicism.

A revealing paradox emerged from the pages of the *American Catholic Tribune* and the proceedings of the congresses: Rudd and his colleagues argued that the "Catholic Church alone [could] break the color line."

Addressing Protestant blacks, who attended the congresses as honored guests, they contended that the church universal transcended the divisive particularities of nationality and race. Yet the delegates to the congresses protested vigorously against discrimination from white Catholics. Thus, on the one hand, they held up the image of the age-old church of Rome, which had "in her early history," as Robert Ruffin of Boston remarked to the third congress, "blacks . . . holding most exalted positions." He went on to list saints Monica, Felicita, Perpetua, Augustine, Basil, Cyprian, Moses, Benedict the Moor, and Cyril, "all of whom . . . were of pure Ethiopian blood."[10] On the other hand, the same congress challenged the exclusion of black children over twelve years of age from Catholic schools. The delegates appointed a committee to gather reports of discrimination, circulate questionnaires among American bishops on the matter, and report their findings to the pope in Rome.

The tension revealed in the congresses between the ideal of church universalism and the reality of racial discrimination broke into outright conflict a generation later in the case of the Federated Colored Catholics. This organization of black Catholic laymen and laywomen was founded in 1917 by Thomas Wyatt Turner, a descendant of Catholic slaves from southern Maryland who taught as a professor of biology first at Howard University and then at Hampton Institute. Turner, like Rudd before him, combined a deep commitment to Catholicism with a dedication to active protest for racial justice. The Federated Colored Catholics organized black Catholics nationally, developed black leadership locally, and protested discrimination within and without the church. Initially, Turner enjoyed the friendship and cooperation of two white Jesuits, Father William Markoe and Father John La Farge, pioneers in the apostolate of interracial justice. But eventually Turner broke with the two priests over the basic purpose and direction of the organization he had founded. He intended it primarily as an organization of black Catholics united to achieve equality within the church; the two priests wanted it to serve as a forum for interracial cooperation and rejected the black identity of the group as reverse racism. When Father Markoe engineered a change in the name of the journal of the Federated Colored Catholics from the *Chronicle* to the *Interracial Review*, a change symbolic of the shift in overall direction toward interacialism, the organization split in two. Turner's faction, diminished in numbers and influence, lasted until the mid 1950s. In this case the model of universalism seemed ill-suited to accommodate forms of racial independence and activism, a problem exacerbated institutionally by the paucity of black clergy, which made black Catholics seem like wards of a white institution.

The model of religion transcending race, as illustrated in the black Catholic experience, seemed to founder on a paradox. Dan Rudd had argued that blacks should convert to Catholicism because it breaks down the color line. The church knows no race. The universalism of the church was construed as evidence for the truth claims of Catholicism. When confronted by contradictory evidence—acts of discrimination by fellow Catholics and Catholic institutions—black Catholics looked beyond America to the teachings and example of the church universal. While some white Catholics might be prejudiced, the Catholic Church extended around the world, embracing dark-skinned peoples in Africa and Asia. While individual priests might be bigots, the sacraments worked *ex opere operato*, independent of the disposition of the priest. The mass and popular devotion linked black Catholics to the timeless, cosmopolitan church of Rome, which was one, holy, apostolic, and catholic. And yet, the tension remained. Black Catholics knew all too painfully that race did matter in the church in America.

For the majority of black Protestants, this tension was solved long ago by forming separate black churches and denominations. Black Catholics might have done the same had they been willing, like the Polish National Church, for example, to go into schism. And with the Imani Temple movement led by Father (later Bishop) George Stallings, some did. But for the vast majority this move went against the very grain of their Catholic identity.

The rhetorical effectiveness of this model depended upon the recognition that the fundamental relationship between universalism and particularity is an antinomy. That is, without the recognition of cultural, racial, and ethnic particularity there can be no true universalism—a position embraced explicitly by the Catholic Church in the twentieth-century proposal of enculturation. Universalism needs to include all; otherwise it simply means the hegemony of the dominant group. On the other hand, particularity, with no reference to a universal dimension of cross-cultural and interethnic community, becomes in my third model a "race religion" to a degree not foreseen by Rudd in his disputes with his black Protestant colleagues.

IDENTIFYING RELIGIOUS/RACIAL ORIGINS

Beginning in the late nineteenth century small groups of African Americans invented new myths of their religious and racial origins in which religion and race became conflated. While varied in teaching and structure, various groups of self-described Jews and Muslims held in common myths of origin that redefined the history of African Americans. In 1896, William S. Crowdy founded the Church of God and Saints of Christ, in Lawrence, Kansas. Crowdy included a number of Jewish rituals in the observances of his congregation, which continued to practice Christianity as well. Significantly, he asserted that black people were descended from the ten lost tribes of Israel. Other congregations, such as Prophet F. S. Cherry's Church of the Living God—Pillar and Ground of Truth for All Nations in Philadelphia, also adopted Jewish customs and, in Cherry's case, mounted caustic attacks against Christian clergy. As Yvonne Chireau has perceptively noted: "Many of the early black Jewish groups encouraged their followers to make a conscious break with certain aspects of their heritage while retaining others. Name transformation, or the rejection of the terms 'Negro' and 'black' in favor of 'Hebrew,' was one strategy by which some blacks signified Judaism as a racial classification."[11]

In the 1920s Wentworth A. Matthew formed around a nucleus of West Indian immigrants the Commandment Keepers Congregation of the Living God, for years Harlem's largest congregation of black Jews. The Commandment Keepers believed that African Americans were Ethiopian Jews, or Falashas, who had been stripped of their true religion by slavery. Judaism was the ancestral heritage of the Ethiopians, whereas Christianity was the religion of the Gentiles, that is, whites. The Commandment Keepers rejected Christianity as the religion of a corrupt white society. They condemned emotionally expressive worship as "niggerition." Moral restraint and dignity presumably distinguished the behavior of the Ethiopian Hebrew from the immorality and self-indulgence of the "typical" Negro.

Black Muslim groups resembled black Jews in the rejection of Negro identity as pejoratively defined by whites and in their invention of a new religious-racial identity for African Americans. The original religion of black people, they claimed, was Islam. In 1913, Timothy Drew founded the Moorish Science Temple in Newark, New Jersey. The Noble Drew Ali, as his followers called him, taught that African Americans were not Negroes but Asiatics. Their original home was Morocco; their true nationality was Moorish American. To symbolize recovery of their true identity, members of the Moorish Science Temple received new names and identity cards issued by Noble Drew Ali. Knowledge of their true origins and their true religious selves, Ali taught, would empower them to overcome racial oppression. The Moorish Science Temple survived Ali's death in 1929 only to be eclipsed by another esoteric Muslim group that would in time gain much more notoriety.

In 1930, W. D. Fard began teaching poor blacks in Detroit that they were members of a Muslim "lost-found tribe of Shabbazz" and that salvation for black people lay in knowledge of self. Fard left the movement in 1934 to the leadership of Elijah Poole, renamed Elijah Muhammad, who guided the Nation of Islam for the next forty years. The Nation taught that the black man was the original man and that his religion was Islam. White people were a race of devils, the product of a black scientist's malicious genetic experiment. Heresy in orthodox Muslim eyes, this teaching seemed to Messenger Elijah's disciples a plausible explanation for endemic white racism and an effective antidote to the myth of black inferiority. The hortatory power of this rhetoric (especially as articulated by Malcolm X) lay in its expression of black rage over the injustices perpetrated against black people. It was then a "rhetoric of rage" that served, moreover, as a warning to whites to cease the oppression or face the consequences. (Unless they accept Martin, as Malcolm assured Coretta Scott King in Selma, they have to deal with me.)

Black Muslims castigated black Christians for accepting the "white man's religion" and denounced the black church for keeping black Americans ignorant of their true identity. Like black Jews, the Nation of Islam rejected behavior associated with popular black culture and disciplined its membership to observe strict dietary and social regulations. Moreover, black Muslims insisted on a new national as well as religious identity. Elijah Muhammad taught his followers to reject the rituals of American civic membership, such as saluting the flag, voting, and registering for the draft. Claiming to constitute a black nation, the black Muslims demanded that the federal government set aside a separate section of the country for black people in compensation for the unpaid labor of their slave ancestors.

In effect, black Jews and black Muslims solved a problem that had long troubled black Christians: the racist attitudes and behavior of white Christians. From slavery days on, black Christians had resisted the temptation to identify Christianity as a religion for whites by distinguishing true Christianity, which preached the equality of all races, from false Christianity, which countenanced slavery and discrimination against black people. There were always those, however, who failed to see the distinction and who scorned Christianity as the religion of the oppressors. Given the history of white brutality against blacks, how could blacks accept the same religion as whites? Alienated from their own nation by a history of slavery, disfranchisement, and discrimination, how could black people consider themselves American? Given the pejorative definition of black people, how could they identify themselves with that definition? So black Muslims and black Jews created new religious and racial origins and identities, newly imagined homelands, new racial religions. However, doing so required them to deny significant aspects of their own history as African Americans. For most black Americans, this was too high a price to pay. Judith Weisenfeld in a perceptive essay argues forthrightly that one of the devastating results of racism, or, as she puts it, "the persistent location of evil in blackness," has been its effect upon African American individuals and communities, leading in the case of the Nation of Islam to a "drive to shuffle hierarchies in order to attempt to exercise power over others."[12]

James Baldwin, whom Weisenfeld quotes on internalized racism, expressed a similar fear about the Nation of Islam in *The Fire Next Time*. Understandable as the appeal of the Nation's rhetoric of rage might be, for a people whose humanity and personhood had been so persistently denigrated, ultimately its narrative sacrificed too much black history and black humanity. Pondering his experience of visiting the Messenger Elijah Muhammad at his home in Chicago, Baldwin wondered, in the vengeful future predicted by the Nation: "What will happen to all that beauty?" And then, in a powerful statement, the penultimate sentence of the book, he presented a poignant possibility of interracial community. "If we— and now I mean the relatively conscious whites and the relatively conscious blacks, who must, like lovers, insist on, or create, the consciousness of the others—do not falter in our duty now, we may be able, handful that we are, to end the racial nightmare, and achieve our country, and change the history of the world."

SEARCHING FOR COMMUNITY

I began this essay by quoting Howard Thurman, and I want to conclude my discussion of four ways of relating religion to race with a model that he not only articulated but managed to build, a model of community across racial and religious lines. I don't mean to present him as without context: the thickening ties of ecumenical Protestantism in the twentieth century and the growth of interracial movements and structures. But I do see Thurman as the foremost articulator and representative of this wider movement.

Howard Thurman was born in 1900 in Daytona, Florida, and died in 1981 in San Francisco, California. As a child Thurman experienced a profound mystical intuition into the unity of all being, which provided a powerful focal point for his vision of community. As he recalled it much later:

As a boy in Florida, I walked along the beach of the Atlantic in the quiet stillness that can only be completely felt when the murmur of the ocean is stilled and the tides move stealthily along the shore. I held my breath against the night and watched the stars etch their brightness on the face of the darkened canopy of the heavens. I had the sense that all things, the sand, the sea, the stars, the night, and I were *one* lung through which all of life breathed. Not only was I aware of a vast rhythm enveloping all, but I was a part of it and it was a part of me.[13]

He remembered this experience as one of the primary, defining moments of his life.

In 1926 Thurman enrolled in Rochester Theological Seminary (now Colgate-Rochester) and after graduation accepted a call to serve as minister of a black Baptist church in Oberlin, Ohio. His preaching attracted a steady stream of white visitors, Oberlin professors, students, a mixed congregation of auditors who did not become members. At this point Thurman decided that he needed to cultivate an inner life of prayer and meditation, hoping to connect on an experiential level with the needs of his congregation. This inward turn was reinforced by Thurman's encounter with a small book, *Finding the Trail of Life* (1926), written by the Quaker mystic Rufus Jones. Recognizing a kindred spirit, Thurman took a leave of absence to do an independent study program at Haverford College with Jones in the spring of 1929. Under the tutelage of Jones, Thurman read widely on mystical experience and developed an interest in Meister Eckhart and Francis of Assisi. Returning to the South, he took up a position as professor of religion and director of religious life at Morehouse and Spellman Colleges, and in 1932 he accepted an appointment as dean of the chapel at Howard University in Washington DC. From this position Thurman began to establish a national reputation.

Three years later Thurman and his wife, Sue Bailey Thurman, accepted an invitation to travel to India and Burma on a good-will tour sponsored by the Christian Student Movement of India and Burma. The trip proved to be a catalyst for the Thurmans' future vocations. Like other African Americans before them, the Thurmans made the pilgrimage to visit Gandhi, who questioned them closely about the racial discrimination that divided American Christians. Important as the visit to Gandhi and also to Tagore was for the Thurmans, the experience of India pushed them toward a deeper and clearer realization of the interrelatedness of all people and a vision of creating a religious fellowship that would cut across all barriers to common life.

It would take several years for this inner vision to take external shape. Back at Howard, Thurman received a letter of inquiry from Alfred Fisk, a Presbyterian minister in San Francisco. Fisk was looking for a black ministerial student or a young minister to take a part-time position as co-pastor of a church in a black neighborhood in San Francisco. Thurman began to consider that the letter might be a call to him personally. In 1944 Fisk and Thurman, white Presbyterian and black Baptist, became co-founders and co-pastors of the Church for the Fellowship of All Peoples. For the next nine years Thurman worked to create a new kind of community committed to the ideal that religious experience should be a force of unity rather than division among people willing to embrace diversity and so be enriched by it.

Thurman experimented with the Sunday worship service, incorporating a weekly period of guided meditation and reflective silence. The congregation decided to become independent rather than place itself under the authority of any one denomination whose doctrinal definitions might restrict Fellowship Church's ideal of inclusiveness. A nationwide network of affiliate or associate members was formed out of supporters of the Fellowship ideal. Thurman traveled extensively, lecturing and preaching to support the church and to spread its mission. He was a mesmerizing preacher whose voice and presence powerfully articulated his vision of interracial religious community. Many of his sermons and meditations formed the bases for books. After nine years Thurman left San Francisco to become dean of the chapel at Boston University, where he continued to preach community until his retirement in 1965. Returning to San Francisco, he chaired the Howard Thurman Educational Trust, a charitable and educational foundation, until his death in 1981.

Thurman's vision of community was based upon his profound awareness of the unity of all created being. Community, he insisted, is embedded in the very structure of life itself. The drive toward community is the drive toward completion or wholeness, what he called "whole-feeling." Wholeness, Thurman firmly believed, is the goal toward which all the myriad forms of life, from the simplest to the most complex, struggle. And completion or wholeness consists in community. Community is the goal of life, intended by life's author.

For humans, community is the source of identity, for within each person the inner law of life ineluctably searches for wholeness and fulfillment. The denial of community assails persons at the very foundation of their sense of identity. Historically, the drive for wholeness and community of black people has suffered sustained attack from the denial of their full membership in American society. When discrimination and racism intervened to destroy community, they frustrated the very thrust of life itself. Eventually, if the thrust toward wholeness embedded in life is to be fulfilled, racial separateness must yield to human community. Thurman did not shrink from accepting the logical extension of his vision of community: ultimately the black church as a separate institution would be required to yield to interracial community.

Critics of Thurman argued that the liberal character of his theology and his privileging of religious experience over doctrinal formulations and denominational identity relegated his impact to the extent of his personal influence upon others. His charismatic presence and preaching did not yield any sustained institutional or social change. When he was asked late in life why he had not lead a social movement, he replied that he was not a movement man, that his talent lay in articulating the central importance of universal religious experience for personal and social integrity. Thurman's rhetoric of community seemed to its critics to be vague, visionary, long on idealism and short on practical program. His defenders argued that Thurman led by example and by offering counsel as a board member of the Fellowship of Reconciliation, the Congress of Racial Equality, and the National Association for the Advancement of Colored People. Whitney Young, Vernon Jordan, and Martin Luther King Jr. acknowledged, as did many others, the influence of Howard Thurman upon their lives.

CONCLUSION

I have sketched out four models by which black Americans have related religion and race. To summarize:

1. Redeeming the religion of the master casts the history of African Americans against the backdrop of biblical narrative, especially the story of Exodus, in order to fashion a map of meaning for black people as a specially chosen people whose destiny is "to save the soul of the nation." Institutionalized in the large black Protestant denominations and their institutions, known collectively as the Black Church, the religious rhetoric of this model takes the form of the classic jeremiad. Martin Luther King Jr. recapitulated this rhetorical tradition during the civil rights movement of the 1960s.

2. Erasing the color line emphasizes the capacity of religion to transcend racial categories by articulating the universalism and inclusiveness of Christianity historically and globally as an argument against the

racially exclusive practice of Christian clergy and churches in the United States. The religious rhetoric of this model attempts to negotiate the tension between the universal and the particular by urging the universal church to embrace enculturation and to implement it institutionally, pastorally, and liturgically.

3. Identifying religious/racial origins collapses categories of race and religion into new myths of origin that counter the myth of black inferiority perpetuated within American society. Arguing for black self-worth and self-definition, this model takes institutional form in separatist structures. Symbolically abandoning the dominant national and religious identities that have excluded black people from full inclusion in the nation, this model rejects America and Christianity. Its rhetoric of rage expresses the pent-up anger of black Americans at their condition in the United States and offers a biting critique of the racist deeds of white Americans, sometimes couched in apocalyptic language. The most articulate spokesman of this model was Malcolm X.

4. Searching for community emphasizes religion as an ecumenical force for overcoming all divisions, including racial, ethnic, and religious divisions themselves. This model takes institutional form in ecumenical fellowship. Its rhetoric focuses on religious experience as a primary human experience that takes priority over differences of doctrine, denomination, race, and culture. Howard Thurman was a major voice for this model.

I've proposed these models to elucidate the variety of ways in which black Americans have struggled religiously to create maps of meaning, identity, and hope in the midst of the absurdity and brutality of slavery and racial discrimination, persistently supported by appeals to Christianity. These are in the end models of transformation intended to change attitudes and behaviors based upon the belief that religion has the power to affect the conditions of African Americans in a society that consistently and continuously identified them as inferior, not only different, but as pejoratively other. My students ask me, "Which of these models do you choose?" I answer: "None of them. Each has its advantages and its deficits. What I do choose is to admire and to embrace the wisdom and courage of people who, amid circumstances so bleak that the only appropriate response seemed despair, kept alive their hope and asserted their humanity." These models represent the cries and whispers, the shouts of anger, the hopes and aspirations of people who survived and even transcended the injustices that circumscribed their lives.

NOTES

[1] Gomes Eannes de Azurara [Zurara], *Chronicle of the Discovery and Conquest of Guinea*, trans. Charles R. Beazley and Edgar Prestage, 2 vols. (London: Hakluyt Society, 1896, 1899) I: 50–51, 81–82, 84–85.

[2] David W. Wills, "The Central Themes of American Religious History: Pluralism, Puritanism, and the Encounter of Black and White," in *African American Religion: Interpretive Essays in History and Culture*, ed. Timothy E. Fulop and Albert J. Raboteau, 7–20 (New York: Routledge, 1997).

[3] Howard Thurman, *Deep River: An Interpretation of Negro Spirituals* (Mills College, CA: The Eucalyptus Press, 1945), 17.

[4] Peter Kalm, *Travels into North America*, 2nd ed., reprinted in vol. 13 of *A General Collection of the Best and Most Interesting Voyages and Travels*, ed. John Pinkerton (London, 1812), 503.

[5] Appeal to Governor Thomas Gage and the Massachusetts General Court, May 25, 1774, Collection of the Massachusetts Historical Society, 5th ser., 3 (1877), 432–33.

[6] See Albert J. Raboteau, *Slave Religion: The "Invisible Institution" in the Antebellum South* (New York: Oxford University Press, 1978), 141, 307 and sources cited there.

[7] Absalom Jones, *A Thanksgiving Sermon Preached January 1, 1808, in St. Thomas's, or the African Episcopal Church, Philadelphia: An Account of the Abolition of the African Slave Trade* (Philadelphia, 1808), 18.

[8] Charles Davenport, cited in Raboteau, *Slave Religion*, 304.

[9] Pierre Landry, "From Slavery to Freedom," unpublished memoirs, cited in Charles Bathelemy Rousseve, *The Negro in Louisiana* (New Orleans, LA: Xavier University Press, 1937), 39.

[10] *Three Catholic Afro-American Congresses* (Cincinnati: American Catholic Tribune, 1893; reprint, New York: Arno Press, 1978), 141–42.

[11] Yvonne Chireau and Nathaniel Deutsch, eds., *Black Zion: African American Religious Encounters with Judaism* (New York: Oxford University Press, 2001), 21.

[12] Judith Weisenfeld, "Difference as Evil," in *The Courage to Hope: From Black Suffering to Human Redemption*, ed. Quinton Hosford Dixie and Cornel West (Boston: Beacon Press, 1999), 98.

[13] Howard Thurman, *With Head and Heart: The Autobiography of Howard Thurman* (New York: Harcourt Brace Jovanovich, 1979), 225–26.

Chapter 2

The Difficulty of Our Situation

The Oblate Sisters of Providence in Antebellum Society

DIANE BATTS MORROW

Black and free in a slave society that privileged only whiteness, female in a male dominated society, Roman Catholic in a Protestant society, and pursuing religious vocations in a society doubting the virtue of all black women, the Oblate Sisters of Providence proved exceptional in the antebellum southern United States. Organized in 1828, the Oblate Sisters dedicated themselves as "a Religious society of Coloured Women established in Baltimore with the [approval] of the Most Reverend Archbishop, [who] renounce the world to consecrate themselves to God, and to the Christian education of young girls of color."[1]

Historically, black people have used their spiritual resources to assert their personal worth. Whether slave or free, black people in the Protestant tradition used religion, both as individuals and collectively in congregations, to counter the attacks of a white society denying black humanity. The founding of the Oblate community provided a new example of black religious piety. The Oblate Sisters of Providence distinguished themselves by their collective profession and practice of spirituality as the first black women to pursue religious communal life in the Roman Catholic tradition. This chapter examines how the Oblate Sisters, in publicly professing themselves as—and in wearing the habits of—women religious both challenged and responded to social attitudes about race and gender in the pursuit of their pioneering mission.

Two streams of immigration that met in Baltimore in the 1790s made possible the formation of the Oblate Sisters almost forty years later. As the see, or official seat, of the first diocese of the Roman Catholic Church formed in the United States in 1789, Baltimore provided a logical haven for Catholics fleeing revolutions in France and the Caribbean. The French Sulpician priests arrived in Baltimore in 1791 to educate young men for the priesthood. Beginning in 1793, black as well as white refugees fled the slave revolution in the French Caribbean colony of St. Domingue—now Haiti—to several port cities in the United States.[2] In Baltimore, shared traditions attracted Sulpicians and San Domingan exiles to each other, bound together by their French language, cultural heritage, and profession of the Roman Catholic faith. In 1796 the Sulpician priests organized Sunday religious instruction for the black San Domingan refugees, who met in their seminary chapel.

In 1827 Sulpician priest James Hector Joubert assumed direction of Sunday religious training for the black children and proposed a school to improve religious instruction. To staff the school Joubert approached Caribbean emigrants Elizabeth Clarisse Lange and Marie Magdelaine Balas, two educated women of color and experienced teachers who conducted a school for children of their race in their home. During their first meeting Lange and Balas informed Joubert of their decade-long desire to become sisters. That these two black Catholic women persisted in their religious vocations for ten years before fulfillment reveals much about them. With neither external acknowledgment nor official encouragement, Lange and Balas relied exclusively on their internal commitment to their religious vocations, based on their faith that God would provide. After consulting with Archbishop James Whitfield of Baltimore, Joubert concluded that a black sisterhood would suit his purposes as well.[3]

Segments of the Baltimore Catholic community objected to the pending Oblate foundation almost immediately. From 1789 through the 1830s, the church in the South formed the foundation of American Roman Catholicism. Indeed, the Catholic Church in the United States retained the imprint of its southern origins throughout the nineteenth century. As did their Protestant counterparts, Roman Catholic clergy and women religious not only tolerated the institution of slavery, but also actively participated in and profited from the ownership and sale of human chattel. Several distinguished prelates, societies of priests, and at least nine congregations of women religious held slave property.[4] The antebellum Roman Catholic Church's acceptance of racism and the institution of slavery necessarily affected its attitude and policies toward black people. Archbishop Whitfield approved the establishment of the Oblate community of black women religious in 1829. Nevertheless, constituencies within the church disapproved of the black Oblate Sisters.

On 17 June 1829, Father James Joubert visited Archbishop Whitfield to confide his concern about the coalescing opposition to the establishment of the colored religious community, scorned by some as "a profanation of the habit." Joubert noted, "These good girls . . . admitted to me that after all they had heard said, only through obedience would they be determined to take the religious habit." Joubert further revealed: "I had myself heard much talk. I knew already that many persons who had approved the idea of a school for pupils disapproved very strongly that of forming a religious house, and could not think of the idea of seeing these poor girls (colored girls) wearing the religious habit and constituting a religious community." The outcry against the idea of black sisters had come to Whitfield's attention, who, according to Joubert, "knew very much himself, even more than I did, and he advised me not to be in the least discouraged."[5]

On 2 July 1829, James Joubert received the professions of the four charter members of the Oblate Sisters of Providence: Elizabeth Lange, Marie Balas, Rosine Boegue, and Therese Duchemin. They pledged themselves to a life of service and faithful observance of the vows of poverty, chastity, and obedience. The term *oblate* means "one offered" or "made over to God."[6] Lange became the first mother superior, and Joubert the first spiritual director of the Oblate sisterhood.

Sister Mary Elizabeth Lange served as mother superior of the Oblates from 1828 to 1832 and again from 1835 to 1841. She then joined the Oblate staff at St. Mary's Seminary until 1850. When she returned to the convent from the seminary, Lange became novice mistress from 1850 until 1855, assistant superior from 1857, and from 1858 director of an Oblate school at Fells Point in east Baltimore. Her personal qualities, example, and leadership, incorporated in the Oblate communal identity, fortified the sisterhood in its encounters with trials, challenges, and rejection throughout its first half-century.

Father James Joubert validated this first community of African American Catholic sisters in the eyes of the institutional church. Without benefit of guiding precedent he deftly negotiated uncharted paths to legitimize the Oblate community as a congregation of sisters. Joubert secured diocesan approbation of the Oblate Rule from Archbishop James Whitfield. He then orchestrated papal recognition of the black Oblate Sisters as a community of women religious. Joubert promoted the Oblate cause and advanced their mission in the frequently hostile environment of the antebellum South and the American Roman Catholic Church.

During their first decade the Oblate Sisters addressed the racial dimension of their exceptional position within southern church and society. In 1835 Louis Deluol, superior of the Sulpician Seminary, requested two Oblate Sisters to manage the domestic affairs of the seminary household. Oblate Superior Mary Lange responded to this request with a letter reflecting her clear understanding of both the promise and the perils of the Oblate community's status:

> We do not conceal the difficulty of our situation [a]s persons of color and religious at the same time, and we wish to conciliate these two qualities in such a manner as not to appear too arrogant on the one hand and on the other, not to miss the respect which is due to the state we have embraced and the holy habit which we have the honor to wear. Our intention in consenting to your request is not to neglect the religious profession which we have embraced.[7]

Oblate experience with clerical disapproval of the concept of a black sisterhood in 1829 had prompted Lange's concerns about full recognition of and respect for the Oblate Sisters' religious status at the seminary. Objections to the Oblate foundation expressed within the white Baltimore Catholic community—even among the Sulpician priests—had dismayed the four charter Oblate members. Consequently, Lange insisted on the guaranteed integrity of the Oblate religious state as a precondition to the sisters' employment at the seminary. She further requested separation of the sisters from the other seminary servants—slave and free—in an effort to reserve for the Oblate Sisters a distinctive social position based on their status as women religious. Lange responded to a routine request for traditional domestic services with a nontraditional manifesto defining the Oblate Sisters' religious, racial, and social positions as they understood them.

The Oblate Sisters fulfilled religious vocations in a slaveholding society that denied the virtue of all black women—slave or free. Antebellum American society ostracized black women beyond the pale of the social construction of gender. From the early days of slavery white public thought considered black women the opposite of women of virtue, the idealized social construct of white middle-class women. The image of black women as the sexually promiscuous Jezebel became fixed in the white public consciousness. Negative stereotypes of black women remained so widespread in American culture that long after the abolition of slavery in 1865 a white observer accurately represented public sentiment when she stated in 1904, "I cannot imagine such a creation as a virtuous black woman."[8] Only the equally dysfunctional slave stereotype of black women as Mammy, the asexual caretaker devoted to the nurture of her white family to the neglect of her own, challenged the Jezebel image of black women in white public opinion.[9]

Refusing to accept such social condemnation, the Oblate Sisters demonstrated self-empowerment by defining themselves primarily in terms of their disciplined exercise of piety and virtue. As teachers, the Oblate Sisters effectively countered the Mammy stereotype's neglect of her own offspring with their collective devotion to the intellectual, spiritual, and social nurture of black children. In dedicating themselves to the religious state, the Oblate Sisters offered their lives to God. Arrayed in religious garb, the raiment of women of virtue, these black women became "brides of Christ." As women religious, the Oblate Sisters at least partially transcended their social marginalization in claiming "the respect which is due to the state we have embraced and the holy habit which we have the honor to wear," the same respect, virtue, and honor normally reserved for white middle-class women exclusively.

Two aspects of Oblate spirituality established during their first decade resonate with racial meaning. From 1833 the Oblate Sisters claimed St. Benedict the Moor as the fourth special patron of their house, after the Blessed Virgin Mary, St. Joseph, and St. Frances of Rome.[10] This designation represents the only explicit element of African identity in their spirituality, as historian Cyprian Davis has noted.[11] The animosity surrounding their formation plausibly explains why the Oblate Sisters postponed claiming this black saint formally as a community patron until after inferred papal recognition had secured their status as women religious in antebellum Baltimore.

On 2 July 1830 Oblate spiritual director James Joubert, the four charter Oblate members, and the three Oblate novices enrolled in the Association of Holy Slavery of the Mother of God, receiving the symbolic chain of membership. Future Oblate members were to enroll in the association the day they received their habits. Oblate affiliation with this devotional society initially appears problematic for black sisters in the context of the antebellum South. However, their allegiance to this devotional society conformed completely to the centrality of devotion to the Blessed Virgin in the Oblate charism. Davis treats this association as a development from seventeenth-century French devotional practices and states that the metaphor "holy slavery" enjoyed widespread usage in church devotional circles. Theologian Thaddeus Posey asserts that "to freely give oneself to a slavery that would secure a constant union with Christ was in complete harmony with the Oblate Rule."[12]

Oblate membership in the Association of Holy Slavery of the Mother of God represented no embrace of slavery as the classic model of the abused of the black community, but rather a conversion—if not subversion—of the specific secular connotations of the institution of slavery in the antebellum South. The spiritual slavery with which the Oblate Sisters associated differed critically from its social analogue of involuntary subjugation to an owner, both in its voluntary nature and sole purpose

of personal spiritual benefit. Oblate membership in this devotional society reflected the degree to which these black sisters successfully
dissociated themselves spiritually—if not physically—from their immediate social context to divest the term *slavery* of its dehumanizing
connotations.

The Oblate community further sought to divest the institution of slavery of its dehumanizing faculty in their membership policy. Of the forty
women who entered the Oblate novitiate in the antebellum period, eight
had risen from slave origins.[13] The Oblate Sisters of Providence did not
consider a candidate's previous condition of servitude a liability for Oblate membership. The Oblate Rule did not explicitly address the issue of
slavery. The general requirement that candidates "be free from debts
and detained in the world by no hindrance whatsoever"[14] commonly
appeared in the regulations of religious congregations. Only in the context of the racial identity of the Oblate Sisters did this requirement mean
that candidates had to be free black women.

It hardly proves surprising that the Oblate Sisters neither expressed
abolitionist sentiments nor engaged in antislavery activities, whatever
their private feelings about slavery might have been. Oblate silence about
slavery occurred within the context of an American Roman Catholic
Church whose clergy and hierarchy not only engaged in slaveholding
but also frequently and vociferously defended the institution of slavery.
As a religious society within the Roman Catholic Church, the Oblate
Sisters—and all sisterhoods—adhered to official church policy of nonin-
tervention in social and political matters. The Oblate Rule required that
"[the sisters] will not take the liberty of condemning others, though these
may be really wrong. They will endeavor as much as possible to live at
peace with everyone; they must strive to conciliate the goodwill of all."[15]
Clearly this policy referred to the obligation of the Oblate membership
to maintain the goodwill of the parents of their pupils; nevertheless, it
applied with equal validity to Oblate abstention from public debate about
social and political issues confronting antebellum society.

The Christian education of young girls of color formed the principal
purpose of the Oblate Sisters of Providence, equal to their determination
to consecrate themselves to God. The Oblate School for Colored Girls
opened in 1828 and offered its black patrons a solid common-school education. The Oblate curriculum, advertised in the national Catholic
directory for the first time in 1834, offered courses in religion, "English,
French, Cyphering and Writing, Sewing in all its branches, Embroidery,
Washing and Ironing."[16] In addition to common school and domestic
instruction, the Oblate teaching ministry required the sisters to instill in
their pupils "certain principles of virtue becoming their situation: the

love of labor and of order . . . , a [careful avoidance of unsupervised male company], that innocent bashfulness which is the principal ornament of their sex, and that exterior modesty which is the surest preservative of virtue."[17] The emphasis on feminine virtues in three of the four listed principles typifies the philosophy influencing not only convent schools, but also all nineteenth-century education for women.

Significantly, the Oblate Sisters taught these values of respectability to black girls in defiance of antebellum American society's exclusion of black women from its social construction of gender. No surviving evidence suggests that the antebellum Oblate school curriculum explicitly addressed the racial identity of its clientele. Nevertheless, in offering a solid Catholic education to black girls, the Oblate Sisters taught their pupils values and ideals beyond those that white society thought either appropriate or possible for black women.

Oblate insistence on "the respect which is due to the state we have embraced and the holy habit which we have the honor to wear" and their teaching emphasis on respectability for their pupils conformed to what historian Evelyn Brooks Higginbotham has identified as the politics of respectability:

> By claiming respectability through their manners and morals, poor black women boldly asserted the will and agency to define themselves outside the parameters of prevailing racist discourses. . . . Respectability was perceived as a weapon against such assumptions, since it was used to expose race relations as socially constructed rather than derived by evolutionary law or divine judgment.[18]

The 1840s began auspiciously for the Oblate Sisters of Providence. Yet, by 1844, the Oblate Sisters were encountering a series of crises that threatened their very survival. From the late 1830s the declining health of their beloved spiritual director, James Joubert, haunted the Oblate community like some inexorable specter. His bouts of sickness caused Joubert to relinquish his responsibilities as Oblate spiritual director to Sulpician colleagues Edward Damphoux or John Hickey, often for weeks at a time.[19] By July 1842 Joubert's illnesses had become so frequent that the Oblate annalist commented, "Father Director was very sick, as he always is at this time."[20] On 15 June 1843 Joubert came to the Oblate convent for a ten-day visit that extended until 4 July. At his departure the sisters noted anxiously, "We do not know when we will have the pleasure of seeing him again."[21] By 29 October Joubert was "ever between life and death."[22] On 5 November 1843, James Hector Joubert died, mourned by the entire Oblate community. On 7 November, the day of his funeral, the sisters and the schoolchildren stood at the cemetery in the bitter cold "until they had entirely finished covering the grave." They observed that "the weather was gloomy and seemed in some way to share our affliction."[23]

The Oblate Sisters had realized the newly precarious nature of their position within the Baltimore religious community even before Joubert's death. On 24 July 1842, with Joubert sick and no other priest available to celebrate mass in their chapel, all the Oblate Sisters had had to go out to mass, a portent of things to come. On 20 August 1843 the Oblate annalist noted, "Since July 30th until today there has been nothing in the chapel because of the absence of Father Hickey."[24] By 3 September 1843, diocesan authorities assigned John Hickey, who had essentially functioned as Joubert's surrogate in ministering to the Oblate community since 1841, to the Baltimore Cathedral as assistant rector. On 10 September 1843 the Oblate annalist reported: "There is still nothing in the Chapel, and we may well believe that this will continue, since we have not the same confessor. May God's will be done."[25] Two days later a priest celebrated mass in the chapel "in order to consume the Host of the Monstrance."[26] Between 12 September and the end of the year—5 December excepted—priests said mass in the Oblate chapel, not to accommodate the sisters or their needs as a religious community, but only as required by church law to maintain the Blessed Sacrament in authorized houses of worship.

In 1843 the church observed the feast of St. Benedict the Moor on 8 October. Traditionally, the Oblate community had celebrated the feast of St. Benedict, their one patron saint of African descent, with appropriate pomp and solemnity. The sisters, who had had no Mass in their chapel since 12 September, observed that "today, the feast of St. Benedict, Father Superior of the Seminary [Deluol] had the goodness to procure a Mass for us, but it was said, not so much for St. Benedict, as to renew the consecrated Host."[27] It boded ill for the Oblate community and Baltimore's black Catholics, who venerated St. Benedict as one of their own, that the local clergy neglected this feast in 1843. From 1835 through 1842 Deluol himself had sung a high mass in the Oblate chapel on St. Benedict's feast day; in 1843 he did not even attend the modest observance of this major patronal feast day for black Catholics. When, on 29 October 1843, the Sulpician priest Augustin Verot said mass in the Oblate chapel, again "in order to renew the Host," the sisters requested that Verot have "the goodness to give a little instruction after the Gospel."[28] They thus asserted their legitimate claim as a religious community to customary pastoral care, a right recently withheld from them by Baltimore's clergy.

On 8 November 1843, the day following Joubert's funeral, Louis Deluol met with the Oblate Sisters of Providence. The Oblate annalist reported that after conferring privately with Oblate Superior Therese Duchemin, Deluol

> assured us of his protection and that he was ready to do everything that depended on him for our welfare. He also recommended us to pray to the Good God that He would make it clear as to what he would have to do. All the Sisters were very grateful to him, for they had been very uneasy in the belief that he would not consent to take care of the house. They thanked him for his goodness and felt more at ease.

The sisters maintained, "His visit was for us as would be that of a consoling angel."[29]

However, little in Deluol's remarks provided substantive grounds for rejoicing. His cryptic request that the sisters entreat God to inform Deluol of "what he would have to do" for their benefit hardly reflected conviction and a clear sense of purpose or commitment on Deluol's part. Only in the context of the clerical neglect they had recently experienced could the Oblate Sisters find comfort in this interview. In contrast to their detailed and hopeful account of this meeting on 8 November 1843, Deluol reported simply in his diary, "At 4:30 I went to the Providence convent, where I had not gone since 9 March. Saw all the professed Sisters."[30]

On 5 December 1843, the month anniversary of Joubert's death, Deluol celebrated a commemorative mass in the Oblate chapel that many people attended. After mass Deluol, whom the sisters called "our present superior and protector,"[31] attended to some affairs of the convent. Evidently Deluol noted neither the mass nor the meeting in his diary. The Oblate *Annals* or diary itself ceased for all of 1844, all of 1845—save three isolated entries—and all of 1846. In effect, in the words of Oblate historian Sister Theresa Catherine Willigman, "Of the sorrow and deep distress of the Sisters in the years following we draw a veil."[32]

From late 1843 through 1847 the Oblate Sisters of Providence confronted a series of crises—the death of co-founder James Joubert, the first departures and dismissal of professed members, and apparent desertion by church authorities. The sisters persevered in their observance of religious life and the conduct of their school without benefit of official clerical sponsorship. Few contemporary sources counteract the vacuum of information about the Oblate Sisters created by the discontinuation of the Oblate *Annals* during the critical middle years of the 1840s. However, some glimmers of the Oblate experience penetrate the veil of silence in which the sisters enveloped themselves. Louis Deluol mentioned the Oblate Sisters in his diary throughout the 1840s. Furthermore, several later nineteenth-century sources, including the Oblate Sisters themselves, reconstructed various aspects of the critical 1844–47 period in Oblate history and both elaborated upon and corroborated Deluol's limited information.

Louis Deluol, partisan of the Americanist faction in the Sulpician community, remained indifferent to the interests and concerns of black people. He owned or had owned slaves and had equivocated on the issue of slavery. He proclaimed his personal feelings "most violently opposed" to slavery, yet cautioned that "if we want to be right we must act from principle and not from feeling."[33] He then repeated the American church's official position accommodating the institution of slavery.

In 1839 Deluol had corresponded with Sister Margaret George, treasurer of the Sisters of Charity of St. Joseph, Emmitsburg. Cynically casting his directions as "a nubbin of theology for you," he advised her that she could sell two of her community's slaves at a premium "without doing an injustice to anybody." In another reference to the sale of the "yellow boys" [mulattoes], Deluol opined, "pity that you did not send them down ten or twelve days sooner—They would have brought $75 to $100 more."[34] Neither principle nor feeling but racism and profit-seeking prompted Deluol to conclude that the sale of black children as chattel property produced no "injustice to anybody." The institution of slavery, not a conviction of the humanity of black people, informed the American cultural values Deluol had so eagerly embraced.

The ambivalence of the Roman Catholic Church toward sisterhoods with service, not contemplative, ministries informed the experience of the Oblate Sisters of Providence and other communities of women religious in the United States who engaged in teaching or care of the sick, indigent, or orphaned with particular intensity in the 1840s. The wave of European immigrants arriving in the United States in the 1840s included priests who "required time and experience before they could balance ascetic practices with the needs of the American sisters whom they directed." Under the influence of immigrant spiritual directors following "the practice of looking to Europe for models of excellence while despising native creations," several individual members of American communities of women religious, like Oblate Sister Therese Duchemin, "wanted to be genuine religious rather than members of a half-caste group which was neither religious nor lay." Such sisters "sometimes endured crises of conscience when living in communities in which it was impossible to carry out cloister rules."[35]

James Joubert, a long-time Baltimore resident, had personally favored a service ministry for women religious and had also accommodated the realities of the Oblate southern American milieu. As spiritual director of the Oblate Sisters of Providence, Joubert had secured the Oblate Sisters in their active orientation. But Joubert's declining health, especially after 1841, had circumscribed his effective functioning as Oblate spiritual director. His death in 1843 and the subsequent alienation of the Sulpician priests from the Oblate community exposed the Oblate Sisters to the guidance of the Redemptorist priests, an order established in Baltimore only since 1840 and unfamiliar with American culture.

Limited to masses in their chapel only "once a month for renewal of the Sacred Species and also when a stranger pass[ed] through the city who[m] charity would induce to offer the Holy Sacrifice for us,"[36] the Oblate Sisters increasingly went out for mass. Between 1842 and 1845 they made the distant trek to St. James Church, located at Aisquith and Eager Streets, more than a half-hour walk from their convent and in the charge of Redemptorist priests.[37] Although founded by Alphonsus Liguori in Naples, Italy, in 1732, the Redemptorists had flourished in German-speaking countries. The order followed German emigrants to America and established a mission in Baltimore in 1840.[38]

Initial Oblate contact with the Redemptorists occurred in July 1843 when Louis Gillet, a Belgian Redemptorist and gifted preacher who spoke French exclusively, celebrated two masses in the Oblate chapel. Gillet preached for an hour to the sisters on the obligations of the religious profession. Oblate Superior and annalist Sister Therese Duchemin noted, "He explained to us very well what a spouse of Jesus Christ must do in order to remain faithful to her divine Spouse."[39]

A source generally considered Duchemin herself later recorded a personal, if third person, account of her spiritual struggle:

> Although belonging already to a religious Society, she had for a long time felt the desire of consecrating herself to God in a religious order of strict observance . . . she placed herself under the guidance of a religious, the Reverend Father Schackert. . . .
>
> It was therefore, that she discovered to him everything that passed in her soul. . . . Her Director, instead of sending her to a convent already established, as she wished, decided upon sending her to the Reverend Father Gillet, another Redemptorist who had charge of the parish of Monroe.[40]

On 9 September 1845 Sister Marie Therese Duchemin left the Oblate community for Michigan, armed with the permission, blessings, and letters of introduction from her confessor, the Redemptorist Superior Peter Czackert, and the Sulpician Superior Louis Deluol.[41]

Duchemin's departure precipitated two other defections from the Oblate community in 1845: Sister Ann Constance and Sister Stanislaus.[42] Writing later, Willigman revealed the reactions of the Oblate Sisters to this unanticipated rupture in their community:

> In 1845 Sister Therese made known that she intended to sever her connection with the Order, as from the state of affairs she did not know what the result would be. It must be said to the credit of the Sisters that they were willing to put up with all their trials, and it was far from their intention to give up. The Community numbered then fourteen Sisters, but only three were of the same opinion. Sisters Therese, Ann Constance, and Stanislaus had their plans fixed in secret, and only at the last minute did they make them known. Everything had been arranged and the place of their next establishment decided upon. There was a mantle of good feeling and charity shown by the Superior, Sister Louisa [Noel], who said Sister Therese's motives were to serve God in greater perfection than in the present Community. But all had not the same opinion of her leaving. Superiority had a great share in the separation.[43]

Issues of ethnicity, religion, and race inhered in this internal rupture in the Oblate community in 1845. Certainly the withdrawal of French Sulpician support for their community compounded the problems, stresses, and uncertainties confronting the Oblate Sisters after Joubert's death in 1843. Duchemin left the Oblate community in part because "from the state of affairs she did not know what the outcome would be."[44] The German Redemptorist priests had arrived in Baltimore only in 1840, their mandate directed them to provide pastoral care for immigrant European populations, and the Redemptorist contingent in Baltimore comprised immigrant priests exclusively. Redemptorist lack of familiarity with United States culture from a racial perspective benefitted the Oblate Sisters; not yet acculturated to racist influences, the newly immigrant priests perceived people of color as human beings fully deserving of pastoral care.

Issues of religion compounded the impact of this ethnic transition in clerical guidance on Oblate Sister Therese Duchemin individually. Duchemin had become personally conflicted about her status as a "true religious" in the Oblate community and individually more militantly Francophile than the other Oblate Sisters, even before her initial contact with the Redemptorists. The vulnerable Duchemin evidently inferred from the spiritual guidance of Redemptorists Louis Gillet and Peter Czackert—who delivered messages of spiritual discipline through the medium of the French language—encouragement to pursue a different religious experience. Initially, she sought membership in a "regular" religious congregation in Europe before agreeing to join a new service sisterhood.[45]

Issues of race intruded in the form of the racism of diocesan authorities Archbishop Samuel Eccleston and Deluol, indifferent to the fate of the Oblate Sisters of Providence as a religious community because of the racial identity of its members. Their lack of confidence and support for the Oblate Sisters served as a catalyst rupturing the Oblate community. On 13 October 1844 Deluol had noted in his diary that "someone had written to Belgium to have Sister Therese, an Oblate, taken in at a convent of Religious Sisters." On 22 November 1844 he reported, "Sister Therese, an Oblate, told me that she saw Father Louis [Gillet], but she did not get much satisfaction from him."[46] These entries in Deluol's diary documented Sister Therese Duchemin's increasing alienation from the Oblate community, her determination to sever her ties to it, and Deluol's awareness of both. Had Deluol felt genuinely protective of the integrity and welfare of the Oblate community, he certainly would have informed the sisters of Duchemin's disaffection and attempted to mediate their differences, rather than merely expediting Duchemin's departure in 1845.

The Oblate Sisters faced another crisis with the withdrawal of support for their continued existence by Baltimore's diocesan authorities and clergy in the middle years of the 1840s. The sisters characterized their condition during these years as "in a pitiable state." Keenly feeling the spiritual "deprivation of all the consolations they had enjoyed," the sisters "resigned their cares to God and his Divine Providence."[47] The indifference and inaction with which Baltimore's episcopal authorities—Sulpician Archbishop Samuel Eccleston and Sulpician Vicar-General Louis Deluol—responded to the black Oblate community's loss of its spiritual director in 1843 contrasted starkly to their expressed concern and sense of obligation toward the communities of white women religious as late as 1849. When the impetus from Sulpician headquarters in France for the American Sulpicians to restrict themselves to their original mission to train seminarians arose in 1845 and actual implementation of the retrenchment policy began in the spring of 1849,[48] Eccleston maintained to French Sulpician authorities that the traditional Sulpician direction of the Sisters of Charity obligated the order to continue this relationship until appropriately replaced.[49] No extant evidence indicated that either Eccleston or Deluol expressed such concern or initiated such efforts on the Oblate Sisters' behalf between 1844 and 1847.

Writing in 1900, chronicler L. W. Reilly presented a Redemptorist perspective on the clerical neglect of the Oblate community between 1843 and 1847:

> But a storm was gathering that threatened the very existence of the Institute [Oblate community]. Archbishop Eccleston was not well disposed to it. Several other clergymen who had formerly viewed the formation of the society with approval now entertained doubts of its utility. Some even expressed the opinion that "good servants were needed," hinting at the dissolution of the community. The death of the founder they thought available as an opportunity to destroy his work. If no one else would take it up, it must perish.
>
> The Sulpitians [sic] did not care to keep up the responsibility of the Sisterhood in view of the disfavor with the diocesan authorities into which it had fallen. They accordingly withdrew from its direction.[50]

Although Reilly identified only Samuel Eccleston by name, Louis Deluol could well have numbered among the unnamed "several other clergymen" opposed to the Oblate community. Sulpicians Samuel Eccleston and Louis Deluol constituted "the diocesan authorities" at this time. As Eccleston's former professor, confessor, and current confidant, Deluol exerted so much influence over the archbishop that at times "it was never really clear which of the two was running the archdiocese."[51] From the beginning of the Oblate Sisters in 1828, both Eccleston and Deluol had remained personally indifferent, if not hostile, to this community of black women religious. Between his elevation to the episcopacy of Baltimore in 1834 and the year 1848, Eccleston had visited the Oblate premises only once, when his obligations as presiding prelate of the archdiocese undoubtedly required that he dedicate the new Oblate chapel in 1836. Louis Deluol's semi-annual celebrations of mass in the Oblate chapel likewise may have reflected less any personal interest in the Oblate community than an obligatory performance of his duties as vicar-general. After Joubert's death the Oblate Sisters "had been very uneasy in the belief that he [Deluol] would not consent to take care of the house."[52] The sisters had correctly intuited Deluol's ambivalence toward them.

The Oblate Sisters of Providence responded to their twin crises of internal community rupture and external alienation by diocesan authorities

with commendable fortitude. In 1845 the sisters themselves characterized their condition since 1843—and would remain so until October
1847—as "abandoned or apparently so, if the world was consulted, but
not by God, for since the establishment of the community not once has
Almighty God ceased to bestow His gifts and graces, not withstanding
our unworthiness."[53] Although "by degrees it appeared that everything
was falling, the school decreased, sad was it to think on the future state
of the community," still the sisters were "willing to put up with all their
trials and it was far from their intention to give up."[54] Willigman recalled that "one great consolation was left them . . . namely the presence
of Our Lord in the Blessed Sacrament in the Tabernacle. Their dear
Chapel was their refuge in trial."[55]

Contemporary observers verified the Oblate community's spiritual integrity during this critical period. On 19 April 1844 Deluol himself
reported, "I went to the Oblates and for five hours examined them; I
found them better disposed than I had expected."[56] The Redemptorist
priest Louis Gillet recalled that in 1844 the Oblate Sisters, "then entirely
abandoned," and "whose vows had not been renewed for a long time,"
were nevertheless "living still in community."[57] Before departing for New
Orleans in 1847, former Redemptorist Superior Peter Czackert enjoined
fellow Redemptorist Thaddeus Anwander to do all in his power to help
the Oblate Sisters, "for they were good, holy, simple souls and good religious."[58] The spiritual worthiness of the Oblate Sisters of Providence
had manifested itself clearly to those who would see it.

However much diocesan authorities may have concluded that the
Oblate community must perish after Joubert's death if no one else would
take it up, the Oblate Sisters themselves refused to give up. Because the
sisters constituted a diocesan community of women religious, their archbishop retained the authority to disband them. Archbishop Samuel
Eccleston had withheld ministerial support from the Oblate community
between Joubert's death in November 1843 and October 1847; however,
he had not mandated their dissolution. Unconvinced of the spiritual fervor and commitment of these black women religious, Eccleston may have
assumed that a policy of neglect alone would effect Oblate disintegra-
tion. Furthermore, the inferred papal recognition of the Oblate
community probably stayed Eccleston's hand.[59] Between 1843 and 1846,
as Eccleston contended with papal inquiries about his own mental competence and fitness for office, he may have refrained from provoking
Roman authorities further by initiating the dissolution of a presumed
papally recognized diocesan community.

However, by October 1847 the Oblate Sisters of Providence still persisted and diocesan authorities evidently determined to proceed against

them. No extant official correspondence or proclamation documented this decision, but on 7 October 1847 Louis Deluol maintained to Father Alexander Czvitkovicz, a Redemptorist priest, that the Oblate Sisters' "purpose has failed, and we can't hope to preserve it."[60]

Three days later, on 10 October, John Neumann, who had replaced Peter Czackert as Redemptorist superior in America early in 1847, delegated Thaddeus Anwander "to take charge of the Oblate Sisters, then in a very bad condition of abandonment, for it was unfortunately the wish of high Ecclesiastical authority that the Sisters should dissolve and disband."[61] Anwander immediately sought appointment as spiritual director of the Oblate Sisters from Archbishop Eccleston, who initially refused the young priest's request. Had Eccleston resolved to disband the Oblate community only because he could find no cleric willing to direct them, as some sources maintain, he would not have refused the very offer of what he allegedly sought.[62] Anwander responded to Eccleston's laconic refusal, "Cui bono?" (To whose good?) by dropping to his knees and pleading with the archbishop for his blessing and permission to try. Eccleston relented, and Anwander left his audience with the archbishop the newly appointed spiritual director of the Oblate Sisters of Providence.[63]

Born in 1823, Thaddeus Anwander had enjoyed a privileged youth in a wealthy farm family in Bavaria. He entered the Redemptorist novitiate in Freiburg in 1841, responded favorably to Father Alexander Czvitkovicz's recruitment efforts for the American missions in 1843, arrived in New York in 1845, and immediately set out for Baltimore.[64] Ordained a priest in December 1846, Anwander was serving as pastor of St. James Church in Baltimore when Neumann proposed that he assume the additional responsibility of directing the Oblate Sisters. Extraordinary powers of persuasion, if not divine inspiration, enabled Anwander to convert Eccleston from his determination to disband the Oblate Sisters. Perhaps just once, in the earnest, pleading eyes of the young priest on his knees before him, Eccleston fathomed the spiritual worth of the first permanent community of African American women religious.

Finally, the Oblate Sisters of Providence had acted on their own behalf. Between 1843 and 1847 they steadfastly observed religious community life, strictly adhered to their vows and community rule, and faithfully attended mass and confession—no longer in the security and convenience of their own chapel but out in distant, public churches. The Oblate Sisters' commitment to their religious state first attracted the notice, then the interest, and finally the admiration of individual priests of the Redemptorist order, who observed the sisters at St. James and St. Alphonsus churches.

In successfully sustaining their internal spiritual integrity during the critical middle years of the 1840s, the Oblate Sisters of Providence precipitated the series of events that effected their revalidation as a legitimate religious constituency by diocesan authorities in Baltimore.

On 7 October 1847 Louis Deluol had accurately informed Redemptorist priest Alexander Czvitkovicz that something had failed. But the failure did not reside with the Oblate Sisters, as Deluol asserted. The failure of the years 1844 through 1847 proved to be that of diocesan authorities to attend the spiritual needs of the Oblate community and the black Catholic laity because of their racial identity. In reflecting on the critical middle years of the 1840s in the Oblate experience, author Grace Sherwood observed, "It had been a wearying, soul trying four years since Father Joubert's death, endured with not only patience but honor! All the doubt, all the disagreement about the Oblates were from without. Within were steadfastness, devotion to the community life, quiet hope that all was not lost. It is a superb story."[65]

In religious life women functioned in permanent association in an exclusively female environment and claimed spirituality—not marriage and maternity—as the primary determinant of their identity. In forming a community of women religious, the Oblate Sisters demonstrated that moral virtue and spiritual fervor among black people occurred not in isolation, but permeated the population sufficiently to motivate a group of black women to claim religious piety as their primary identity. As an institution the Oblate Sisters bore witness to the virtue and spirituality of black women.

Black female agency proved the hallmark of the antebellum Oblate experience. In the signal act of institutionalizing themselves as a community of women religious within the Roman Catholic Church, the Oblate Sisters of Providence converted their religious status into an effective counteridentity with which to resist, to defy, and ultimately to transcend the restrictions and social controls white antebellum society sought to impose on them, predicated on their identity as black women. By their very existence the Oblate Sisters of Providence challenged the American Roman Catholic Church to revise its conventional views of black moral and intellectual capacities and to accommodate a black institutional presence.

NOTES

[1] *The Original Rule and Constitutions of the Oblate Sisters of Providence*, English manuscript copy, Box 41, Archives of the Oblate Sisters of Providence (hereafter cited as AOSP).

[2] John T. Gillard, *Colored Catholics in the United States* (Baltimore: The Josephite Press, 1941), 79–80.

[3] *A Translation of The Original Diary of the Oblate Sisters of Providence*, typescript copy (hereafter cited as *Annals*), 1.

[4] Richard R. Duncan, "Catholics and the Church in the Antebellum Upper South," in *Catholics in the Old South: Essays on Church and Culture*, ed. Randall M. Miller and Jon Wakelyn (Macon, GA: Mercer University Press, 1983), 90; Cyprian Davis, O.S.B., *The History of Black Catholics in the United States* (New York: Crossroad, 1990), 43, 38–39; Barbara Misner, *"Highly Respectable and Accomplished Ladies": Catholic Women Religious in America, 1790–1850* (New York: Garland Publishing, 1988), 75–88.

[5] *Annals* 1:5, AOSP.

[6] Davis, *The History of Black Catholics*, 100; *New Catholic Encyclopedia* (1967), s.v. "Oblates."

[7] *Annals* 1:38–39, AOSP.

[8] Evelyn Brooks Higginbotham, "African American Women's History and the Metalanguage of Race," *Signs* 17, no. 2 (Winter 1992): 264.

[9] For thoughtful treatments of white society's derogation of black women's morality, see Angela Y. Davis, "Reflections on the Black Woman's Role in the Community of Slaves," *The Black Scholar* 3 (December 1971): 3–15; Deborah Gray White, *Ar'n't I a Woman?: Female Slaves in the Antebellum South* (New York: W. W. Norton & Co., 1985), 27–61; Elizabeth Fox-Genovese, *Within the Plantation Household: Black and White Women in the Old South* (Chapel Hill: University of North Carolina Press, 1985), 192–241; Patricia Morton, *Disfigured Images: The Historical Assault on Afro-American Women* (New York: Praeger, 1991), 1–25; Gerda Lerner, ed., *Black Women in White America: A Documentary History* (New York: Vintage Books, 1972), 47–53, 150–71; Darlene Clark Hine, "Rape and the Inner Lives of Black Women: Thoughts on the Culture of Dissemblance," in *HineSight: Black Women and the Re-Construction of American History*, ed. Darlene Clark Hine (New York: Carlson Publishing, 1994), 37–47 (reprinted from *Signs* 14 [Summer 1989]); Paula Giddings, *When and Where I Enter: The Impact of Black Women on Race and Sex in America* (New York: William Morrow, 1984), 31–55; Evelyn Brooks Higginbotham, "African American Women's History and the Metalanguage of Race," *Signs* 17, no. 2 (Winter 1992): 256–66.

[10] *Annals* 1:26, 32, 45, 46, 59, AOSP.

[11] Davis, *The History of Black Catholics*, 101.

[12] *Annals* 1:9; Davis, *The History of Black Catholics*, 100; Thaddeus Posey, "Praying in the Shadows: The Oblate Sisters of Providence, A Look at Nineteenth-Century Black Spirituality," *U.S. Catholic Historian* 12, no.1 (Winter 1994): 25.

[13] "Where He Leads," commemorative pamphlet, n.d., 11, AOSP; *Manumission Documents*, Box 21, AOSP; *Marie Germain: St. Peter's Pro-Cathedral Baptisms*, 1812–19, M1511-5, p. 230, AAB microfilm, MdHR.

[14] *Original Rule*, AOSP.

[15] Ibid.

[16] *Metropolitan Catholic Calendar and Laity's Directory* (Baltimore: Fielding Lucas, 1834), 65–71; *Original Rule*, AOSP.

[17] *Original Rule*, AOSP.

[18] Evelyn Brooks Higginbotham, *Righteous Discontent: The Women's Movement in the Black Baptist Church* (Cambridge: Harvard University Press, 1993), 192.

[19] *Annals* 1:57, 66–67, 74, 77, 79, 85, 87, 92–96; *Annals* 2: 25 August 1842; 30 October 1842; 20 November 1842; 18 December 1842; 22 January 1843; *Annals* 2: 26 February 1843; 1, 5, 9, 15, 19 March 1843; 9, 13, 23 April 1843; 25, 28, May 1843; 8, 14 September 1843; 8, 15, 29 October 1843; 1, 5 November 1843.

[20] *Annals* 1:95.

[21] *Annals* 2: 15 June 1843.

[22] Ibid., 29 October 1843.

[23] Ibid., 7 November 1843.

[24] Ibid., 20 August 1843.

[25] Ibid., 10 September 1843.

[26] Ibid., 12 September 1843; French text of incomplete English translation for 3 September 1843; *Cathedral Records from the Beginning of Catholicity in Baltimore to the Present Time* (Baltimore: The Catholic Mirror Publishing Company, 1906), 65.

[27] Quote taken from *Annals* 2: 8 October 1843; 9 October 1842; *Annals* 1:32, 37, 42–43, 45, 51, 59, 71, 79, 86.

[28] *Annals* 2: 29 October 1843.

[29] Ibid., 8 November 1843.

[30] "Excerpts from Louis R. Deluol's Diary concerning the Oblate Sisters of Providence," comp. John W. Bowen, S.S. (Baltimore: Sulpician Archives) [hereafter cited as SAB], 8 November 1843.

[31] *Annals* 2: 5 December 1843 (French text).

[32] Sister M. Theresa Catherine Willigman, O.S.P., "A Few Facts Relating to the Oblate Sisters of Providence of Baltimore, Maryland," typescript copy, 6, AOSP.

[33] Quotes taken from Deluol to Charles Carroll's granddaughter, n.d., RG 24, Box 9, SAB; for Deluol's ownership of slaves, see "Article of Agreement," RG 1, Box 7, SAB, cited in Loretta M. Butler, *History of Black Catholics in the Archdiocese of Washington, D.C. 1634–1898: A Select Bibliography of Works Located in Maryland and Washington, D.C. Archives and Libraries* (Washington DC: Office of Black Catholics of the Archdiocese of Washington, 1984), 8.

[34] Daughters of Charity—St. Joseph Provincial House, Emmitsburg, Maryland, Letters III, Deluol to George, 15 November 1839 and 28 November 1839, cited in Misner, *"Highly Respectable and Accomplished Ladies,"* 78–79.

[35] All quotes taken from Mary Ewens, O.P., *The Role of the Nun in Nineteenth-Century America* (Salem, NH: Ayer Company Publishers, 1984), 34, 107, 118, 206; Misner, *"Highly Respectable and Accomplished Ladies,"* 101–2.

[36] *Annals* 2: under date 1847.

[37] Grace Sherwood, *The Oblates' Hundred and One Years* (New York: Macmillan, 1931), 109–10, 114; Thomas Spalding, *The Premier See: A History of the Archdiocese of Baltimore, 1789–1989* (Baltimore: The Johns Hopkins University Press, 1989), 137–38.

[38] *Annals* 1:95; *Annals* 2: 14, 21 July 1843; Spalding, *The Premier See*, 137.

[39] *Annals* 1:116–17.

[40] Father Schakert is Peter Czackert, variously spelled Chakert or Tchackert. M. Rosalita Kelly, I.H.M., *No Greater Service: The History of the Congregation of the Sisters, Servants of the Immaculate Heart of Mary, Monroe, Michigan, 1845–1945* (Detroit: Congregation of the Sisters of the Immaculate Heart, 1948), 45.

[41] Ibid., 45–46; M. Immaculata Gillespie, C.I.M., *Mother M. Theresa Maxis Duchemin* (Scranton, PA: Marywood College, 1945), 27.

[42] *Annals* 2: 9 September 1845, 1847.

[43] M. Theresa Catherine Willigman, O.S.P., "Memories of Sister Theresa Duchemin," typescript copy, n.d. 3–4, AOSP.

[44] Ibid., 3.

[45] *Annals* 2: 9 September 1845; under date 1847; Willigman, "Memories," 4, AOSP.

[46] Deluol's Diary, 13 October 1844, 22 November 1844, SAB.

[47] Willigman, "Memories," 3, AOSP.

[48] Charles G. Herbermann, *The Sulpicians in the United States* (New York: The Encyclopedia Press, 1916), 236; Spalding, *The Premier See*, 148–49; Sherwood, *The Oblates' Hundred and One Years*, 117; Christopher J. Kauffman, *Tradition and Transformation in Catholic Culture: The Priests of Saint Sulpice in the United States from 1791 to the Present* (New York: Macmillan, 1988), 127–29.

[49] Eccleston to De Courson, 5 August 1849, RG 29, Box 8, SAB.

[50] L. W. Reilly, "A Famous Convent of Colored Sisters," *Annales Congregationis SS. Redemptoris* (Provinciae Americanae, Supplementum, Pars II, 1903), 109–10.

[51] Spalding, *The Premier See*, 128.

[52] *Annals* 2: 8 November 1843.

[53] *Annals* 2: 9 September 1845.

[54] Ibid., 3 June 1847; Willigman, "Memories," 3, AOSP.

[55] M. Theresa Catherine Willigman, O.S.P., "First Foundress of the Oblates," typescript copy, n.d., 13, AOSP.

[56] Deluol's Diary, 19 April 1844, SAB.

[57] Sister Maria Alma, C.I.M., *The Reverend Louis Florent Gillet: His Life, Letters, and Conferences* (Philadelphia: The Dolphin Press, 1940), 136.

[58] Anwander to Sourin, 27 March 1876, AOSP.

[59] *Metropolitan Catholic Calendar and Laity's Directory*, 69–70.

[60] Deluol's Diary, 7 October 1847, SAB.

[61] Anwander to Sourin, 27 March 1876, AOSP.

[62] Sherwood, *The Oblates' Hundred and One Years*, 114–16; Michael J. Curley, C.SS.R., *Venerable John Neumann, C.SS.R.: Fourth Bishop of Philadelphia* (Washington DC: The Catholic University of America Press, 1952), 134.

[63] Deluol's Diary, 7 October 1847; Willigman, "A Few Facts," 6–7, 3; Reilly, "A Famous Convent of Colored Sisters," 111; Spalding, *The Premier See*, 149.

[64] Sherwood, *The Oblates' Hundred and One Years*, 112–14.

[65] Ibid., 118.

Chapter 3

Henriette Delille

Servant of Slaves, Witness to the Poor

CYPRIAN DAVIS, O.S.B.

Henriette Delille was born in 1812 in New Orleans. She was born into a city that Gwendolyn Midlo Hall called the most African city in America.[1] We could also call New Orleans a Latin city, a Catholic city, a slave center, and a city of easy virtue. Founded in 1718, New Orleans was named in honor of Philippe, the duke of Orléans. The city was begun by the Company of the Indies, which was the commercial organization that owned and exploited the territory of Louisiana. Pierre LeMoyne and Jean-Baptiste LeMoyne were the two Canadian adventurers and explorers who helped create both the Louisiana Colony and the city of New Orleans. Pierre is better known by the patent of nobility that made him the Sieur d'Iberville and his brother, Jean-Baptiste, who was also ennobled, was better known as the Sieur de Bienville.

Both the colony and New Orleans itself were a financial headache for France. Compelled to search for settlers, the French government was reduced to rounding up criminals and prostitutes from Paris and elsewhere to be sent to populate both the colony and the city of New Orleans. Although in the beginning many Native Americans were reduced to slavery for the colonists, it was the importation of African slaves, beginning in 1717, that grew in number and extent as the agricultural demands increased.[2]

France lost its colony to Spain at the close of the Seven Years' War (1756–63) and Louisiana passed to Spanish control. Although the population remained French speaking, the governing council was the *cabildo*, the officials were Spanish, and the legal system was Spanish. The Spanish left their mark, especially regarding the church. In 1801 Spain returned Louisiana to France. Thomas Jefferson, third president of the United States, wanted the port of New Orleans, one of the largest in the

47

South, for the United States. Napoleon realized that he could not defend New Orleans against the British, and in 1803 he sold Louisiana to the United States for almost fifteen million dollars.

When Henriette Delille was born, New Orleans had been American for almost a decade. At the time of the purchase Louisiana had a total of approximately thirty-six thousand people: thirteen thousand slaves, seventeen hundred free blacks, and twenty-one thousand whites. Henriette was born a free woman of color. Thanks to the extensive paper trail left by the bureaucracy of French and Spanish officialdom, combined with the sacramental registers of the Catholic Church, we are able to trace the lineage of at least one-half of the genealogy of Henriette Delille. Notaries in eighteenth-century Europe were lawyers who registered a wide variety of legal acts, both financial and commercial. To buy or sell land, to buy and sell slaves, to draw up the provisions of a will, and to witness contractual arrangements, one had to appear and register the action before a notary. The record was placed within the notarial bindings according to dates and names; these are now kept in the notarial archives both in the city of New Orleans and in the provincial archives. Thanks to the extensive array of legal papers pertaining to the life and activity of Henriette Delille, the details of her life and works can be pieced together.

THE FAMILY

Henriette Delille was the great-great-granddaughter of an African slave woman whose name was Nanette. Nanette had three children by her owner, Claude Joseph Villars Dubreuil. He was one of the richest landowners in Louisiana. Much of his land later became part of the city of New Orleans. Originally from Dijon in France, he arrived in Louisiana in 1718 and received a concession of land from Bienville.

Dubreuil, who was also an engineer, was responsible for digging the first canals and the construction of levees as well as the construction of the third convent for the Ursuline nuns, which in time was converted into the bishop's residence and now houses the present-day ecclesiastical archives. He was one of the first to cultivate indigo, plant sugar cane, and raise tobacco. When Dubreuil died in 1757, he had become one of the most important figures in early New Orleans history.[3]

On October 1, 1770, Nanette came before the notary, Andres Almonaster y Roxas. She had in her hand a piece of paper, known as the *carta de libertad*. This piece of paper—the certificate of freedom—showed that she had been freed from slavery in 1763 by Claude Joseph Villars

Dubreuil, the son of Claude senior, the father of Nanette's children. The act drawn up before the notary Andres Almonaster announced that she was buying her daughter, named Cécile, and Cécile's children, Henriette and Narcisse. Legally, they would still be slaves until she could free them.[4]

Under Spanish law a slave could avail himself or herself of a provision known as *coartación*, meaning that the slave had the right to ask the owner for a price for his or her freedom. If the owner refused, the court could order a third party to make the assessment. Once the price for freedom was obtained, the slave could work to raise the funds for the *carta de libertad* or borrow money to pay the price.[5] This is what Nanette had done. Once freed, Nanette raised twenty-eight hundred livres (two thousand and some dollars) for her daughter and two of her grandchildren. She was a very resourceful woman.

Cécile was the great-grandmother of Henriette Delille. She died in 1815, when Henriette was two or three years old. Her grandmother, the daughter of Cécile, was Henriette Laveau. Some have suggested that she was related to the famous Marie Laveau. Marie Josephe or Josephine was the mother of Henriette, one of eight children born to Henriette Laveau.

The family of Henriette Delille belonged to that section of the Louisiana population known as the free people of color. These were the descendants of black slaves and white slave owners. The slave owners very often freed their children or enabled them to obtain their freedom. Many of these children were light skinned. In a city like New Orleans the movement from bondage to freedom was as simple as crossing a very narrow line. In other words, one could speak of a kind of twilight zone in which those in servitude lived very much like those already freed. These slaves who lived on their own with or without permission simply passed over into the world of freedom.

The free people of color formed a group among themselves. They were often entrepreneurs, shop owners, craftsmen, tavern keepers, tailors, musicians, morticians, hunters, and sailors. Many free women of color were peddlers, cooks, laundry women, dressmakers, housekeepers, and also prostitutes. In a sense they were the backbone of the local economy, and many owned land. Henriette Delille's family owned a large amount of property in the French Quarter. Not a few free people of color were wealthy. Thomy Lafon, one of the best-known philanthropists in the nineteenth century, was a good example of a free man of color who gave much of his money to charity, including to the Sisters of the Holy Family. Finally, the free people of color often owned slaves, that is, one or two domestics or servants.[6]

It is strange to talk about blacks owning slaves or even freed slaves being slave owners. The recent novel *The Known World* by Edward Jones gives us a picture of slaveholding blacks and their mentality.[7] Historians have noted that slaveholding by free blacks was often the result of one of three factors: First, free blacks sought to purchase the freedom of their children or grandchildren, as was the case with Nanette. As will be explained later, it was not easy to manumit a slave. Often enough a man or woman who was free would purchase a spouse from the slave owner. Legally, the spouse became the slave of the future bride or groom but also a wife or a husband with whom they could marry and raise a family. Oftentimes the legal condition of the husband or wife might not be generally known.

Another reason for free blacks to own slaves was that from time to time when difficult situations developed with white slave owners, slaves sought a black person to purchase them in order to improve their condition. Finally, it was also the case that blacks owned slaves for the same reason that whites owned slaves: they used them, they exploited their labor; they purchased them for a price and improved them physically and sold them for a higher price. This was speculation in human merchandise.

Many free women of color had an alliance with well-to-do white men. In Louisiana the system was known as *plaçage*. An arrangement was made between a young woman of color—beautiful and perhaps very cultured—and a white gentleman. Although marriage was legally prohibited, this arrangement or alliance was more than a casual affair. The young woman and the children sometimes lived with the white gentleman. There was no recognition by law or blessing by the church, but in this Catholic city the situation was not considered either immoral or shameful.[8]

This was the situation of practically all of Henriette Delille's male ancestors in each generation. It was the case of Cécile Bonille, Henriette Delille's sister. Cécile had an alliance with Samuel Hart, a wealthy Jewish merchant in New Orleans. She was eighteen when she began life together with Samuel Hart, who was then fifty-three. He had four children by Cécile. He died in 1832, leaving a large amount of money to Cécile. Although the law recognized the right of natural children to have some claim on the inheritance of their father, the woman did not necessarily have this right. Samuel Hart's family in Europe contested the will successfully, but Cécile was able to win a comfortable settlement, thanks to the effort of her attorney, John Slidell, the future Confederate statesman.

Marie Josephe (also known as Josephine) had three children by different fathers. Clever and resourceful, despite the fact that she could not write, she bought and sold several slaves. At one point she was declared insane and given a guardian but was later released. She died in 1848. Her illiteracy did not prevent her from owning property and profiting therefrom.

Juan Bonille, the father of Cécile, was living in Cuba when she drew up her will in 1841, just before she died about the age of twenty-eight. Marie Josephe had a son, named Jean Delille, Henriette's older brother, who lived much of his life as a planter in St. Martinville. About all that is known about the father of Jean Delille and Henriette Delille is that he was named Jean Delille. Who was he? Was he white? Why does he not figure in all of the legal papers drawn up before the notaries that present a picture of Henriette's family? He appears only once, and that is on the marriage record of Jean Delille, who was married in St. Martinville on December 28, 1830.[9]

There is good reason to believe that Jean Delille, the father of Jean and Henriette, was Jean-Baptiste Delille-Sarpy, from a well-known family of merchants in the Louisiana colony who were originally from southern France near the Spanish frontier. The Sarpy family had many brothers, and many were named John. The Sarpy family also used many variations of Delille-Sarpy. All were involved in some business venture. Some were wealthy; others were not very well off. What is certain is that Henriette Delille did know who her father was, but that her father played no real part in the life of the family.

Henriette Delille's family was typical of a family of free people of color. They were not poor, and they owned and perhaps trafficked in the buying and selling of slaves. They were related in one way or another to most of the extended families of the free people of color throughout New Orleans. From all indications they were not deeply religious. The notarial archives are filled with extensive legal papers listing the names of Henriette Delille, her immediate family, and the large extended family who signed and counter-signed the documents and gradually revealed the outlines of this rather unusual extensive family.

THE VOCATION

In 1836, when Henriette was in her twenty-fifth year, she evidently had some kind of religious experience. She wrote in French on the fly leaf of one of the small book of devotions that she had in her possession a fervent declaration of her relationship to God. First there is the statement that the book was hers and then the date: "This book belongs to henriette [sic] Delille. May 2nd, 1836." Then she continues in French: "I hope in God. I love. I wish to live and to die for God." It does not seem that this is simply a pious thought or a short pious prayer. The statements are not balanced but are short, concise declarations about life and death. If one believes in God and then hopes in God, the next statement would logically read "I love God," but it does not; it is simply "I love."

There is a tear in the fly leaf. Part of the verb "to wish" is illegible. The presumption is that the verb is "to wish" because the text has *je v—*. The likely word is *veux;* however, it could just as well be *je vais*, that is, "I am going to. . . ." Thus, the text could read, "I wish to love and die for God." It could also be "I am going to live and die for God." In other words, it could be a statement of intent. In my opinion there is reason enough to see a young woman almost twenty-five years old declaring her undying love for God and the intention to give her life and to love unto death. It is now her vocation. This written statement could very well be a written covenant with God and the result of a mystical experience. Written into her book of meditations, she would have before her this written covenant, this statement of undying love for God and her experience of God.

We know little about the early years of Henriette Delille. The notarial acts give some idea of the family's financial and real-estate transactions. We do know that she was the youngest of the family of Marie Josephe Dias, and that she was close to her half-sister, Cécile, who died in 1841. Henriette's mother died in 1848.

It is not clear where Henriette received her education, as education for young people of color was uncertain and informal in pre–Civil War New Orleans. At the end of the eighteenth century the Ursuline nuns permitted girls of color to receive religious instruction in their school as long as they were taught separately from the white students. They even went so far as to permit legitimate daughters of a white father and a quadroon mother to receive an education in their school. Michael Portier, who became bishop of Mobile in 1826, reported back to France that he gave religious instruction to young people of color. A certain Sister Ste-Marthe Fontière, a religious sister from a community known as Les Dames Hospitalières from Belley in France, came to New Orleans with eight other women in 1823. Sister Ste-Marthe began a school on St. Claude Street for young girls of color that same year. In the beginning she had as many as eighty pupils. By 1826,the St. Claude School was in financial difficulty, and by 1831 Sister Ste-Marthe returned to France. She came back to New Orleans the following year. It is not clear whether she gave the school to the bishop of New Orleans or sold it. What is clear is that another remarkable woman, Marie Jeanne Aliquot, a recent arrival from a rather well-known family from the south of France, acquired another building known as the Collège of Orléans, which was turned into the new St. Claude School. She had a sister who was a member of the Ursuline nuns. A determined woman, at times a difficult woman, and a controversial figure, but totally devoted to black people, both slave and free, she acquired the college and opened another school for young girls of color. Mlle. Aliquot sold the school to the Ursuline nuns, who in turn sold it to the Sisters of Mount Carmel, also originally from France. By 1839, although the St. Claude School was the object of discord and anger among Aliquot, the Ursulines, and the Carmelite Sisters, there were still nearly eighty students in the school. At that time Henriette Delille was twenty-nine years old. More than likely, she had been a student at the St. Claude School, and, in fact, she may have been teaching at the school.

When in 1836 Henriette Delille inscribed a dedication in one of her books, she may not have realized that she had started on the road of her lifelong vocation. The book she inscribed was a work in French by the Countess de Carcado, a very devout noblewoman who had written many works of devotion. The work entitled *The Soul United to Jesus Christ in the Most Holy Sacrament of the Altar*, first published in Paris in 1830, was typical of the devotional literature of the time.[10] It is also a reminder that in this period most people did not receive communion daily. Thus they visited the Blessed Sacrament and adored Christ in the Eucharist. Seemingly, at this time the young Henriette Delille was living a life of greater devotion and deeper prayer.

Another written text reveals the increasing devotion of this young woman. The earliest document in the archives of the Sisters of the Holy Family is a notebook in French containing the list of names and donors. The year 1859 has been placed at the beginning of the list. The purpose of the list of names is not clear. Certainly these are names of those who gave offerings of money. Some of the names are of persons we recognize. This list, however, is not as important as another text written in the middle of this little notebook. This text, also written in French and in the handwriting of Henriette Delille, follows here:

> The Rules and Regulations
> For the Congregation of the Sisters
> Of the Presentation of the Blessed Virgin
> Mary under the invocation of Mary V.S.P.
> Founded in New Orleans
> The 21st of November 1836.

For the purpose
1. to care for the sick
2. to succor the poor
3. to instruct the ignorant.

There are three chapters; "chapter two" as a heading is omitted by inadvertence. The first chapter lists the officials who form the council. The second chapter describes the spirit of the community and its purpose, and the third chapter describes the religious practices. The Presentation of the Blessed Virgin is a devotion based on an apocryphal biblical text widespread in eighteenth-century piety. As a child Mary was supposed to have been given over to be raised in the Temple in Jerusalem where she lived and prayed during her girlhood. These sisters renewed their consecration every year on November 24, the Feast of the Presentation.

At first glance this would seem to be the rules for a community of religious sisters. Further examination makes it clear that this is the description of a community of pious women who did not live together, had no religious vows, and were often married with a family. They were laywomen who gathered together on specific occasions, who ministered to the poor, and who supported one another.

The *Catholic Directory* of 1850 documents the existence of three charitable associations of laypersons in New Orleans: the society of the Ladies of Providence *(les dames de providence)*, the young Ladies of Providence *(les demoiselles de providence)*, and finally, "an association of colored persons, for the nursing of the sick and destitute."[11] This unnamed charitable association was the Sisters of the Presentation. In 1836, in the same year in which Henriette made known her desire to give herself totally to God, she began not a religious community but a society of pious women, the first of its kind among black people in Louisiana. The two white communities of pious laywomen, the Ladies of Providence, had a structure that was almost identical to the structure and activity of the Sisters of the Presentation.

Two years after the commencement of the Sisters of the Presentation, Henriette Delille appears in three records related to the sacraments and the instruction of slaves and former slaves. In January 1838, in St. Mary's Church, she signed the register as witness to the marriage of Jean Garièhr, a free black, and Loiza, the slave of a Monsieur Latour. Two months later, in March, Henriette witnessed a marriage between a French national, born in Le Havre, France, and a native of New Orleans whose mother was named Gaudin and was born in Haiti. The entry indicates that the marriage was between a French man who was white and a woman of color of Haitian origin. The priest who witnessed it was a P. Amand. For reasons that are not quite clear, these records signed by P. Amand were kept separate from the others. This suggests that the records dealt with delicate matters such as the marriage between a white person (in this instance a French man) and a person of color (in this instance a woman named Gaudin originally from Haiti). Juliette Gaudin, whose mother was originally from Haiti, was a constant companion of Henriette when she began the religious community.[12]

The following month Henriette acted as the sponsor of Marie Thérèse Dagon, who had been baptized by Père Rousselon, who also acted as godfather. Henriette signed as godmother. The baptism took place in the chapel of the St. Claude Convent, the house of the Carmelite sisters and the school. Marie Thérèse was fifteen years old.[13] Presumably, Henriette had instructed her. Moreover, she was perhaps a student at the school where Henriette was teaching and where Rousselon was at the time the chaplain. What we have here is the certitude that Henriette Delille was working as a witness for the baptism and the marriage of slaves and people of color. This would be her future ministry. It is also clear that Henriette was already working with Père Rousselon.

THE BEGINNING OF RELIGIOUS LIFE

Etienne Rousselon was originally from Lyons in southern France. Born in 1800, he was ordained a priest in 1827. He was rector in the minor seminary in Lyons and a close friend of Antoine Blanc (who later was named bishop of New Orleans), whom he served as vicar general.[14] Rousselon came to the United States in 1837, and in 1841 Bishop Blanc began plans to build the church of St. Augustine in the Trémé neighborhood just outside the French Quarter. It was an area that was growing in numbers. Here Henriette Delille and her constant companion, Juliette Gaudin, and later Josephine Charles, would begin their religious life not far from the church, which opened its doors in 1842.

In the meantime, Antoine Blanc, now bishop of New Orleans, had written to the Congregation of the Propaganda requesting that Henriette and the Sisters of the Presentation, a "certain group of pious women, called to works of piety, in serving the sick, assisting the dying, and teaching adolescent girls, etc., under the title of the Congregation of the Presentation of the Blessed Virgin Mary . . . be affiliated to the congregation which exists in Rome . . . under the title of the Annunciation." This group of pious women was thereby affiliated with the Sodality of the

Annunciation in Rome. In this way the status of the sodality was placed on solid ground as one of the oldest sodalities in Louisiana.[15]

The Sisters of the Holy Family would always look to the year 1842 as the date of its foundation as a religious community, according to oral tradition. Even though there seems to be no documentary evidence that points to a beginning in the year 1842, it is clearly evident that between 1842 and 1851 there was a gradual development from a group of pious women to the creation of a religious congregation. The movement from a group of pious women to a religious congregation is the trajectory of many religious orders of women.

Henriette and Juliette began their religious life with a small dwelling on St. Bernard Street but quickly moved to a provisional dwelling on Hospital Street, which would later be called Bayou Road. Juliette Gaudin, born in Cuba in 1808, was four years older than Henriette. Her mother, Marie Thérèse Lacardonie, a free woman of color, was born in Haiti and died in New Orleans in 1837. Juliette's father, Pierre Gaudin, born in the southwest of France, was a schoolteacher in New Orleans. Her parents were not married. Juliette was well educated and was a faithful friend of Henriette. Josephine Charles, a free woman of color from New Orleans, joined the foundation house on Bayou Road in 1843. She would be the organizer of the Sisters of the Holy Family after the death of Henriette.[16]

From 1845 to 1860 the names of the three women, Henriette, Juliette, and Josephine, began to appear as sponsors for slaves of all ages, for free people of color, and as witnesses to marriages of slaves at St. Augustine, St. Mary's, and also the cathedral. By 1847 the charitable work of these three women was backed by an organization of men and women who would be known as the Association of the Holy Family. In the beginning Henriette Delille served as president. The organization opened a building known as the Hospice of the Society of the Holy Family. While the existence of the association raises questions that at present cannot be answered, the documents seem to indicate that the management of the association moved away from control by Henriette Delille. It seems that the Sisters of the Presentation might have developed into the association and have become more than a group of pious women.

THE CONSTITUTIONS AND RULES

The earliest printed text in the archives of the Holy Family is a leaflet entitled "Provisional Constitutions of the Sisters of the Holy Family."[17] This text was approved in 1876 by Archbishop Perché and signed by

Gilbert Raymond, the vicar general, as administrator. What is important about this printed text is that it gives the earliest definite date for the foundation of the Sisters of the Holy Family. The text reads:

> They [the sisters] shall have a total devotion for the Sovereign Pontiff; and they shall recognize after the Sovereign Pontiff, Monseigneur Blanc, archbishop of New Orleans and their venerated Vicar General, Monsieur Rousselon, as the beloved founders of their little community nearly 25 years ago.[18]

Twenty-five years earlier would have been 1851. Thus in 1851 the Sisters of the Holy Family were founded by Bishop Blanc and Père Rousselon. One might wish that the name of Henriette Delille had been added to that of the bishop and the vicar general, but her will states clearly her position in the foundation of the Sisters of the Holy Family.

One of the troubling issues in this foundation has been the question of novitiate and vows. The earliest histories of the Sisters of the Holy Family state that Henriette made her novitiate with the Religious of the Sacred Heart in St. James Parish. Unfortunately, there are no documents to corroborate this assertion. Although the sisters had many slaves, it would be unlikely that Henriette would have been placed in the community itself. It is possible that the community created an informal situation that could have served as a novitiate and that Henriette returned to New Orleans to make her vows. The earliest histories recount that both Juliette and Josephine made their vows with Henriette. It is more likely that the three women made their vows as private vows and that they were repeated later as public religious vows.

There is no question, however, that by 1851 these three women were living in a convent as religious women. Unfortunately, there are no documents that describe the details of their religious life. We have no sense of a horarium or of common prayer, or even of a habit. In fact, we know that the black sisters wore no religious habit on the streets of New Orleans until the 1870s. What we do have is a collection of about seventy-four books published between 1807 and 1859 that are now in the archives, books that seemingly were part of the original library of the nascent community in the time of Henriette Delille. Some of the books have the names of either Henriette Delille (about four) or Juliette Gaudin (about twenty). No books bear the name of Josephine Charles. All are in French with the exception of two liturgical books. A large folio-size bible written in the classical French of the seventeenth century (the translation of Isaac Le Maistre de Sacy) was probably used for oral reading for common prayer and at table. A small copy of the New

Testament in Latin, bound with a Latin translation of *The Imitation of Christ* with no name inscribed therein, may very well have been a personal copy belonging to Juliette. Many of the works of spirituality, including those by St. Teresa of Avila and St. Francis de Sales, have the name of Juliette on the inside cover. At some time or another the books with the name of Père Rousselon became part of the original collection. What is most important is that the collection of books that seemed to have been part of the original library collection before the Civil War reveals a level of spirituality and education equal to the collection of any other French-speaking community in pre–Civil War New Orleans.

THE THREE WILLS OF HENRIETTE DELILLE

In May 1851 Henriette Delille lay ill in the provisional convent located at the time on Condé Street (Chartres Street today). The notary, Octave de Armas, arrived at her bedside accompanied by several male witnesses to draw up a will. Henriette bequeathed all of the property on Bayou Road, that is, the convent, which was in her name, to Antoine Blanc, the archbishop of New Orleans, and to his successors. She declared that this property was for the religious instruction of "the poor and the ignorant," a work known as "the Children of the Holy Family." She bequeathed to her brother, Jean Delille, living at St. Martinville, her slave named Betsy along with the sum of $867. She left her linens, household furnishings, and other items to Juliette Gaudin.

This first will drawn up by Henriette reveals three important facts. First, she was the leader in whose name the convent on Bayou Road was constructed. Second, the work for the poor and the ignorant was begun by her initiative and was to continue under the authority of the archbishop. Finally, and perhaps most surprising, Henriette owned a slave named Betsy. This is the first indication that she owned a slave. It seems certain that Betsy did not live on Bayou Road. Either she lived on her own or was already in St. Martinville.[19]

A year and a half later, in 1852, Henriette drew up a second will. Once again she bequeathed to Archbishop Blanc the property on Bayou Road and the work that she had founded for the poor and the ignorant of "population of color." She stipulated that Juliette Gaudin was to have the right to live there for the rest of her life. She again made mention of linens and other furnishings, which were to go to Juliette. She made her brother "her sole heir and universal legatee." She granted liberty to Betsy; nevertheless, Betsy was to remain in the service of Jean, Henriette's brother, "up to the day when she could be freed without being bound to leave Louisiana."[20]

Although Betsy had been freed by Henriette, this could not go into effect because by 1852 freed slaves in Louisiana had to leave the state under penalty of being re-enslaved. There is no evidence as to the identity of Betsy; more than likely, Betsy was a slave that Henriette acquired, perhaps at the request of Betsy herself. By this time Louisiana, like many other Southern states, wished to curtail the number of freed slaves in order to minimize their influence on the slave population in the state. As elsewhere, Louisiana introduced several measures to drive out the freed black population. If Betsy was a woman of considerable age or with a number of dependents, the prospect of pulling up stakes and leaving Louisiana might have been a considerable burden. Henriette's stipulation regarding the status of Betsy was more than likely in keeping with the desire of Betsy herself.

In 1860 Henriette drew up her last will on December 10. In less than two weeks South Carolina would secede from the Union and the nation would move into the Civil War. Archbishop Blanc had died, and his successor had not yet been named. Still, Henriette confirmed the fact that she had founded her work, and she mentioned again the personal linens and furnishings to be left to Juliette; there was no mention of Josephine. Finally, she left instructions that Jean was to free her slave Betsy. At this time it was no longer possible to manumit a slave. It may be that Henriette felt that at this critical juncture, on the verge of war, slavery would not last. Can one say that this third will, drawn up by a woman who was in very bad health, was most of all a statement of hope?

In the census of 1850 the records indicate that two persons lived on Bayou Road: Henriette and Juliette. Within ten years the scene had changed completely. The census for 1860 names seven persons living on Bayou Road. The list with the names spelled by the census takers follows:

Juliette Godin	49	Sisters of Charity
Henriette De Lyle	60	Superior
Josephine Charles	36	Sisters of Charity
Josephine Vecque	57	
Suzanne Navarre	27	
Henriette Fazende	57	
Orfise Romain	46	

In the left margin is written: "Asylum for blind and Destitute Negroes. By the Sisters of Charity." Juliette's birthplace is given as Cuba; for

Henriette, Josephine Charles, Josephine Vecque, Henriette Fazende, and Orfise Romain, Louisiana; finally, for Suzanne Navarre, New York. The age of Henriette was given as sixty; in fact, she was fifty, but her state of health had aged her considerably. Juliette's age was given as forty-nine, although she was fifty-two. Josephine Charles was listed as thirty-six years old, but in reality she was about fifty.

Four black women who were ex-slaves under the care of the women identified as Sisters of Charity were listed as living in the house next door.

Name	Age	Race	Origin
Ant__I_zette	60	Black	St. Domingue
Julie Beau__ois	40	Black	St. Domingue
Marianne	90	Black	Louisiana
Charlotte	115	Black	Guinea

The census records of 1860 provide a concrete example of the ministry that Henriette had begun and had fought so hard to maintain. Here, less than a year before the Civil War, there were four new members of a religious community, already named the Sisters of Charity by the people themselves. Later the title would be Sisters of the Holy Family.

In many ways Henriette Delille is an elusive figure. We have no letters from her, no written notes or memos, nothing of flesh and blood to reveal her humanity, her feelings, or her intimate thoughts. Only two letters remain from her very young niece, living at the time in Chicago. The first was written in the summer of 1860 and the second in January of 1861. She mentions the imminent war and the call for peace, the desire to see Henriette, who was both cousin and godmother, whose wisdom and advice she so badly needed. Her name was Ella Bell. Her grandmother was the half-sister of Henriette Delille's mother.

To the surprise of many, the port of New Orleans was captured by the Union Navy in April 1862, and as a result, New Orleans became an occupied city. The reaction of whites was consternation, bitterness, and dismay. They were faced with economic ruin and social catastrophe. On the other hand, the slaves very quickly rallied to the Union cause. The more radical shift among the free people of color developed more slowly. Rousselon wrote lurid accounts of how the whites were suffering in his letters to Jean-Marie Odin, the newly appointed archbishop of New Orleans, who was in Europe at the beginning of the Civil War. He predicted that the slaves would rise up and massacre their former masters. His attitude was typical of the feeling of the white Catholics and the Catholic clergy. There was seemingly no sympathy for or interest in the plight of the slaves or the feelings of the free people of color. At this time only one priest championed the cause of the black population. This was Claude Pascal Maistre (1820–75), the pastor of St. Rose of Lima Church. Maistre would later be suspended by Archbishop Odin.

There is no indication of how the fledgling community of Henriette Delille reacted during this time, whether or not it was in solidarity with the cause of the blacks of New Orleans. Nor do its members emerge as sympathizers with the white population. More than likely they passed over to the cause of the free people of color. Growing more radical every day, aligning themselves with the Union army quartered in the city, the former Louisiana National Guard became an all-black regiment under General Butler. These soldiers were from the same milieu as were the sisters and their pupils.

It was in the midst of turmoil, confusion, and bitterness that Henriette Delille slipped quietly away on November 17, 1862. Her death was not recorded in the municipal records, but the register of the cemetery indicated that she died of tuberculosis. Her obituary did appear in the Catholic newspapers. It was duly noted that she had begun her work about 1850.

Henriette Delille lived and died in a time of trial and trouble, of poverty and pain. In a time when human dignity and human freedom were sacrificed in the slave market, she made her choices. From the time of her youth she recognized where God was calling her, and she chose not to follow the moral ambivalence chosen by women of her race and class. In a world where life was cheap and success was material advancement, she chose the gospel values of charity and justice. At the end of her short life she made it clear that the religious family that became the Sisters of the Holy Family was her idea, her work, and her inspiration. As she said, "I am going to live and die for God." And so she did.

NOTES

[1] Gwendolyn Midlo Hall, "The Formation of Afro-Creole Culture," in *Creole New Orleans: Race and Americanization*, ed. Arnold Hirsch and Joseph Logsdon (Baton Rouge: Louisiana State University Press, 1992), 58.

[2] Gwendolyn Midlo Hall, *Africans in Colonial Louisiana: The Development of Afro-Creole Culture in the Eighteenth Century* (Baton Rouge: Louisiana State University Press, 1952), 5–8.

[3] Henry P. Dart, "The Career of Dubreuil in French Louisiana," *Louisiana Historical Quarterly* 18 (1935): 267–331.

[4] Notarial Archives of New Orleans (hereafter NONA)/Almonaster y Roxas, 1770, October 1, 205b–7a (four pages).

[5] Judith Kelleher Shafer, *Slavery, the Civil Law, and the Supreme Court of Louisiana* (Baton Rouge: Louisiana State University, 1994), 2–3.

[6] Kimberly Hanger, *Bounded Lives, Bounded Places, Free Black Society in Colonial New Orleans. 1769–1803* (Durham, NC: Duke University Press, 1997); see also "Avenues to Freedom. Open to New Orleans' Black Population, 1769–1779," *Louisiana History* 31 (1990): 237–64.

[7] Edward P. Jones, *The Known World* (New York: Harper Collins/Amistad Press, 2003).

[8] Henry E. Sterkx, *The Free Negro in Ante-Bellum Louisiana* (Rutherford, NJ: Fairleigh Dickinson University Press, 1972), 248–51.

[9] St. Martin's Church, *Marriage Records, 1825–1836,* VII, no. 167 (St. Martinville, Louisiana).

[10] This work by the Countess de Carcado is found in the Archives of the Sisters of the Holy Family (SSF Archives). The title of the book is *L'Ame Unie à Jésus Christ dans le très saint sacrament de l'autel,* vol. 2 (Paris: Méquignon Junior Librairie de la Faculté de Théologie, 1830).

[11] *Metropolitan Catholic Almanac and Laity's Directory* (Baltimore: Fielding Lucas, Jr., 1849), 139.

[12] Archives of the Archdiocese of New Orleans (hereafter AANO), *St. Mary Marriages, 1805–1880,* no. 39; for the Amand Letters, see University of Notre Dame Archives, V-4-9.

[13] Ursuline Convent Archives, *Baptismal Register, November 19, 1837—September 14, 1845.*

[14] *Dictionary of Louisiana Biography,* s.v. "Rousselon, Etienne-Jean-François, clergyman, educator, administrator."

[15] University of Notre Dame Archives, V-4–1. Antoine Blanc. August, 1841. Also AANO, Blanc to the Congregation, 13 October 1840, and AANO, Register of the Acts of the New Orleans Diocese, n. 113, February 4, 1841.

[16] AANO. See the lists from the baptismal registers of St. Louis Cathedral.

[17] A copy of the original document is in the Archives of the Holy Family.

[18] SSF Archives, *Constitutions Provisoires des Soeurs de la Sainte Familie.*

[19] NONA, Octave de Armas, 1851, May 23, no. 161. *Testament de Henriette Delille.*

[20] NONA, Octave de Armas, 1852, December 20, 53:378.

Chapter 4

Dealing with Desegregation

*Black and White Responses to the Desegregation
of the Diocese of Raleigh, North Carolina, 1953*

CECILIA A. MOORE

Early Sunday morning, May 31, 1953, Bishop Vincent S. Waters left Nazareth and traveled sixty miles east and south to officially begin the desegregation of the Diocese of Raleigh. His destination was Newton Grove, a small tobacco village of about four hundred citizens, and most of them, both black and white, were Catholic. Newton Grove Catholics knew that the bishop had ordered the closing of the black parish, St. Benedict the Moor, and the integration of the white church, Holy Redeemer, but they had no idea that the bishop himself would preside at the mass that morning.

Less than six years into his episcopacy, Bishop Waters had announced in 1951 that the Diocese of Raleigh would not tolerate segregated parishes or schools.[1] Indeed, from 1945 Waters had begun to introduce Carolina Catholics to the new way of Catholicism that they would practice and lead the South in practicing as well. Stories abound of Waters confirming black and white children together in the Cathedral of the Sacred Heart in Raleigh, of his insisting on having white and black acolytes at masses at which he presided, and of his requiring the diocesan newspaper to cover the activities of black Catholics and their parishes with as much interest as they covered those of white Catholics in the diocese.[2] But nothing could quite prepare the faithful of North Carolina for what would transpire on this late spring morning in Newton Grove.

In the Catholic world North Carolina had been dubbed "the China of America" because it had the smallest Catholic population of any state in the Union.[3] But there were pockets of Catholicism throughout the Tar Heel State where Catholic evangelization had really taken root. Newton

Grove was one of these pockets. The tiny village was almost all Catholic, black and white. Catholics came to be the majority religion in Newton Grove in the late nineteenth century following the conversion of the village's most prominent resident, Dr. John C. Monk, in 1871. Dr. Monk brought most of his family and neighbors with him into the Roman Catholic fold, and he was a founding member of the Church of the Holy Redeemer in Newton Grove. The Church of the Holy Redeemer served all Catholics in the village and surrounding area until 1933, when the Church of St. Benedict the Moor was built right beside it. Holy Redeemer and St. Benedict the Moor shared the same Redemptorists priests, who only had to walk across the yard to get from one to the other.

The logical question is why did such a small community require two churches be built right next to each other? The answer is found in the evangelization strategy the Diocese of Raleigh began to employ in the 1930s.

Frustrated in their attempts to build up the Catholic Church in North Carolina, North Carolina missionaries and Bishop Eugene J. McGuinness determined to try something new and prudent in North Carolina evangelization. And that was to follow the customs of the culture in evangelization. This included respecting the principles of Jim Crow, most particularly racial segregation. They reasoned that if they provided separate churches for blacks and whites, they would have a greater chance of attracting North Carolinians to Catholicism. If Carolinians felt comfortable in Catholic churches, then missionaries would have greater opportunities to present the faith to them. Hence, the foundation of the Church of St. Benedict the Moor. Blacks who had worshiped with whites in Holy Redeemer, though in segregated seating, were presented with their own church and school. So, from 1933 until May 31, 1953, faithful black and white Catholics worshiped every Sunday in their own churches. By 1953 Holy Redeemer had about three hundred members and a parochial school with about seventy-two students, and St. Benedict the Moor had about eighty members and a school with about thirty-two students.[4]

A Virginian by birth and rearing, Vincent Waters knew Southern culture and its traditions and mentality intimately, particularly as they related to race. As a young man he did not question his culture; he simply abided by it. He described the horror he felt the first time he encountered a black person sitting out of place on a Maryland streetcar. When the man sat beside Waters, Waters said he solved the "problem" by getting off the streetcar.[5] Racial avoidance was but one of the tools his culture equipped him with to maintain the separation of the races.

While studying for the priesthood in Rome in the late 1920s, Waters began to question the racial lessons, rules, and practices of his culture.

During this time he experienced a self-identified racial conversion. His racial conversion was inspired by a friendship he made with a black man named Charlie. Charlie was a convert to Catholicism, and he had come to Rome hoping to study for the priesthood. He had tried without success to gain seminary admission in the United States. With just enough money to get to Rome, Charlie continued to pursue his vocation. But he had no better fortune in Rome than in the United States. Eventually he was directed to the North American College. Instead of admission, the rector offered Charlie a job waiting tables in the seminary refectory so he could earn his return fare to the United States. Waters said that when he and other seminarians saw Charlie come to wait on them, "the whole student community got up and gave a cheer" because they had not seen a black person for such a long time.[6] Charlie represented home to them, the United States. Working as their servant, he represented the way they thought things should be, at least as far as their culture taught them.

Vincent and Charlie became friends over books, and they talked about Charlie's particular situation. One book Charlie borrowed was *The Autobiography of the Little Flower.* Waters believed that it was the life of St. Thérèse of Lisieux that inspired Charlie to approach the pope about being admitted to seminary. Charlie determined this would be his last effort; if it proved unsuccessful, he would return home. He wrote the pope a letter explaining his situation and gave it to the pope in a private audience. The next day Charlie received word that he should go the Propaganda Fide seminary where he would be admitted.[7] Waters said, "Meeting a preserving Negro did for me what logic could not do." It was the first time Waters looked at his culture critically and light of the gospel. He observed: "I am a Southerner. I have been prejudiced. I had to get rid of my prejudice to get to be a little more Catholic."

In 1931 Vincent Waters was ordained a priest for the Diocese of Richmond, Virginia.[8] Prior to his consecration as bishop of Raleigh, Waters had spent his priestly career in Virginia, where he worked to bring more blacks into communion with the Roman Catholic Church and to break down the color bar in the church. To this end he became involved in the Catholic Committee for the South, the Catholic Interracial Council, and in his various positions in the Diocese of Richmond he paid special attention to the needs and concerns of African Americans.[9] By the time he was bishop of Raleigh, Waters was firmly convinced that the practice of racial segregation in the Catholic Church was a grave violation of the teachings of the faith, and he was intent on using his episcopal authority to redress this violation.

At the beginning of the year 1951, Waters sent a pastoral letter to the people of North Carolina. He declared:

Christ's Church in the world is Catholic. This means that it is broad as the human race itself. Persons of every race and nation have been Popes, Bishops, Priests, Religious and Laity in this one Church which goes back to Christ, and extends to every corner of the world. All of these various nations and races are in one communion in the Church, receiving the same identical sacraments, and have the same doctrine and discipline as they form, with their head, the one Mystical Body of Christ in the world. The Holy Ghost, the soul of this Body, lives and works in each of them.[10]

He went on to state that racial supremacy "is heresy and should be condemned." These statements served as a prelude to his announcement that "equal rights" were accorded to every race and nationality in the Catholic Church. Practically, this meant that everyone had the right to sit wherever he or she pleased in church buildings and to approach the sacraments without any preference being given to any race or nationality. Waters guaranteed these rights and put the clergy on notice that "pastors are responsible for the observance of this practice." Giving a brief history lesson, the bishop reminded the people that it was only a few years ago that separate churches for blacks and whites had become an established practice in North Carolina. Waters used the letter as an opportunity to praise black Catholic Carolinians for their achievements in education, business, and culture. He said, "We are especially proud of them because they are religious men and women and belong to us, as we do to them, in the Mystical Body of Christ."[11]

The 1951 pastoral and Waters's other efforts at integration were signs of the new Catholic way for North Carolina. With all of this, the bishop's decision to integrate St. Benedict the Moor and Holy Redeemer should not have come as much of a surprise to people, but surprise them it did. The first integrated Mass in Newton Grove, North Carolina gained the attention of national and international secular and religious press and profoundly changed the experience of Catholicism for southern blacks and whites.

The New York Times, New Republic, Time, Newsweek, Christian Century, America, and *Commonweal* all reported on the first integrated Sunday mass at Holy Redeemer Church in Newton Grove on May 31, 1953.[12] Bishop Waters presided at the first mass that morning. On May 27 parishioners of Holy Redeemer and St. Benedict the Moor received letters from Bishop Waters informing them that from that Sunday forward all Masses in Newton Grove would be at Holy Redeemer and that St. Benedict the Moor would be closed.[13] Upon hearing this a group of Holy Redeemer parishioners immediately protested the bishop's decision in their own missive. They sought to explain to Bishop Waters why this decision was imprudent and unfair.

First, they reminded the bishop that he was dealing with southern Catholics. They wrote: "As you are aware, interacial [sic] gatherings are opposed in the South, social and religious and while we are at all times glad and anxious for all races to have advantages, religious and otherwise, we really do oppose them coming to worship."[14] They also pointed out that their parish had grown and was attracting even more converts and that bringing blacks into their church would surely curtail its growth.

Along the same lines they complained that their church was not large enough to accommodate all the whites and all the blacks. They issued a veiled threat to withhold their financial support, saying: "Our members, some of the oldest and most devout have declared they will attend church in other towns; need we add that they are among our staunchest financial supporters? We cannot sit by without voicing our feelings." The parishioners felt Bishop Waters had dropped a "bomb" in their midst, and they were convinced it would be the "ruination" of all they had accomplished in building up their church and school.

Finally, they were devastated by how Waters's decision would be regarded by their fellow white North Carolinians, who already looked down on the Catholics. They pleaded with Waters, writing:

> We have it so hard living by and being acknowledged as equals by our non-Catholic neighbors and business acquaintances who have, as you are aware, always been prejudiced, we feel it an injustice to have to accept this until—maybe that time will come—this be universally accepted in all fields of life and among others in our Faith and all churches. We, the undersigned members of this congregation, plead with you to give your serious consideration.[15]

According to Mrs. Kennon Bowden, president of Holy Redeemer's Holy Family Sodality, Bishop Waters did not respond to their letter. Her husband told a reporter that the parish was "upset the worst I've ever seen anything in my life."[16] And Dr. John C. Monk, the namesake of Newton Grove's first Catholic, told reporters: "We are expecting trouble. There is a strong feeling there might be violence on May 31."[17]

Monk's prediction came true. There was some violence and plenty of anger that Sunday. A group of white Catholic and non-Catholic protesters gathered around the Holy Redeemer Church that Sunday, determined not to leave until Bishop Waters gave them a hearing. According to reports, protesters threw stones at the church and yelled curses and threats to the bishop during mass.[18] Major Sutton, president of the Holy Name

Society and a cradle Catholic (sixty years old) said: "I think I will tear up the church. I say we can all go outside, or beat up the bishop, one or other."[19]

At least one white woman disagreed with the crowd and decided to take her daughter with her into the church for mass. She reportedly said to her daughter: "You don't defy me. You come on in here. Don't disobey the bishop. Come on." Angrily, the girl obeyed her mother. A few moments later the child's father went into the church and dragged his daughter out, saying: "I don't believe in no such thing. . . . I think it's the Communists. They got everybody's skin in their way."[20] Another man declared that the child his wife was carrying would "never come up a Catholic." Most of the Catholics who attended Holy Redeemer that Sunday were black. Many white Catholics and some black Catholics made arrangements to attend other parishes that Sunday, either out of fear for their safety or out of spite for the bishop and his decision. Upon leaving mass that Sunday, a white woman reportedly declared to the crowd gathered outside: "I'm a catholic [sic] and will be one until the day I die. I'm proud of what I've done and I will be back next Sunday if I have to walk. I'm just what I am and no one is going to change me."[21] The crowd responded, "She's crazy."[22] The same reporter remarked on the demeanor of black Catholics at Holy Redeemer that Sunday. He wrote: "Those brave and trusting enough to put in an appearance last Sunday, displayed a calmness that was a beauty to behold. Unruffled, serene, and pleasant-faced, they marched in orderly procession, in and out of the church their bishop had ordered them to attend."[23] The reporter said they gave no indication that anything unusual was happening and that their poise had a sobering effect on the angry crowd. When he asked the black parishioners about their feelings, "they expressed their steadfast faith in God and trust in the wisdom of the bishop" and "their intention to continue in the faith and to come each Sunday for worship at the church of the Holy Redeemer."[24]

After mass the crowd pressed on the rectory where Waters and the priest were. The group tried to storm the door and in the process a priest who was trying to protect the bishop was injured. Waters agreed to speak to the Catholics gathered outside, but he refused to address the non-Catholics. Two by two Catholic protesters were admitted to see the bishop. He listened to their complaints, but he was not swayed by them and held firm to his decision.

News of what happened in Newton Grove spread far and wide rapidly. Religious and secular presses in the United States and internationally reported on the desegregation Sunday, and editorial pages teemed with black and white, Catholic and non-Catholic responses to Newton Grove.

Overwhelmingly, the responses were favorable, and the event was hailed as one of courage and true Christianity and moral leadership. *The Carolinian*, a black newspaper out of Raleigh, North Carolina, wrote: "The average Negro, whether Protestant or Catholic, could not but admire the action of the bishop and the policy of the church he was implementing."[25] While the editors appreciated Waters's principled strike against segregation, they found the authoritarianism that undergirded the move to be troubling and "a show of arbitrary power."[26] In their opinion this was characteristically Catholic, and they would have preferred that the bishop had consulted the people and given them more time to prepare. However, *The Carolinian* concluded, "education in right attitudes can follow as well as precede changes, and sometimes it takes place very rapidly when the learning must follow the change, rather than the change wait on the learning."[27]

A few days later, on June 9, 1953, A. M. Rivera, Jr., a black Catholic, responded to an editorial in the *Durham Morning Sun* that called for North Carolinians to protest any Supreme Court decision to end racial segregation. The editor used the desegregation of the churches in Newton Grove as an example of a move against segregation that merited protest and opposition.[28] Referring to the pending *Brown v. Board of Education* case that the Supreme Court was considering and to the 1896 *Plessy v. Ferguson* decision that declared "separate but equal" accommodations for the races to be constitutional, Rivera greeted what had happened in Newton Grove as a victory for all blacks who suffered under legalized segregation. It was another nail in Jim Crow's coffin.

Blacks were playing in the major leagues (Jackie Robinson, Roy Campanella, Satchel Paige) and even southern minor-league teams were beginning to integrate.[29] Truman had decreed the integration of the armed services of the United States, and now a southern Catholic bishop had started to integrate the church. Rivera declared: "Secretly we all must admire the courage of Bishop Vincent S. Waters, for all of us who have half-heartedly mumbled the Lord's Prayer know that a belief in religion is the belief that before God all human beings have an absolute equality—not a staggered equality, but a complete equality."[30] An editorial in the *Afro* agreed with Rivera and saw in Bishop Waters "a genuine Christian, who is willing to stand up and fight for the doctrine of brotherhood. Unfortunately, men of his caliber are all too few on the American religious scene."[31]

While to some Bishop Waters was a leader of "Christian Democracy," a lover of justice, and a true moral leader, others saw him as a Communist, an enemy of southern culture, and a traitor of white Christianity. Carl E. Gaddy, Sr., of Micro, North Carolina, likened Waters to Soviet

Premier Georgi M. Malenkov and the pope to an absolute dictator.[32] Racial segregation was a principle that white Southerners had lived and died to defend and to preserve for future generations. Mr. Gaddy opined if Newton Grove whites were to remain Catholic, they would have to betray this legacy their ancestors had bequeathed them. The desegregation of the churches in Newton Grove caused white Catholics to betray their heritage. Bitterly Gaddy concluded, "As I see it, there are but two things the good folks in the Catholic Church around Newton Grove can do, worship with the Negroes or go to Hell."[33]

In a similar vein, Dr. H. A. Eldridge of Dunn, North Carolina, accused Bishop Waters of perpetrating a "civil rights maneuver" and of using Newton Grove as a "guinea pig."[34] He warned that "bull-headed . . . 'little Hitlers' posing as Spiritualist leaders should be put back into their rightful place by the rule of the supreme power of our union—the U.S. Supreme Court."[35] Dr. Eldridge, like so many of Waters's opponents, saw the desegregation efforts as a Communist plot against American values and beliefs and practices. He contended, "Very likely this decree originated from the 'cold war' being waged between Communist dictators, Stalin, and Malenkov, and the Catholic director Pope Pius XIV of Rome." But he felt confident that ultimately North Carolinians would not be "brainwashed" into accepting integration in the church or elsewhere.[36]

Bishop Waters's secretary kept scrapbooks of all the letters and newspaper articles he received regarding Newton Grove. But neither the Catholic Marines stationed at Cherry Point, North Carolina, who offered "very direct and physical support to your endeavor," nor the elegant letter of appreciation and admiration on fine stationery that Senator John F. Kennedy sent, nor those who prayed "may the good loving Almighty God punish you, drag your wicked tongue out by the roots" seem to have influenced Waters one way or the other.[37] And, about three weeks after integrating the churches in Newton Grove, the bishop announced his decision to desegregate all Catholic institutions in the diocese.

Once broken free from the chest, it is impossible to discern the race of the human heart. Hearts are all the same. In most art dealing with the Sacred Heart of Jesus, Jesus is depicted holding his heart in his hand or with his heart suspended in the center of his chest. His heart is bleeding, its veins are raised, and it is red and fleshy and surrounded with a wreath of thorns. The Sacred Heart of Jesus calls attention to Jesus' humanity. Jesus' heart, apart from him and without the crown of thorns, is as generic as the heart of any other man or woman. But in spite of its distinctiveness, the human heart is essential for life. When it stops beating life is over. The life of the body ultimately depends upon the heart.

As the body depends upon the heart for life, the heart is also thought to be the seat of human feeling and emotion. The Sacred Heart of Jesus is not a valentine, but it does express the love of Jesus for all people that made it possible for him to sacrifice his life for all.

On the Feast of the Sacred Heart of Jesus, Bishop Waters sent a valentine of sorts to the Diocese of Raleigh. At his request it was delivered at all masses throughout the diocese on Sunday, June 21, 1953, in lieu of a homily. Simply and solemnly Bishop Waters declared, "There is not segregation to be tolerated in any Catholic Church in the Diocese of Raleigh."[38] Priests would carry out the mandate strictly. In order to effect the desegregation, Waters determined that "all special churches for Negroes would be abolished immediately as lending weight to the false notion that the Catholic Church, the Mystical Body of Christ, is divided." And, as he announced in his 1951 pastoral, equal rights would be granted to all Catholics of any race or nationality from that day forward. In addition to "equal rights" in church buildings, Waters also announced that blacks would be admitted to Catholic schools and colleges and would have the right to enjoy the services of any Catholic institutions in the diocese.[39]

Waters was declaring war upon racism in the Diocese of Raleigh. He told his people: "In the Diocese of Raleigh we fight only one enemy, the arch-enemy of God. No matter under what guise he may present himself or what means he might use, there is only one enemy of mankind, of the Church, and of the individual Catholic; that enemy is Satan, the arch-enemy of Christ and His Church."[40] Satan did not appear as a person but in the "Spirit of the World." "The Spirit of the World" sowed seeds of division, hatred, and pride that threatened to choke the seeds of unity, love, and humility that the church planted. The fruits of division, hatred, and pride were manifest in nationalism, racism, classism, ethnic chauvinism, provincialism, and materialism. Waters believed these fruits were allowed to "grow in the human heart" and were in complete opposition to "the love represented by the Sacred pierced Heart of Jesus." Jesus' Sacred Heart represented love for all people. All people had an equal opportunity to receive the love of the Sacred Heart and to return love to the Sacred Heart. The Sacred Heart represented the love that sacrifices itself for the lives of others.

Waters knew the power and symbolism of the theology of the Sacred Heart and the strength of its devotion among Catholics of his day. But he was aware that many who were devoted to the Sacred Heart also bore racism in their hearts. By choosing the imagery and language of the Sacred Heart, he offered a new way for North Carolina Catholics spiritually to confront their culture. Satan had convinced them that they were on the path to salvation. Southern culture and tradition were the tools he used to destroy the body and soul of the church. For the Mystical Body of Christ to be whole and the church to be Catholic, it had to include "all, in one communion, in one bond of love."[41]

Bishop Waters believed racial prejudice was personal, and he likened it to a virus. As a virus attacks the body and compromises its well-being, racism attacks the soul and threatens its ability to recognize the good and to see what is right. But, as a body can be inoculated against a virus and an infected body can be cured, the same is true for souls. Waters admonished North Carolina Catholics, saying, " I revolt against our children infected with this virus, when men and women of good-will everywhere can preserve them from it." Faith was the cure for racism. Waters believed, "The virus will not die out of itself, it has to be killed by being exposed to the light of Faith."[42]

For Waters, faith expressed as love was the only answer. Toleration was not an option. Toleration was negative. Love was positive. He reminded his diocese: "If Christ said love your enemies, we certainly can love our friends. These [blacks] are our friends and members of our own body, the Church. It is our duty as Christians of the early days, not only to love them but to serve them."[43] The requirement for whites to love and serve blacks was surely scandalous to many ears in Catholics churches on June 21, 1953, and certainly to many outside the Catholic Church as well. Bishop Waters was calling for a reversal of centuries of tradition and thought. He was demanding the social equality for blacks that the demand to love entailed, and he was also insisting that whites take on the role of servant in relation to blacks. He insisted that whites had an obligation to help blacks to "get better educational facilities, better opportunities for culture, better living conditions, better jobs, better homes and families, better civic representation and better friendliness in the community." How fulfilling this requirement might make whites feel about themselves or appear to others was of no consequence to the bishop. He just reminded them of Jesus' teaching, "As often as you have done this to the least of my brethren, you have done it to me."[44]

Bishop Waters did not fear what his decision to desegregate the Diocese of Raleigh might mean. He was well aware of the potential for violence both within and without the Catholic community. They had already experienced this at Holy Redeemer in Newton Grove. And, as the protest staged there did not change his course, neither was he deterred by the possibility that diocese-wide desegregation might cause a mass exodus of North Carolinians, white and black, and their money from the church. He did it anyway.

He explained, "As pastor of your souls, I am happy to take the responsibility for evil which might result from different races worshiping together, but I would be unwilling to take any responsibility for those who refuse to worship God with another race." Because he believed that faith expressed as love was the only cure for prejudice, he was relying on love to change the hearts of those who opposed him. Bishop Waters hoped, "I shall be able to convince you if I love you enough, and if you love me you will understand, for God first loved us."[45]

While Bishop Waters used his moral and episcopal authority to initiate an integrated church in North Carolina, everyday black and white Catholics ultimately were responsible for the work of integration. The brave but ordinary black and white Catholics who attended mass in Newton Grove on May 31 accomplished the first act of integration. The very idea of blacks and whites even sitting in close proximity to each other was illegal in many parts of the South, and when not illegal certainly was offensive to the sensibilities of many southern whites and dangerous for many southern blacks, particularly black men. Just two days before this integrated mass, the State of North Carolina executed Raleigh Speller and Clyde Brown in the name of the people of the state. They were found guilty of raping white women.[46] So it is not hard to imagine the fear and anger many black and white Catholics had to come to terms to with in order to walk into the Church of the Holy Redeemer. Most likely they were not conscious that they were playing a role in bringing down Jim Crow, but they were. Most of these Catholics simply wanted to be faithful to the church and to practice the way of Christ. They accomplished this, but in doing so they were taking a stand against what was regarded as legal, natural, right, and Christian in their culture. These men, women, and children became members of the first line in the southern Catholic war against racism.

Black and white Catholic teenagers were the next lines of soldiers in this war. In the fall of 1954, just a couple of months after the *Brown v. Board of Education* decision struck down "separate but equal" public education, Bishop Waters directed that the Catholic high schools in North Carolina admit black students. And in the following year, 1955, Catholic grade school children would begin to do their part to "kill" the virus of racial prejudice when the elementary schools were gradually integrated.

Four years after the desegregation of the Catholic high schools, *The Sign* sent a photojournalist to Cathedral Latin High School in Raleigh to see how integration was working there. Ed Lettau's photographic essay was called "Integration in Action," and it featured a day in the life of Barbara Morgan. Barbara Morgan was a sixteen-year-old black Catholic coed at Cathedral Latin. She and her whole family converted to Catholicism when she was in the second grade, and she and her siblings attended

Catholic schools in Raleigh. Of her experience at Cathedral Latin Morgan was quoted as saying: "I've never had any difficulty with the white students. I think they know I really want a Catholic education."[47]

The photographer captured pictures of Morgan praying in chapel with her classmates, receiving help from a Dominican student, eating with friends in the cafeteria, working in the school library, enjoying records at home with her sisters, playing piano and singing with her family. The pictures were lovely and inspiring, and Morgan had only good things to say about her experience as a student at Cathedral Latin. But the article did not skirt the less than ideal realities of integrated education in the South either. For example, there were not lots of interracial friendships. The article noted that black students tended to eat lunch with one another, and white students tended to eat lunch with one another because their friends tended to be of their own races. School dances were no longer part of the social life of Cathedral Latin students because of concerns of the public outcry that might happen if black and white teenagers enjoyed an evening of dancing together. Miscegenation was still a big fear. And often competing schools would cancel sporting matches with Cathedral Latin because they did not want their students playing black students.[48]

North Carolinians paid a high price to be truly Catholic in the segregated South of the 1950s. The dearest cost was the church's loss of members. Some whites left because they were not willing to pay the social and cultural tax of accepting blacks as their equals. Some blacks left because it was painful to lose the churches that had become their homes and because they did not feel accepted in the integrated churches.[49] However, those who remained in these difficult times offered hope to people, Catholic and non-Catholic, near and far.

Mrs. Doris B. Rice, a member of Our Lady of the Miraculous Medal Church in Greensboro, North Carolina, reflected on the sacrifices that black Catholics in Greensboro were willing to make. She said, "While the Negro Catholics of Greensboro may not be so aggressive for a change, I do think we should 'back up' in whatever way possible our clergy on the stand they have taken to do what is right, and no longer being willing to tolerate what is despicable and not acceptable to God."[50] She and her fellow Greensboro Catholics believed that whatever they might suffer in this effort, it would "have far-reaching effects for, and benefits to Negroes, other religious groups, and minorities." They were ready allies. As far away as South Africa, North Carolina Catholics were offering hope to segregated peoples. A Benedictine priest in South Africa heard of what had happened in Newton Grove and requested a copy of Bishop Waters's pastoral. He said, "As you must have heard racial prejudice and discrimination are sadly evident in this country, and I should like to be able to quote from your pastoral letter when trying to better the state of affairs here."[51] It would not be until the 1970s that southern states like North Carolina would come into full compliance with civil rights legislation that prohibited segregation, and it would not be until the 1990s that South Africa would see apartheid finally ended, but without a doubt black and white North Carolina Catholics, motivated by their faith, made an early and significant contribution to the fight for racial justice in the twentieth century.

NOTES

[1] Vincent S. Waters, "Pastoral Letter to the Diocese of Raleigh, North Carolina," January 29, 1951.

[2] Interviews with Franciscan Handmaids of the Most Pure Heart of Mary, August 2000. These sisters were among the religious working in North Carolina during Bishop Waters's tenure. When I mentioned his name to them, they immediately began telling me stories about things they knew Bishop Waters did to promote integration in North Carolina. I also learned many similar stories from Bradley K. Blake, archivist of the Diocese of Raleigh.

[3] James J. Kavanaugh, "Hope of the Southland," *Extension* (February 21, 1955), 27. Kavanaugh was the auxiliary bishop of Raleigh.

[4] William F. Powers, *Tar Heel Catholics: A History of Catholicism in North Carolina* (Lanham, MD: University Press of America, 2003), 161.

[5] Vincent S. Waters, "How I Lost My Prejudice," *The Catholic Digest* (December 1956), 18.

[6] Ibid., 20.

[7] Ibid., 20. When I first read Bishop Waters's account of his racial conversion, it seemed a bit unbelievable, but I was able to verify that in fact Waters did meet a young black American in Rome who was pursuing a priestly vocation. So impressed was Waters with the sincerity of this man's vocation, he wrote to this bishop in Virginia and advocated that the Diocese of Richmond sponsor the man's vocation. The bishop declined, but the man was ultimately accepted to a seminary in Rome. See Gerald Fogarty, *Commonwealth Catholics: A History of the Catholic Church in Virginia* (Notre Dame, IN: University of Notre Dame Press, 2001).

[8] Waters, "How I Lost My Prejudice," 18.

[9] Fogarty, *Commonwealth Catholics*, 447.

[10] Waters, "Pastoral Letter to the Diocese of Raleigh, North Carolina" (1951).

[11] Ibid.

[12] In addition to these religious and secular national organs, Catholic and African American newspapers across the country also covered the Newton Grove incident and Bishop Waters's pastoral letter of 1953. Among these newspapers

were *The Carolinian, The Richmond Afro-American, The Norfolk Journal and Guide, The Catholic Virginian, The Catholic Interracialist, The Guardian, The Catholic Messenger,* and *The Pittsburgh Courier.* North Carolina papers also carried articles and numerous letters to the editor regarding the matter.

[13] Powers, *Tar Heel Catholics,* 16.

[14] Letter from Parishioners at Holy Redeemer Church to Bishop Vincent S. Waters, 1953.

[15] Ibid.

[16] "Catholics Protest White-Negro Parish," *The New York Times,* May 22, 1953.

[17] Ibid.

[18] James A. Shepherd, "Newton Grove Incident Marks Victory for True 'Christian Democracy,'" newspaper name and date not available; and Burke Davis, "The Bishop Stood His Ground," *New Republic* (August 3, 1953), 10.

[19] Davis, "The Bishop Stood His Ground," 10.

[20] Ibid.

[21] Shepherd, "Newton Grove Incident Marks Victory for True 'Christian Democracy.'"

[22] Ibid.

[23] Ibid.

[24] Ibid.

[25] "Reflections on Newton Grove," *The Carolinian,* June 6, 1953.

[26] Ibid.

[27] Ibid.

[28] A. M. Rivera, letter to the editor, *Durham Morning Sun,* June 9, 1953.

[29] Ibid.

[30] Ibid.

[31] Editorial, "His Kind Too Few," *Afro,* June 13, 1953. There were many *Afro* newspapers (Baltimore, Richmond, Virginia, Washington DC, Philadelphia, and so on). I have not been able to identify which of the *Afro* newspapers published this editorial.

[32] Carl E. Garry, Sr., letter to the editor. I do not have the name of the newspaper or the date of publication.

[33] Ibid.

[34] H. A. Eldridge, M.D., letter to the editor, *Durham-Sun Herald,* June 8, 1953.

[35] Ibid.

[36] Ibid.

[37] Father Robert Heim, C.S.Sp., to The Most Reverend Vincent S. Waters, 1 June 1953; 100% English and an S.A. Nationalist to the Right Reverend V. S. Waters, no date given.

[38] Waters, "Pastoral Letter to the Diocese of Raleigh, North Carolina," June 21, 1953.

[39] Ibid.

[40] Ibid.

[41] Ibid.

[42] Ibid.

[43] Ibid.

[44] Ibid.

[45] Ibid.

[46] "Two Carolina Negroes Executed as Rapists," *Danville Register*, May 20, 1953.

[47] Ed Lettau, "Integration in Action," *The Sign* (November 1958), 16.

[48] Ibid., 17.

[49] Powers, *Tar Heel Catholics*, 22. William Powers argues that the Newton Grove desegregation ultimately destroyed the black and white Catholic community there and that gains from Waters's actions did not make up for the losses. I disagree with this assessment.

[50] Doris B. Rice, "A Personal Opinion," June 24, 1953. I do not have the name of the publication.

[51] Dr. K. F. McMurtie to The Most Reverend The Lord Bishop of Raleigh, North Carolina, June 30, 1953.

Chapter 5

Black Catholic Clergy
and the Struggle for Civil Rights

Winds of Change

KATRINA M. SANDERS

While numerous works have chronicled the contributions of various individuals and organizations to the civil rights movement in the United States, little has been written on the activities of black Catholic clergy and religious during that period.[1] One factor that may have contributed to this neglect is the perception that the Catholic Church did not play a large part in either black or southern history.[2] William D. Broderick argues that prior to World War II the Catholic Church had "relatively little contact" with black Americans in places other than Louisiana.[3] In a 1970 case study on the Catholic Church and black Americans, Broderick found the American Catholic Church to be a predominately "urban church" with which blacks had little contact until they migrated to larger urban centers in the wake of World War II. A 1946 article in *Ebony* magazine supports this claim, noting, "In the years that followed Emancipation, the Catholic Church did little to win over Negro Americans, spent most of its time and talent converting the 'heathen' in foreign lands."[4]

James Finn also notes the lack of interaction between the Catholic Church and blacks. In his work *American Catholics and Social Movements*, Finn observes that although the Catholic Church, "a Church of immigrants," initially focused its attention on establishing various church-related welfare agencies for Catholic immigrants, the focus on welfare agencies waned as those Catholics immigrants attained a "relatively comfortable place" in American society and became "content with the conditions of that society."[5] Black southern communities, which were familiar with the Catholic Church, may have viewed the church as distant and detached. And, they may have associated Catholicism with slave-owning priests, segregated churches, or black priests, who were barred from celebrating mass in white Catholic Churches.[6] By 1960 only 4 percent of thirty-six million Southerners were Catholic, and most of these lived in southern Louisiana.[7] William A. Osborne argues in *Segregated Covenant* that, with the exceptions of Louisiana and San Antonio, the Catholic Church in the South consisted primarily of the descendants of the Irish and, up to the 1950s, was seen as an "alien or minority group institution."[8]

The lack of visibility and prominence of Catholic clergy during civil rights efforts may also contribute to the paucity of information concerning their participation. In the groundbreaking 1990 work *The History of Black Catholics in the United States*, Benedictine monk Cyprian Davis writes:

> By and large Catholics, either black or white, were not in the fore-front of the civil rights movement or among the leadership of the protest organizations. Black priests, unlike many black Protestant clergymen, were not in the vanguard of grass-roots leadership that supported and followed King on the local level. One reason for this, of course, was that few black priests were in leadership positions of any kind in the early sixties. In general, they were neither pastors nor religious superiors. Moreover, the notion that it was unseemly for either clergy or religious to engage in public spectacles like demonstrations was especially strong among Catholics in general.[9]

Although records of their efforts are invisible in civil rights histories, black Catholic clergy and religious did play a significant role in securing civil rights in their communities. Either covertly or overtly, cautiously or loudly, black Catholic clergy and religious contributed as needed to securing civil rights for members of their communities in the rural South and the urban North.

THE CATHOLIC AWAKENING

In 1967 the cardinal archbishop of the Archdiocese of Detroit, John F. Dearden, charged that American Catholics were not doing their part in the fight for social justice:

> American Catholics have yet to show consistent dedication to social justice. In the fight against racism, the Church—again with

notable exceptions—is moving with the rest of the nation in its slow, unsteady advance. And in terms of affecting the political and economic structures in our society in order to remedy inequities, the Church has been a negligible influence.[10]

Dearden's criticism may have been an accurate assessment of the Catholic Church as an institution, but it was not an accurate assessment of Catholic individuals. There were notable exceptions working to secure social justice.

By the 1960s the notion that it was unseemly for Catholic religious to participate in civil rights demonstrations and to concern themselves with American race relations began to change. Catholics, both white and black, became increasingly visible at several civil rights demonstrations. For example, Cardinal Patrick A. O'Boyle, the cardinal archbishop of Washington, was on the official program for the August 28, 1963, March on Washington. O'Boyle gave the invocation at the Lincoln Memorial where Martin Luther King, Jr., later gave his famous "I Have a Dream" speech.[11] Davis comments that this was "the first time, the Catholic church was significantly present at a massive public demonstration under the leadership of black civil rights leaders," but he quickly points out that this demonstration had official, governmental support.[12] Catholics were again highly visible at the march on Selma, Alabama, held in March 1965. That visibility was captured in a photograph that was widely circulated throughout the country. The photograph featured approximately a dozen priest in collars and four nuns in full habit.

It is important to note that while some Catholics were calling for greater participation in civil rights efforts, and while Catholics were becoming more visible in civil rights activities, not all Catholics supported the movement. The response to the Catholic priests and nuns who gathered at Selma was great disapproval from the bishop of Mobile-Birmingham.[13] Osborne notes that "Archbishop Thomas Toolen of the Diocese of Mobile-Birmingham deplored the intrusion of clergy and religious at Selma, declaring that they 'should be home doing God's work.'"[14] Toolen's comments demonstrate that many Catholic officials felt the issue of racial injustice in America was social rather than moral. These officials felt Catholic clergy and religious were responsible for dealing with moral issues, and the government should deal with social issues.[15]

Several factors may have sparked the change in Catholic attitudes. Finn remarks that many Catholics believed Rome, through Vatican Council II, had given them permission to participate in the civil rights movement:

The national ferment aroused by the civil-rights movement and the war on poverty coincided with a general ferment within the Church most publicly signaled by the innovating reign of John XXIII and Vatican Council II. Many Catholics felt that they had been given strong and additional warrants to commit their best efforts to the secular society and to a war on the worst evils of that society.[16]

Initiated by Pope John XXIII, the Second Vatican Council brought bishops together from around the world to pray, to consider, to discuss, and to deliberate about the state of the church. The council, which opened in 1962, sought to address not only internal ecclesial matters of discipline and order, but also the relation of the church to the modern world. Before the council closed in 1965, it issued sixteen documents—constitutions, declarations, and decrees—that made many widespread decisions about the life of the church. In an interview Reverend Theodore K. Parker observed that although Vatican II did not specifically tell Catholics to go out and participate in the civil rights movement, those who were inclined to do so might have taken inspiration from *Gaudium et spes (The Pastoral Constitution on the Church in the Modern World)*.[17] For example, the preface of *Gaudium et spes* takes special notice of the unity and relation of the "whole of humanity," "the whole human family along with the sum of those realities in the midst of which it lives."[18]

More investigation, however, is needed to determine if presumed permission from Rome was the sole impetus that inspired Catholics to become more active in civil rights efforts. This seems doubtful since Rome had reprimanded American Catholics before for their unjust treatment of blacks. Morris MacGregor in his historical study of St. Augustine's Parish in Washington DC writes that in 1904 Cardinal Girolamo Gotti, head of Propaganda Fide,

> bluntly told the new apostolic delegate to the United States, Archbishop Diomede Falconio, that "it has been referred to this Sacred Congregation that in some of the dioceses of the United States the condition of the Catholic negroes [sic], not only in respect to the other faithful but also in respect to their pastors and bishops, is very humiliating and entirely different from that of the whites."[19]

Falconio wanted the Vatican to take steps to "lessen and gradually eliminate such discrimination." In reply, the bishops complained that "Rome was meddling in an extremely sensitive area about which it knew little." But, the Vatican continued to urge Catholics "to be friendly to Negroes, who are called no less than other men to share in all the great benefits of the Redemption." In addition, the Vatican formed a committee to review the American church's treatment of blacks. MacGregor writes that although it is not clear what prompted this and later Vatican interventions on behalf of black Catholics, it seems likely that the black Catholic congresses played a role.[20]

Catholic Church officials also spoke out against discrimination within its community during the late 1950s. In 1958 the American Catholic Bishops issued a pastoral letter entitled "Discrimination and the Christian Conscience." The letter stressed that the "heart of the race question is moral and religious"[21] and that racial segregation could not "be reconciled with the Christian view of our fellow man."[22] In April 1968, after King's assassination, the National Conference of Catholic Bishops issued *A Statement on the National Race Crisis*. It charged that the churches "had failed to change the attitudes of many believers," and agreed that "a white segregationist mentality is largely responsible for the present crisis."[23]

The shift in Catholic attitudes might also be attributed to the Catholic Church's efforts to recruit and maintain black members. Although Pope Leo XIII had pointed out the "fertile field for converts existing among Negroes in America" in 1891, the Catholic Church continued to focus its missionary activity in foreign lands.[24] But this changed to include black Americans after World War II. In 1946 Pope Pius XII asked a black reporter to convey to black Americans his hope for their "well-being, happiness and the ultimate triumph over the handicaps with which they are confronted."[25] During the late 1960s the Catholic Church began to concentrate on maintaining black Catholics as many were leaving the church in the wake of the black power movement:

> The general consensus . . . is that young black Catholics, particularly the educated ones, are leaving the church in large numbers; and that the only issue over which they are leaving is that of race. They are confronting an identity crisis as black Catholics, and they are coming out black rather than Catholic.[26]

STEALING A MEETING

While the Catholic Church as a whole was trying to figure out if and how it would address America's racial problems, black Catholic priests and religious mobilized to address the injustices that they, along with their black brothers and sisters in the laity, experienced. Outraged after the April 4, 1968, assassination of the Reverend Dr. Martin Luther King,

Jr., and the subsequent violence that erupted, Father Herman Porter, a black priest of the Diocese of Rockford, Illinois, sent a letter to all black priests in the country inviting them to assemble privately before the start of an interracial Catholic clergy conference scheduled for April 16–18 in Detroit, Michigan. "The invitation was in response to Chicago Mayor Richard Daly's order 'to shoot to kill' all those engaged in looting."[27] While many of their white counterparts registered for the conference, approximately sixty black priests met to discuss the state of black America.[28] The priests who attended this secret meeting did so in the tradition of their enslaved black ancestors who often stole off in secrecy to learn to read and write. Like their ancestors, they were "stealing a meeting." The meeting lasted well into the night. Davis states: "For many it was a time of painful discovery and sometimes bitter revelation. For all it was either a time of anger or of deep-seated unease."[29]

The black priests eventually settled on their objectives—the most immediate being to "deliver a statement to the American bishops, to let them know the seriousness of the situation facing the Church in the black community."[30] After much discussion and argument, the priests finally agreed on the wording for their statement.[31] That statement to the American bishops began with the sentence, "The Catholic Church in the United States, primarily a white racist institution, has addressed itself primarily to white society and is definitely a part of that society." Davis reports that the statement called for the church to

> heed the new spirit that was sweeping through the black commu-
> nity in the wake of the civil rights movement and the Black Power
> movement. It called for the church to look again at the issue of
> militancy in the matter of rights for black Americans. It called for
> greater control by blacks themselves of the Catholic institutions in
> the black community, and warned that the Church "is rapidly dy-
> ing in the black community. . . . In many areas there is a serious
> defection . . . on the part of black Catholic youth. . . . The black
> community no longer looks to the Catholic Church with hope.[32]

Reverend George Clements, co-coordinator of that secret 1968 meeting, recalls the mood of the priests after that meeting:

> The mood was that we had a job to do. We had to really turn things
> around. We had to really make the church understand how viciously
> evil segregation is and how important it is that the church, of all
> institutions, would reflect that which God made us to be . . . hu-
> man beings and equal. We went out with a mission.[33]

That mood, no doubt, had been influenced by the winds of change
that had been blowing throughout the black community. Although King
had not supported the burgeoning black power movement, his assassination fanned flames that engulfed black America. In *Black Religion and
Black Radicalism: An Interpretation of the Religious History of Afro-American People*, Gayraud Wilmore notes that black power meant

> that only by solidifying ranks through a new consciousness of his-
> tory and culture, building political and economic clout, and being
> willing to legitimize group self-interest and even defensive violence,
> if necessary, could blacks hope to survive the onslaught of repres-
> sion, following in the wake of a retreating white liberalism, and
> take control of their own future.[34]

By the late 1960s the black community was not only dealing with
black power, but its religious leaders were also being introduced to the
notion of black theology. Wilmore describes the emergence of black theology around 1969 in the work of James H. Cone, a young black scholar
with a doctorate in systematic theology. Cone showed "how a radical
but historically accurate exegesis of the biblical story leads to the conclusion that black power is an expression of the gospel in a particular
situation of oppression."[35] Cone also studied other works and found "cor-
relative ideas for the assertion that black power is nothing less than the
affirmation of black being against the nonbeing of white racism."[36] Cone
concluded that black power should not only be seen as "indispensable to
the formulation and praxis of a black theology, it is also essential to a
Christian understanding of freedom and humanity."[37] Wilmore points
out that black clergy utilized Cone's concept of black theology to define
their positions in debates with white clergy and to confront issues that
shaped the reality of black oppression:

> Black Theology is a theology of black liberation. It seeks to plumb
> the black condition in light of God's revelation in Jesus Christ, so
> that the black community can see that the gospel is commensurate
> with the achievement of black humanity. . . . The message of lib-
> eration is the revelation of God as revealed in the incarnation of
> Jesus Christ. Freedom IS the gospel. Jesus is the Liberator![38]

Although black Catholic clergy are not considered to have participated
in the formal construction of black theology, some priests felt connected
to it and the non-Catholic clergymen who supported it.[39] Black Catholic
priests also supported the quest for black power. For example, seven

black priests serving the Archdiocese of Chicago chastised the Catholic Church for "suspicious disdain" of black militants. A position paper that was made public after having been circulated among three hundred priests noted: "The militants, whether we like it or not, are *de facto* in touch with grass roots in the black community. They are composed of the intellectuals, the students, and the middle class blacks." Moreover, the paper stated, the church has failed to realize that the "power center has moved away from the 'docile, agreeable, middle-aged black leaders' with whom the Church had preferred to deal."[40]

It is important to point out that black power was not the sole influence on black Catholic activism. In *Black Catholic Protest and the Federated Colored Catholics, 1917–1933*, Marilyn Wenzke Nickels recounts the efforts of black Catholics, who organized themselves in the late nineteenth century to address racial injustices in the church and in society. From 1889 to 1894, black Catholic laity met in assembly as the Catholic Afro-American Congress, and although the Congress movement dissolved, in 1917 a grassroots meeting of black Catholics resulted in the formation of the Federated Colored Catholics.[41] That same spirit of protest manifested itself as the priests left the secret meeting in Detroit in 1968. They had a job to do. Each priest, however, understood that "doing something" meant different things for different communities. Since the issues blacks faced in the North were often different than issues blacks faced in the South, black priests used a variety of tactics to help secure civil rights and promote black power in their communities. The efforts of Reverend August Thompson are but one example.

August Thompson was ordained in 1957 at St. Louis Cathedral, New Orleans, Louisiana, as a diocesan (secular) priest for the Diocese of Alexandria, Louisiana.[42] Having grown up in rural Baldwin, Louisiana, Thompson understood the realities and social restriction under which blacks in the state lived. That knowledge worked to his benefit when he found himself ministering to a black community in Concordia Parish, Louisiana, during the mid 1960s and early 1970s. Located in northeast Louisiana along the Mississippi River, Concordia Parish was known for its Ku Klux Klan activity. Yet Thompson, who had also attended the 1968 Detroit meeting, was resolved to empower blacks in this community. To do so, he utilized tactics that were subdued in nature. For example, Thompson noted that every time blacks, "as quiet as they tried to keep it," sought legal action against discriminatory practices in the schools, Klan harassment of the parties involved increased. Thompson soon realized that the white notaries were alerting the Klan every time blacks attempted to have documents notarized that indicated their legal intents. So Thompson became a notary, and blacks who wished to file complaints against the schools and other institutions in the area could then go to him to have their documents notarized. Since parishioners often visited their priest, little suspicion was aroused.[43]

Thompson's interest in empowering blacks preceded the Detroit 1968 meeting. He had explored the cooperative movement and studied at the International School of Cooperatives in Nova Scotia. He became a member of the board of directors of the Southern Consumers Cooperative (SCC) in 1962 and in 1969 became its president. The SCC's goal was to help poor black farmers achieve property ownership, especially of the land on which they worked, and to reap the profits from that land. The SCC, which started in Lafayette Parish, Louisiana, owned a bakery and a loan company similar to a credit union, and it provided a limited program on consumer education.[44]

Thompson also utilized the SCC to help promote civil rights efforts in Concordia. The black community in Ferriday, a town in Concordia Parish, wanted to bring the Head Start program to the area, but officials—like many others throughout the South—declined the project because of its integrated nature.[45] Thompson and the SCC applied for a grant from the War on Poverty through the Economic Opportunity Act and received $25,000 to start a Head Start program in Ferriday.[46] Thompson notes that when the whites in Ferriday saw how successful the program was, and how much money was being brought into the black community, they became angry. He notes: "Blacks were making more money than ever before—cashing $300 paychecks. The local leaders in Ferriday weren't going to have that, and they told the banks not to cash the checks." The following year, Ferriday officials took over the Head Start program.[47]

Thompson also utilized the SCC to teach black farmers and the community leadership skills. Thompson saw how hard the black Concordia sweet potato farmers worked only to have whites make the profit. He notes that before the SCC, "whites bought the potatoes from blacks at a very low price, then took the potatoes and sold them at much higher prices." With the help of the SCC black farmers began to learn about business, buy trucks, and started driving their products to markets in the north. They cut out the middle man.[48]

In 1969 Thompson continued to show blacks how to utilize the legal system when he was transferred to central Louisiana's Prompt Succor Church in Mansura. In 1971 Wilbert Jean Oliver, a black man, approached Thompson for help. Oliver's mother, Martha Pierre Oliver, had died in a nearby hospital on August 17, 1971, and he wanted to give her a proper funeral. Oliver asked the white-owned Escude Funeral Home—the only funeral home in town—to handle arrangements. Escude agreed to embalm the body but wouldn't handle the wake on its premises because Mrs. Oliver was black. Oliver was deeply hurt by Escude's refusal because his mother was "the community midwife and had delivered and nursed some of the Escude children and was considered a family friend," as noted in her obituary. Oliver wanted to fight Escude's decision and told Thompson of his desire. Thompson searched for a lawyer to take the case, and finally approached the Southern Poverty Law Center. The center took the case and won it. The 1973 case, a federal class-action suit, set a precedent and sent a warning that funeral homes that discriminated would be fined.[49]

Black Catholic clergy in the North were also working to empower blacks in their communities. Reverend George Clements, a co-organizer of the 1968 Detroit meeting, is an example. Clements, probably most widely known as the priest who adopted four boys during the 1980s, was ordained in 1957 as a secular or diocesan priest of the Archdiocese of Chicago. Clements, a native Chicagoan, was pastor at Holy Angels in 1962 when black identity consciousness was rising and rebellions were erupting across the country.[50] The rebellions that began in Watts in 1965 spread in 1967 to other cities including Newark, New York, Buffalo, Milwaukee, Atlanta, and Boston.[51]

Clements focused on building black pride and black power to direct the anger that was prevalent throughout the community. One way he accomplished this was to make his parish self-sufficient. Although Holy Angels was located in a poor area of Chicago and was threatened with closure, Clements knew that the parish was "capable of really surviving." In an interview he recalled these events:

At that time, Holy Angels was being subsidized at about $100,000 per year. My first day there, I got up and told people that we were not going to accept that subsidy anymore. That we were going to send that money back and that we were going to make it on our own. They kind of looked at me as if I was crazy. Then, I told them, symbolically what we are going to do is what is going to happen here at this Mass. I said, here is the unique feature of this Mass, we are counting the collection right now in front of you.[52]

Because the sum of this first collection was "very paltry," Clements said that he told the congregation:

Now, what you've got to understand is that before I go down there and beg those white folks, I'm going to resign. We are taking up another collection right now. For those of you who have any ideas

get them out of your mind because I've already told the ushers before
this Mass to lock all the doors, so nobody is getting out of here.[53]

The second collection, Clements said, was "much better." He then told
parishioners, "I think one more go around will do it." The third collection contained "a fairly significant amount of money," and Clements
said:

> Now be prepared to go through this every Sunday until we start
> collecting what we can because I know what you have. . . . I grew
> up here . . . so you can play all of that poor man with white folks if
> you want to, but it is not going to go with me. These poor Protes-
> tant churches around here, if they can survive without some sugar
> daddy down at the chancery office downtown, we definitely can![54]

Although some might characterize Clements's actions as a form of
extortion, the goal of getting blacks in his community to understand that
they could be self-reliant was clear. That spirit also carried over into the
parish school, which eventually became "top-notch" and the largest black
Catholic school in the country, with more than thirteen hundred students and over one thousand youngsters on the waiting list.[55]

The social demographics in Clements's parish were dramatically different than those of the parish where Thompson ministered. Clements
remembers the parish community as being composed of people who were
"inclined to be activists." In trying to direct this community, Clements
also brought them into contact with the larger black community, the
Black Panthers, in particular. He implemented the Panthers' breakfast
program at Holy Angels School. And Clements organized the Afro-American Police League. Here he describes some of the conditions that blacks
were facing in Chicago:

> We were having the racial riots . . . and just a lot of unrest through-
> out the whole city, when it came to race. So, I decided that the only
> group of people . . . who could legitimately carry guns were the
> police. So, I decided to start an organization of black policemen.
> We called it the Afro-American Police League. This organization
> was set up specifically to work on behalf of the black community.
> Our motto was that we protect and serve, but the ones that we
> protect and serve first are our own, our own black people.[56]

Clements made other efforts to incorporate the black community
within the church. For example, like many blacks, he wanted to pay a

special tribute to the late Dr. King. Clements did so by removing a statue of Saint Anthony at Holy Angels and erecting an altar in honor of "St. Martin Luther King, Jr." This sparked a conflict with Cardinal John Cody, cardinal archbishop of the Archdiocese of Chicago. "Of course the Cardinal immediately got furious with that" and telephoned "screaming and yelling on the phone saying, 'take it down and it better be down immediately.'" The two men debated the issue heatedly. Clements says that "the cardinal argued that saints were proclaimed through 'veneration, beatification, and canonization according to canon law' and that the Catholic Church could not make a Protestant minister a saint." Clements recalls that he countered with the medieval practice of proclaiming saints through the acclamation of the people. The cardinal maintained his position; so did Clements. Finally, the priest suggested that if the altar was to be removed, then the cardinal should send someone to do it. The cardinal never did, and the statue remained in its place at the church.[57]

The debate between Clements and the cardinal raises questions about the oath of obedience that priests take, but this cannot be explored within the confines of this paper. More research is needed on the repercussions clergy faced for their efforts to empower blacks. Thompson maintains that diocesan priests had more flexibility than priests belonging to religious orders or institutes in their efforts to promote civil rights and black power.[58] Thompson explains that although he ministered in the South, he felt "freer to say what he wanted" because he was a diocesan priest. "If you weren't a diocesan priest and you were in an order, they could ship you to New Guinea." He does note, however, that there were bishops in the South who used "veiled threats" of excommunication against priests and sisters.[59]

Clements's comments coincide with those of Thompson:

I could not have done virtually any of these things that I was doing, primarily because in an order you are assigned wherever the order wants to send you. I could just see if I was an order priest working in Chicago and that the superior of the order got ticked off, it would be very easy for him to say, "We're sending you over to Africa," and there would be nothing I could do because of the vow of obedience. No, I could never have done what I did as an order priest.[60]

Yet, superiors in the dioceses did try to control the activities of black priests and often reprimanded them.[61] Clements states:

Yes, I was called in and put on the carpet by the Cardinal over and over again. He threatened me with suspension. He said I was deviant, I was just unruly, I was subversive, radical, and all that stuff. Actually, the only reason that he didn't come down on me really hard was because I had so many of the other priests backing me, as well as [black Protestant] ministers. In fact, I had more ministers than I had priests. We were kind of like a solid group working together, so it was very difficult for him or even for the diocese to really come down on me. The big thing, of course, that they always held over the head of pastors, especially black pastors in the black community, was the whole money issue. They'd say, "We'll take away your subsidy." Well, they couldn't do that with us [at Holy Angels].[62]

CLOSING COMMENTS

Although black Catholic clergy are not reflected in the several histories and studies of the civil rights movement, evidence clearly shows that black Catholic priests did contribute to the black struggle for racial equality and social justice in America. The brief treatment presented here of the work of Fathers August Thompson and George Clements to secure civil rights in society and justice in the church for blacks only scratches the surface of Catholic participation in the civil rights and black power movements. To be sure, black religious sisters and brothers, white clergy, white religious sisters and brothers, and Catholic organizations also participated in varying degrees in these movements. Research on these overlooked efforts is essential for a more holistic understanding of (1) civil rights and social justice efforts and ideologies within the black Catholic community; (2) black impact on the Catholic Church; and (3) the Catholic Church's impact on American race relations.

NOTES

[1] For more information on the contributions of various individuals and organizations to civil rights efforts, see Charles M. Payne, *I've Got the Light of Freedom: The Organizing Tradition and the Mississippi Freedom Struggle* (Berkeley and Los Angeles: University of California, 1995); John Egerton, *Speak Now Against the Day: The Generation before the Civil Rights Movement in the South* (Chapel Hill: University of North Carolina Press, 1995); and Aldon D. Morris, *The Origins of the Civil Rights Movement: Black Communities Organizing for Change* (New York: Simon and Schuster/The Free Press, 1984); John M. Glenn, *Highlander: No Ordinary School, 1932–1963* (Knoxville: University of Tennessee

Press, 1996); Cheryl Lynn Greenberg, *Circle of Trust: Remembering SNCC* (Piscataway, NJ: Rutgers University Press, 1998); John A. Salmond, *My Mind Set on Freedom: A History of the Civil Rights Movement* (Chicago: Ivan R. Dee, 1998); Andrew M. Manis, *A Fire You Can't Put Out: The Civil Rights Life of Birmingham's Reverend Fred Shuttlesworth* (Tuscaloosa: University of Alabama Press, 1999); and Glenda Alice Rabby, *The Pain and the Promise: The Struggle for Civil Rights in Tallahassee, Florida* (Athens: University of Georgia Press, 2000).

[2] For a discussion of the Catholic Church as unrelated to black America, see "7 Negro Priests Criticize Church," *The New York Times*, February 18, 1968.

[3] William D. Broderick, "Case Study: The Catholic Church and Black Americans in 1970," *Black Catholic Clergy Caucus Papers*, box MX1–D, Josephite Archives, Baltimore, Maryland. Louisiana's large number of black Catholics can be traced to the transference of the colony from France to Spain in 1762. In 1789 Spain issued the Spanish Black Code. The code for the Louisiana Colony required all slaves to be baptized Catholic and instructed in the faith. Spain ceded Louisiana back to France in 1800. See Ronald L. Sharps, "Black Catholics in the United States: A Historical Chronology," *U.S. Catholic Historian* 12, no. 1 (Winter 1994): 119–41.

[4] "Converts of Color: Catholic Church Finds Equality Policy Wins Negro Followers," *Ebony* (March 1946), 31.

[5] James Finn, "American Catholics and Social Movements," in *Contemporary Catholicism in the United States,* ed. Philip Gleason, 127–46 (Notre Dame, IN: University of Notre Dame Press, 1969), 132, 133.

[6] "We Have Had to Accept Rejection—Can You?" *The New York Times*, May 25, 1969.

[7] William A. Osborne, *The Segregated Covenant: Race Relations and American Catholics* (New York: Herder and Herder, 1967), 15.

[8] Ibid.

[9] Cyprian Davis, *The History of Black Catholics in the United States* (New York: Crossroad, 1990), 256.

[10] Cited in Finn, "American Catholics and Social Movements," 132.

[11] To see the official program, go to http://www.africanamericans/com/MarchonWashington.htm.

[12] Davis, *The History of Black Catholics in the United States*, 256.

[13] Ibid.

[14] Osborne, *The Segregated Covenant*, 15.

[15] Telephone interview with Fr. August Thompson, April 2, 2004.

[16] Finn, "American Catholics and Social Movements," 135.

[17] Telephone interview with Fr. Theodore K. Parker, O.S.C., May 3, 2004.

[18] *Gaudium et spes* means "the joy and the hope." Available online.

[19] Morris J. MacGregor, *The Emergence of a Black Catholic Community: St. Augustine's in Washington* (Washington DC: The Catholic University of America Press, 1999), 148.

[20] Ibid., 149.

[21] "Current Trends in Negro Education and Shorter Papers, Section A: Discrimination and the Christian Conscience," *The Journal of Negro Education* 28, no. 1 (Winter 1959): 67.

[22] Ibid., 68.

[23] "Case Study: The Catholic Church and Black Americans in 1970," 8.

[24] "Converts of Color," *Ebony* (March 1946), 31.

[25] Ibid.

[26] "Case Study: The Catholic Church and Black Americans in 1970," 8.

[27] Davis, *The History of Black Catholics in the United States*, 257.

[28] Ibid.

[29] Ibid.

[30] Interview with George Clements, Washington DC, January 6, 2004.

[31] Priests interviewed for this project agree that several heated arguments occurred during this meeting.

[32] Davis, *The History of Black Catholics in the United States,* 258.

[33] Interview with George Clements, Washington DC, January 6, 2004.

[34] Gayraud S. Wilmore, *Black Religion and Black Radicalism: An Interpretation of the Religious History of Afro-American People,* 2nd ed. (Maryknoll, NY: Orbis Books, 1983), 194.

[35] Ibid., 214.

[36] Ibid.

[37] Ibid.

[38] Ibid., 215.

[39] "Black Religion Seeks Own Theology," *The New York Times*, January 30, 1971.

[40] "7 Negro Priests Criticize Church."

[41] Marilyn Wenzke Nickels, *Black Catholic Protest and the Federated Colored Catholics, 1917–1933* (New York: Garland Publishing, 1988), 1.

[42] Interview with August Thompson, Maryhill, Louisiana, July 21, 2003.

[43] Ibid.

[44] "At Prompt Succor Church, Mansura: Father August Thompson: One Man with Courage," *Alexandria Daily Town Talk, Alexandria-Pineville*, January 8, 1972; and interview with August Thompson, Maryhill, Louisiana, July 21, 2003.

[45] See *America's War on Poverty: Given a Chance,* Part 2 (Alexandria, VA: PBS Video), 1995.

[46] "At Prompt Succor Church, Mansura: Father August Thompson: One Man with Courage"; and interview with August Thompson, Maryhill, Louisiana, July 21, 2003. For more on the War on Poverty and Head Start, see Catherine J. Ross, "Early Skirmishes with Poverty: The Historical Roots of Head Start," in *Project Head Start: A Legacy of the War on Poverty*, ed. Edward Zigler and Jeanette Valentine, 21–42 (New York: Collier Macmillan Publishing, 1979); and Edward Zigler and Karen Anderson, "An Idea Whose Time Had Come: The Intellectual and Political Climate for Head Start," in Zigler and Valentine, *Project Head Start*, 3–19.

[47] Interview with August Thompson, Maryhill, Louisiana, July 21, 2003.

[48] Ibid.

[49] Interview with August Thompson, Maryhill, Louisiana, July 21, 2003.

[50] Interview with George Clements, Washington DC, January 6, 2004.

[51] For more information on the riots, see Jeffrey C. Stewart, *1001 Things Everyone Should Know About African American History* (New York: Doubleday, 1996).

[52] Interview with George Clements, Washington DC, January 6, 2004.

[53] Ibid.

[54] Ibid.

[55] Ibid.

[56] Ibid. Clements's memories have been echoed by several other priests interviewed for this project.

[57] Interview with George Clements, Washington DC, January 6, 2004.

[58] According to John Deedy, there are roughly one hundred religious orders of men within the Catholic Church. Some of these orders specialize in preaching, some in education, others in missionary work (see *The Catholic Fact Book* [Chicago: Thomas More Press, 1986], 235). Secular or diocesan clergy belong to a particular diocese, an ecclesial geographic designation—for example, Los Angeles, New York, or Chicago—and spend most of their priesthood there.

[59] Interviews with August Thompson and other black priests at the University of Notre Dame, Notre Dame, Indiana , March 11–13, 2003.

[60] Interview with George Clements, Washington DC, January 6, 2004.

[61] The comment was made by several black priests at the University of Notre Dame, Notre Dame, Indiana, March 11–13, 2003.

[62] Interview with George Clements, Washington DC, January 6, 2004.

PART II

THEOLOGICAL AND ETHICAL REFLECTION

Chapter 6

Theology at the Crossroads

A Meditation on the Blues

M. SHAWN COPELAND

For the message about the cross is foolishness to those who are perishing, but to us who are being saved it is the power of God. . . . Christ [is] the power of God and the wisdom of God. (1 Cor 1:18, 24)

In Africa the cross is of two roads intersecting to flow into each other, to nourish each other. The earthly and the spirit worlds meet at right angles, and everything that is most important happens at the spot where they meet, which is neither solely of one world nor the other.[1]

> I went down to the crossroads / fell down on my
>   knees
> I went down to the crossroads / fell down on my
>   knees
> Asked the Lord above for mercy / save poor Bob
>   if you please
>
> Standing at the crossroads / I tried to flag a ride
> Standing at the crossroads / I tried to flag a ride
> Ain't nobody seem to know me / everybody pass
>   me by[2]

Crossroads sit literally at a distance from city and village, often removed from the familiar and customary. Figuratively, crossroads not only evoke potentiality, openings, and creativity but also improbability,

97

caution, even chaos. The woman or man standing at a crossroads cannot but expect risk. Such negotiation requires sensitivity to situations and opportunities, skill in recognizing and interpreting crucial signs and communications, competence in discerning knowledge of good and evil, of truth and falsehood. For the lessons of the crossroads seldom forgive; here doors open or close, futures face foreclosure, chance revises choice. Because the crossroads insinuate revelation and insight as well as disorientation and danger, appeals to divine intervention as well as manifestations of divine presence and power are associated with this juncture of deliberation, turning, and decision. Thus, crossroads signify a place or moment of deep imposing mystery, of access to dense and opaque power.

Crossroads imagery appears in the mythos, legends, and folklore of nearly all cultures. In the black Atlantic world the sign of the crossroads merges with the ancient BaKongo "sign of the cross" to express in ideograph the point of contact and passage between this world and the world of spiritual realities. Visually, when traced in sand, chalked on shrine floors, or painted on vestments, the BaKongo ideograph conflates with the cross of Jesus of Nazareth, compressing and compounding numinous powers. While the Kongo cross neither signifies nor bears any relation to the cross of Jesus of Nazareth, its meaning overlaps Christian interpretation.[3] Indeed, no Christian can glimpse these two simple intersecting lines (+) without thinking of the cross of Jesus, his passage, mediation, and communication.

In African American expressive aesthetics, the multiple meanings of cross and crossroads condense in the blues, in the creativity, style or "cool" (meaning appropriate conduct), power or *àshe* of the blues player. Keenly attuned to the indistinguishable yearnings of Saturday night and Sunday morning, the blues are jagged, raw, liminal, bursting with *eros*, shocking, yet true. The blues reverberate the depth of sorrow and hurt experienced by women and men who live hidden and in uncommon faithfulness in the shadows at the crossroads.

DOWN AT THE CROSSROADS

A theology, black and Catholic, must go down to the crossroads, to listen to and learn from black vernacular culture, to the blues.[4] By engaging in dialectical conversation with this music, theology places black vernacular culture at the heart of its mediation of the Christian message. Doing so will have profound ramifications not for theology or black vernacular culture alone, but rather for *all* human life, especially whenever life is threatened by force, coercion, and cynicism. For the blues narrate and authenticate human feeling, desire, and hope. Blues songs and sounds are the precious gift of black folk to anyone who may be, as folklorist Alan Lomax once declared, "utterly miserable, physically exhausted, totally humiliated [and] overwhelmed by feelings of helplessness, [and] dare [not] complain or talk back, because [one's] fate" rests in the hands of implacable power.[5]

The blues rise from the musings and moaning of enslaved Africans in response to their "peculiar experience" in the new world. These critical, aesthetic, healing songs and sounds "did not just happen," Ollie Stewart states. "There is a history to the birth and form of our music. [The blues contain] every element of life—[not just sex, but] religion, romance, tragedy, faith, hope and primitive abandon—brought together and paid for at a tremendous price."[6] Literary critic Houston Baker maintains that the blues synthesize "work songs, group seculars, field hollers, sacred harmonies, proverbial wisdom, folk philosophy, political commentary, humor, elegiac lament, and much more."[7] This music and moaning bristle with motion and meaning, fuse geography and suffering, recall journeys and transformation, pulsate with the spiritual dynamism of black religion. The blues generate a force field in which differences resolve or dissolve, understanding tests and plucks multiple meanings. And, while the blues form neither a set of propositions nor a reductive interpretation of the black lifeworld, theologian James Cone writes perceptively that the blues are "the essential ingredients that define the *essence* of the black experience. . . . The blues [are] a state mind in relation to the Truth of black experience."[8]

To sing the blues is to meet, deal with, endure adversity, and come back struttin'. Singing the blues transcends the music itself, for the lyrics mediate being human in crossroads conditions:

> I'm goin' down to the river, sit down and begin to
>   cry,
> If the blues overtake me, I'll drink that old river dry.
>
> I got the world in a jug, and the stopper's in my
>   hand.
>
> Yuh can read my letters but yuh sho cain't read my
>   mind.
> When you think I'm laughin', laughin' just to keep
>   from cryin.
>
> If you see me coming, better open up your door,
> I ain't no stranger, I have been here before.

When a theology goes down to the crossroads it risks encounter with new wisdom found at the heart of black vernacular culture. Here theology must sit beside and listen to children, women and men, who live in the shadow of poverty and want and fear. Here theology takes on "the mark of invisibility . . . [the] visible racial mark"[9]; here theology becomes black and Catholic.

CROSSING THE RIVER

The blues recount the black struggle to cross the river of racism, certainly, but as that river rushes over the rapids of imperial domination all of us—irrespective of cultural, racial-ethnic identity, or religion—are caught in its current. From the crossroads, here is what a black Catholic theology sees:

[In a given year] 3.5 million people, 1.35 million of them children, are likely to experience homelessness.[10]

In 2003, children under the age of 18 accounted for 39 % of the homeless population; 42 % of these children were under the age of five. [The National Law Center Study on Homelessness and Poverty] found that unaccompanied minors comprised 5 % of the urban homeless population. However, in other cities and especially in rural areas, the numbers of children experiencing homelessness are much higher. [And] in 2004, 25 % of homeless were ages 25 to 34; the same study found percentages of homeless persons aged 55 to 64 at 6 %.[11]

Poverty and the lack of affordable housing are the principal causes of family homelessness. While the number of poor people decreased every year between 1993 and 2000, in recent years the number and percentage of poor people has increased. The percentage of poor people has risen from 11.3 % of the population in 2000 to 12.1 % in 2002 [according to the U.S. House of Representatives], and by 2004 the number of poor people grew by 4.3 million from 2000. Today, 35.2 % of persons living in poverty are children; in fact, the 2004 poverty rate of 17.8 % for children under 18 years old is significantly higher than the poverty rate for any other age group (U.S. Bureau of the Census, 2005).[12]

Over the last twenty years, 65 million children, women, and men have contracted AIDS. 28 million of them are dead, including 15 million in Sub-Saharan Africa. 14 million children have lost at least one parent to AIDS and/or AIDS-related illnesses.[13]

Between 1980 and 1990, the prison population in the U.S. increased by about 130 percent. In 2002, the U. S. state and federal prison and local jail population exceeded 2.2 million.[14] If that number were to include all the women and men and youth on parole or on probation, then the figure rises to roughly 5.1 million.[15] In 1995, The Sentencing Project documented that the United States and Russia lead the world in "incarceration rates 6–10 times that of most industrialized nations."[16]

Such is the jagged human pain, the blues cry that black Catholic theology sees and hears sitting at the crossroads.

THEOLOGICAL IMPERATIVES

How might black Catholic theologians, exegetes, historians, ethicists, and scholars bring our critical intellectual work to bear on such national and global problems? How might our theological and scholarly work support and participate in creative resistance against vicious spiraling cultural and social decline? How will we open the word of God so that those women and men so severely burdened by urgent and relentless dilemmas may rise up in courage with hope to deal with their circumstances? How ought we to respond to the massive scale of the imprisonment of our brothers and sisters, and what can we do in response to the stress and distress that this causes their families and loved ones? How ought we address the coarsening of the values of the dominant culture, the commodification and commercialization of human flesh and life?

To address adequately the decline of the U.S. cultural and social matrix, black Catholic theology must be at once critically political and deeply mystical. For those who assume that the components of black expressive vernacular culture are too shallow or insufficient for theology or theory, recall that W. E. B. DuBois in *Souls of Black Folk* drew on and privileged that very culture as a key signifier of black life.[17] From the crossroads of that culture, a black Catholic theology troubles explicitly metaphysical and philosophical questions; poses an epistemology rooted in differenti-

ated human experience that pursues the transcendental; and clarifies
moral choice.

As political, black Catholic theology must engage three imperatives.
First, it must rethink Christian theological and social praxis from the
crossroads, that is, standing beside ordinary women and men and children who live the blues. All theology has the responsibility "to influence
the cultural context, to translate the word of God [and] project it into
new mentalities and new situations."[18] But no theology can provide authentic influence if theologians yield to bias, preferring arrogant ignorance
of the historical, cultural, and social experience of the many peoples—
especially, the new immigrants—who make the United States their new
home. A black Catholic theology shaped by the blues strives to transform imagination, understanding, and judgment as well as to encourage
new choices and cultivate new practices for our ecclesial life and for
our society. This theology commits itself intentionally to dialogue with
new immigrants, their histories and cultures, events and happenings.
This theology regards difference as vital for authentic community in
church and in society; it advocates for the flourishing of all human
persons.

Second, black Catholic theology must come to terms with the
Enlightenment's other and enervating dimension. Historian of religions
Charles Long analyzed the Enlightenment's paradoxical and absolutizing
impact on humanity when he wrote:

> In some sense all modern colonized peoples are products of this
> period, for within the heteronomous context of the Enlightenment
> the basis for modern racist theory, capitalism, humanitarianism
> and Christianity may be located. The Enlightenment, true to its
> name and symbolic reference, attempted to overcome the opaque-
> ness of the concrete forms of human life and nature. Its analytical
> methods dissected reality for the sake of knowledge and relegated
> the sheer depths of the real to the arena of unknowability. It is this
> seeing through rather than "standing before" and "coming to terms
> with," which is the hallmark of this cultural orientation.[19]

The blues come from the brutal realities of the underside of the Enlightenment, an underside distorted by uncritical commitment to
autonomy, power, acquisitiveness, control, and indifference. Restless yet
purposeful, supple yet disciplined, repetitive yet dialogical, the blues
rightly suspect "fixity as a function of power."[20] Thus, the blues wonder
and wander in order to shine a blue light in the dark and turn theology

toward a different sensibility, one which is capacious, compassionate, and improvisational. The blues demand of theology a prophetic criticism that contests all arbitrary uses of power or coercion, that challenges individual acquisitive materialism, that repudiates any and every attempt to undermine humanity's very humanness, and that cherishes the lives of ordinary everyday children and women and men of *all* cultures and races.

Third, a black Catholic theology must read the "signs of the times" and offer an analysis, that reaches well beyond any sectarian or cultural or racial-ethnic or interest group (even the theologian's own) in order to collaborate in healing the social whole. This theology must participate in designing a blueprint for human flourishing through commitment to a common human good. Above all, this theology must take its bearings by the dangerous memory of the life-death-resurrection of Jesus of Nazareth. If Jesus' prophetic praxis reveals his passion for God and for us in the midst of a concrete human setup, the cross discloses its radical risk—the resurrection in its audacious, ironic, blues-transcendental hope.

SEEING IN THE DARK

If in its theoretic, pastoral, and moral mediation, a black Catholic theology is to rise to the level of its times, to address adequately the decline of the cultural and social matrix, that theology must be deeply mystical. At the crossroads, theology plunges into the dark, and here it is blinded to insight by the luminosity of the transcendent God. Theology must learn to see in the dark.

Theology emerges from God's gracious act of mercy at our wrestling for meaning in our human condition. Oral tradition tells us that blues, too, come from such wrestling. W. C. Handy, the dance orchestra leader, recalls falling asleep as he waited for a long-delayed train in a depot in tiny Tutwiler, Mississippi. Handy woke to the sight of a thin, ragged black man sliding a knife against the strings of a guitar and singing that he was "goin' where the Southern cross the Dog." The man repeated the line three times, responding with his instrument. Intrigued, Handy asked what the line meant. The man explained that the tracks of the Yazoo & Mississippi Valley Railroad, called the Yellow Dog by locals, crossed the tracks of the Southern Railroad in the town of Moorehead. The musician was headed there; he put his journey into a song. Handy is reported to have commented that this was "the weirdest music" he had ever heard. It was the blues.

Versions of this story function as legend and may have circulated long before Handy's Mississippi encounter. The story helps to explain the genius and astonishing virtuosity of great blues musicians.[21] For instance, bluesman Tommy Johnson told an interviewer that in order to learn to play the blues, you go down to the crossroads about midnight with your guitar; there you will meet a strange, big black man who will take your guitar and tune it, play a few songs, give it back to you, then, the black man drifts away into midnight black.

If the blues function as a trope for theology, then the black Catholic theologian must take on the identity of the blues musician. As Romare Bearden, that dazzling *griot* of the aesthetic, encourages: "You must become a blues singer—only you find the rhythm and catch it good and you structure it as you go along—then the song is you."[22] Like the blues musician, the black theologian is steeped in a desire and an excellence. Like the blues musician, the theologian is sensitive to structure, idiom, and rhythm. Like the blues musician, the theologian is disciplined, but crosses boundaries in creative search of an authentic blue note.

That blue note, the work of the black Catholic theologian, rises as the theologian goes down to the cross(roads) and steps into the dark and unknown. There the theologian may meet a ragged, poor, dark man of uncertain race and origin, who will take the theologian's mind and heart, tune them, then give them back for service to a suffering and crucified community. The word of God possesses and remakes the theologian in the word's own desire and concern, makes the theologian's body a body for the service of others. In this luminous darkness prayer is attention and reverence; it is loving utterance of heart and tongue and pen. In this luminous darkness the theologian falls in love with God.

Here in the darkness of God, the theologian accepts the gift of vocation—to bear the *mythos*, desires, sorrows, struggle, and hope of God's black peoples. Yet black Catholic theology, like the blues, is problematical, fluid, inventive, and the darkness illuminates new intersections, new switches, new tracks. Like the blues musician, the theologian hungers for, seeks out, and wanders into (ecclesial, academic, social) community for dialogue, conversation, even argument with peers, with others, with the very form of theology itself.[23] Black Catholic theology moves back and forth between affirmation and negation, similarity and dissimilarity in clarifying and interpreting the human condition in light of divine salvation.

Yet perhaps especially in the darkness of God, the theologian has no assurance of academic recognition, of ecclesial appreciation, of public affirmation. Here in the darkness of God the theologian learns to wait—

wait for understanding, wait for words, wait for flower and fruit. Wait. Here in the darkness of God the dark theologian learns intimate lessons of sacrifice, suffering, and pain. Here in the darkness of God the theologian learns to respond humbly to the uncommon calling of black Catholic theology with uncommon faithfulness.

THE SIGN OF THE CROSS

This meditation on the blues began with three epigrams that traced verbally the sign of the crossroads—X. The passage line out of the womb of Africa ends in the bluesground of America (\) and intersects with the wisdom line that culminates in the cross of Jesus of Nazareth (/). "For the message about the cross is foolishness to those who are perishing, but to us who are being saved it is the power of God. . . . Christ [is] the power of God and the wisdom of God" (1 Cor 1:18, 24). The cross leads us to the blues, to the moans and songs of struggling people and the blues lead us back to the cross, to the unyielding commitment of Jesus of Nazareth to the reign of God. The risks of the crossroads, of the crossing sign, of the "sign of the cross" are many and they are significant, but the reward is a pearl of great price. And in the dark cloud that rolls across the crossroads and descends upon the cross, those who wait are likely to glimpse a bloodied dark man of uncertain race and origin, who will reach down from the cross and tune their hearts to the sound of the gospel train that runs from here to heaven again.

NOTES

[1] Michael Ventura, *Shadow Dancing in the USA* (New York: St. Martin's Press, 1984), 110.

[2] Robert Johnson, "Cross Road Blues," *Robert Johnson: King of the Delta Blues Singers* (King of Spades Music, BMI, 1937; Sony Music, 1961).

[3] Robert Farris Thompson, *Flash of the Spirit: African and Afro-American Art and Philosophy* (New York: Random House, 1983), 108.

[4] Some readers may ask, "Why not rap?" Certainly, rap in its early years provided serious critique of the dominant cultural and social matrix and its impact upon black lives. The force of gangsta rap clouds this beginning with brutal and raw imagery and lyrics that are misogynist, vulgar, and obscene. Meditating on the blues is an act of black *ressourcement*.

[5] Alan Lomax, *The Land Where the Blues Began* (New York: Bantam Doubleday/Dell Publishing, 1993), 274.

[6] Ollie Stewart, "What Price Jazz?" *The Chicago Defender*, April 7, 1934, cited in Jon Michael Spencer, *Blues and Evil* (Knoxville: University of Tennessee Press, 1993), xxvi.

[7] Houston A. Baker, Jr., *Blues, Ideology, and Afro-American Literature: A Vernacular Theory* (Chicago: University of Chicago Press, 1984), 5.

[8] James H. Cone, *The Spirituals and the Blues: An Interpretation* (1972; Maryknoll, NY: Orbis Books, 1991), 102.

[9] Fred Moten, *In the Break: The Aesthetics of the Black Radical Tradition* (Minneapolis: University of Minnesota Press, 2003), 68.

[10] National Coalition for the Homeless, "How Many People Experience Homelessness?" Available on the nationalhomeless.org website.

[11] National Coalition for the Homeless, "Who Is Homeless"? Available on the nationalhomeless.org website.

[12] National Coalition for the Homeless, "Homeless Families with Children." Available on the nationalhomeless.org website.

[13] Worldwide HIV & AIDS Statistics. Available on the www.avert.org website.

[14] Alan Elsner, "If US Plays Global Prison Rating Game, It Ought to Play by Its Own Rules," *Christian Science Monitor*, March 4, 2004. Available online.

[15] Angela Davis, "Race and Criminalization: Black Americans and the Punishment Industry," in *The House That Race Built: Black Americans, U. S. Terrain*, ed. Wahneema Lubiano (New York: Pantheon Books, 1997), 267.

[16] The Sentencing Project, "Report Summary: Americans Behind Bars: U.S. and International Rates of Incarceration" (1995). Available on the sentencingproject.org website.

[17] W. E. B. Du Bois, *The Souls of Black Folk* (1903; New York: Modern Library, 2003).

[18] Bernard Lonergan, "Theology in Its New Context," in *A Second Collection by Bernard J. F. Lonergan, S.J.,* ed. William F. J. Ryan and Bernard J. Tyrrell (Philadelphia: Westminster Press, 1974), 62.

[19] Charles H. Long, "Structural Similarities and Dissimilarities in Black and African Theologies," *The Journal of Religious Thought* 33 (Fall-Winter 1975): 19.

[20] Baker, *Blues, Ideology, and Afro-American Literature*, 202.

[21] "What Is the Blues?" Available on the pbs.org website. This account also appears in W. C. Handy, *Father of the Blues*, ed. Arna Bontemps (New York: Macmillan, 1941). The musician who wakes Handy from sleep in an empty train depot slides a knife against the strings of his guitar. If African American expressive aesthetics condenses the creativity, grace, style, and *àshe* of the Yoruba *orisha* Eshu or Eshu-Elegba in the blues musician, then the knife may well signify a presence more powerful than Handy grasped. Robert Farris Thompson observes that iconic representations of Eshu, especially as paired male and female figures, often displayed the *orisha*'s attributes, such an upright knife upon the head as a sign of Eshu's power (*Flash of the Spirit*, 20). Is it mere happenstance that a knife as an implement of *àshe*, of the powerfully "weird" surfaces in the story told by W. C. Handy of the first time he heard the blues?

[22] Maureen Mullarkey, "Finding the Tone: Romare Bearden's Monotypes and Robert Blackgurn's Printmaking Workshop." Available on the marueenmullarkey .com website.

[23] See Albert Murray, "Improvisation and the Creative Process," in *The Jazz Cadence of American Culture*, ed. Robert G. O'Meally (New York: Columbia University Press, 1998), 113.

Chapter 7

Daniel A. Rudd and His
American Catholic Tribune

Faithful and Prophetic in Passing on the Tradition

LaREINE-MARIE MOSELY, S.N.D.

Uncommon faithfulness characterized the life and mission of Daniel A. Rudd, an African American Catholic layman who published the *American Catholic Tribune*, a newspaper whose aim was to promote black Catholic life.[1] Rudd was also the founder of the black Catholic congress movement.[2] Through the *ACT* and the five congresses of the nineteenth century, Rudd wielded tremendous influence throughout the black Catholic community and beyond.

Despite the various manifestations of white supremacy and the consistent ecclesial neglect that many African American Catholics faced in the last four decades of the nineteenth century, Rudd was motivated to rally the African American community of his day to take a long and hard look at the Roman Catholic Church as a possible religious home. What prompted this unusual perspective? Rudd genuinely believed in the Catholic Church's wide purview and compassionate care for persons most in need. He reasoned that it would not be difficult for the priests, bishops, and religious to see the needs of black Catholics and to respond to them in the spirit of Jesus Christ. So, after working in the public sector in newspaper journalism in the early years of the 1880s, Rudd decided to edit and publish his own paper with black Catholics in mind.

Dom Cyprian Davis, O.S.B., the author of the seminal book *The History of Black Catholics in the United States* and the premier authority on black Catholic history, has written considerably about Rudd and his passion for his own people and for the Catholic Church that he so loved. Rudd was well endowed with gifts of nature and grace, and he used these gifts for the good of the people of God. In this essay I argue that

108

Rudd's acute experience of the *sensus fidelium*, "the sense of the faithful," allowed him to be a quintessential leader whose life and mission would long be admired. The faithful who influenced and were responsible for Rudd's ongoing faith formation played an essential role in his life. The extant copies of the *ACT* and the proceedings of the nineteenth-century black Catholic congresses testify to the fact that the word of God that Rudd heard, the tradition or "living and lived faith" that was handed on to him, and the multiple traditions that he engaged in had both communal and personal effects. Personally, Rudd knew the word of scripture, the deposit of faith, and the experience of the traditions to be invitations directed to him in a unique manner. Rudd's history bears out the conjecture that in a significant way he embraced the various dimensions of his God-given faith and responded by animating this faith through the venues of the *American Catholic Tribune* and the colored Catholic congresses.

THE *SENSUS FIDELIUM*, TRADITION, TRADITION, AND TRADITIONS

The thesis of this chapter is that Daniel Rudd and the wider black Catholic community that influenced and surrounded him possessed a unique understanding of their role as members of the living and breathing body of Christ. Because there is limited information about Rudd's family members and his black Catholic confreres, this work focuses on Rudd alone. Nevertheless, the principle of communion holds a signature place in Catholicism's self-understanding and lived reality, thus necessitating that Rudd be placed within his communal context.[3] To be sure, Rudd was influenced by white Catholics who were formative in his faith development, but this work accentuates Rudd's belief in himself as an important black subject within the Roman Catholic community who was called to contribute to the life of the church in faithful and distinct ways.[4]

In the aftermath of the Second Vatican Council, greater attention was given to the important and dynamic role of the laity in the church and society. The church's understanding of the *sensus fidelium* is evidence of this significant development. The following excerpt highlights this development:

The council also spoke of the Holy Spirit imparting the gift of faith and bestowing charisms on each Christian. A positive, active, and dynamic understanding of the believer emerged. The teaching of the *sensus fidelium* in particular helped clarify the prophetic duty of the believer to proclaim the word of God. The laity were challenged to deepen their understanding of the faith by prayer, study, discussion, and committed action.[5]

Although it is fair to say that Rudd would most likely not have engaged the language of the *sensus fidelium*, he nevertheless understood this concept quite acutely. He knew himself to be gifted in the areas of civic involvement and newspaper journalism. This prompted him to get involved in the marketplace or secular context. Later Rudd would use these charisms within both secular and religious circles to promote the faith lives of fellow black Catholics and others of African ancestry. Without realizing it, Rudd was ever prophetic as he crafted the *ACT* in a manner that would showcase the Tradition and traditions of Catholicism. Through his fidelity to this "committed action," his and others' understanding of the faith was deepened.

Another way to discuss the manifestations of Rudd's *sensus fidelium* is to engage the language of traditions, tradition, and Tradition. In Yves Congar's classic *Tradition and Traditions: An Historical and Theological Essay,* Congar makes specific distinctions regarding their meanings. The traditions (small "t" and plural) "are determinations, normative in conditions which . . . [are] not contained formally in the canon of Scripture. . . . Their principal concern is worship and discipline."[6] The tradition (small "t" and singular) is "the transmission of the whole Gospel, that is, the whole Christian mystery, in any form . . . in its objective sense as the content transmitted; or as the act of transmitting."[7] Lastly, Tradition (capital "T" and singular) "is the interpretation or meaning given to realities transmitted within the group to which they have been committed, a community living and sharing them."[8] Mindful of Congar's delineations, one can speak of Rudd faithfully transmitting the Tradition through the *ACT* and the Black Catholic Congress movement. His goal was clear: to present the Catholic Church as the logical home for the black community of his day. In this essay special attention is given to the transmission of the Tradition through the *ACT*.

BIOGRAPHICAL INFORMATION

Daniel Rudd was born into slavery in Bardstown, Kentucky, on August 7, 1854, to Elizabeth Frances and Robert Rudd. One of twelve children in this Catholic family, Rudd relocated to Springfield, Ohio, following the Civil War. There he joined his older brother Robert and was intent on acquiring a high school education.[9] Later in life Rudd became involved in promoting racial equality in education and wrote articles and editorials for various newspapers against lynching and racial segregation. Rudd founded and/or edited a number of journals in Ohio before he rolled out the *American Catholic Tribune* in Cincinnati, "the only Catholic Journal Edited and Published by Colored Men."[10]

The *ACT* readership read about Rudd's Catholic roots. St. Joseph, his home parish in Bardstown, Kentucky, held many fond memories for him and was "extremely significant in shaping his Catholic character and perception of the world, especially through his pastor John S. Verdin, S.J., whom he called 'our old instructor.'"[11] Father Verdin was quite successful with his gifted student Rudd. The *ACT* displays in countless ways how Rudd both knew and integrated his life of faith.

The *ACT* included an article from the Philadelphia *Catholic Times*. This article, an obituary of sorts, tells of the death of Rudd's mother, Elizabeth Rudd. Mrs. Rudd's service and devotion to her parish shed light on Rudd's high regard for the church: "Mrs. Rudd, and her family were employed as sextons of St. Joseph's Church for more than sixty-five consecutive years. Elizabeth Smith, was married to Robert Rudd in 1831. Of their offspring twelve in number eight survive to mourn their loss, the father having died in 1865."

DANIEL RUDD, SUBJECT OF THE TRADITION

Mrs. Rudd's obituary testifies to the fact that Daniel Rudd and his siblings experienced their faith in the context of a faithful and devoted Catholic community. Rudd not only learned his catechism, but he undoubtedly understood its significance in the lives of church members. Why else would he include informative articles about the sacraments and other important dimensions of Catholicism?[12]

Like the other black Catholics of his day, Rudd had a genuine love and high regard for one of their own, Father Augustus Tolton, "the most conspicuous Man in America." Tolton was the first self-acknowledged African American priest to serve in the United States, and Rudd honored him by including a large picture of him with a short biography.[13] For Rudd, Tolton was a perfect example that black Catholics could aspire to all things because the Catholic Church was an egalitarian organization based on the equality of all God's children. This sentiment is evident in an engraving present in a limited number of editions of the *ACT* where one could find a picture of a bishop surrounded by what seems to be children of every race. The caption below it read: "The Church Is Mother of All."[14] This is exactly what Rudd knew as the truth to which the leaders and membership of the church aspired. Rudd also included articles about the Blessed Sacrament Sisters, who were founded by Katharine Drexel, and the Oblate Sisters of Providence, who served black children.

With tremendous confidence Daniel Rudd took responsibility for sharing and passing on the faith that had been bequeathed to him. Knowledgeable about Catholicism, he interpreted and conveyed the Tradition in ways that would engage the black community and fill its people with hope and pride. It's hard to imagine that an African American man of his time could have such optimism and hope. These were gifts or charisms with which he had been entrusted and that he used for the promotion and overall benefit of the faith. It has been noted that hyperbole marked the nineteenth-century public writing style. This accounts for some of Rudd's statements that painted the Catholic Church as a faith community that did not exhibit racial prejudice at all. It appears that in a number of writings, Rudd wrote about the Catholic Church that was true to her calling and chose not to emphasize the sinful failures and blind spots of its very human members.

Rudd wanted the world to know that being black and Catholic was neither an anomaly nor an oxymoron. Perhaps he would be surprised to know that over a century later black Catholics in the Untied States would still be affirming their identity and rightful place in the Catholic Church. Theologian M. Shawn Copeland is direct and trenchant when she insists that "the question of identity and identity-formation [that] remains such a sharp point for African American Catholics discloses the pervasive and insidious character of White racist supremacy, as well as the putative normativity and privilege of whiteness."[15]

THE GIFT OF DIVERSITY

It has often been noted that theologian Karl Rahner commented that the post–Vatican II church would be a global church. The shifting numbers of the Catholic Church in the twenty-first century attest to this projection. By looking back at the life, work, and witness of Daniel Rudd, one can begin to anticipate some of the gifts that the church will benefit from when it embraces its diversity.

In addition to his work in the newspaper industry, Rudd also was a lecturer and politician who was keenly aware of the suffering of his sisters and brothers of African ancestry. Knowledgeable of this fact, Rudd was compelled to speak out against lynching, slavery, and oppression of all kinds. Because of his own personal history of being enslaved and the many observations of his keen mind, when Rudd encountered the Tradition his reception was striking, as it is for all of those who hear the word and keep it. What is remarkable is the ingenuity, creativity, and passion that marked the manner in which he transmitted the Tradition through his newspaper not only to his contemporaries but to future generations.

This is particularly evident in how Rudd heard the words of Pope Leo XIII in *Rerum novarum*, the encyclical that inaugurated the Catholic Church's social teachings. His views of Pope Leo XIII were already quite favorable because of Leo XIII's opposition to slavery and the slave trade.[16] So, when *Rerum novarum (On the Condition of Labor)* was issued three years later, in 1891, it is understandable that Rudd heard the words of this encyclical as words that were addressed to himself, as, among other things, a black Catholic. This is the beauty and power of the catholicity and universality of Catholicism. Despite Leo XIII's intention to address problems that had crystallized due to industrial capitalism, his words also spoke to Rudd of the plight of the black community in the United States, which struggled to be educated, find gainful employment, and obtain property.

Perhaps *Rerum novarum*'s significance is based on the fact that it functioned as confirmation to Rudd that the head of the Catholic Church, the pope, would not shy away from the so-called social problem. The pope would address the difficult issues that greatly diminished the quality of life of so many. This boded well for the black community that knew suffering, prejudice, and exclusion. For these reasons Rudd would print *Rerum novarum* in the *ACT* in installments. Undoubtedly emboldened, Rudd would continue in his capacity as editor and publisher of the *American Catholic Tribune*. Rudd's words and overall efforts served to transmit the Tradition in new and innovative ways. Black Catholics in the Untied States past and present owe a debt of gratitude to Rudd for his tireless spirit and work for his community. Through this prophetic work and stance Rudd attested to the fact that "Tradition is not an idle capital, mechanically accumulated: there is development and expansion; it enriches itself from within."[17]

When the Catholic Church recognizes and celebrates its global character, it can attend to and welcome the unique and creative ways the people of God will develop and expand the Tradition, to the glory of God. Daniel Rudd is a case in point. Deeply rooted within the Catholic community he anticipated the spirit of the Second Vatican Council that affirmed and celebrated the presence and gift of the laity. Rudd fulfilled his prophetic duty as editor and publisher of the *American Catholic Tribune.* This newspaper enabled him to reach a significant sector of the society and thereby contribute to the building up of the reign of God.

Rudd was a faithful and gifted black Catholic subject of the Tradition. The words of M. Shawn Copeland capture its spirit:

> In the unfolding of Tradition in African American Catholicism, in its process of traditioning, we meet a subject who consciously and intentionally in word and in deed assumes and affirms personhood and humanity. This subject so values personhood as God's sacred gift that she or he will not yield that gift even to the Church, and is ready in love to rebuke the Church when it fails to reverence and protect creation.[18]

NOTES

[1] Hereafter the *American Catholic Tribune* will be referred to as the *ACT* unless otherwise noted.

[2] Congress of Colored Catholics of the United States, *Three Catholic Afro-American Congresses* (1893; reprint, New York: Arno Press, 1978).

[3] Richard P. McBrien, *Catholicism*, new ed. (San Francisco, CA: HarperSanFrancisco, 1994), 12–14.

[4] M. Shawn Copeland, "Tradition and Traditions of African American Catholicism," *Theological Studies* 61, no. 4 (2000).

[5] J. J. Burkhard, "Sensus Fidelium," *New Catholic Encyclopedia,* 2nd ed. (Detroit: Gale, 2003), 12: 917. Also see *Gale Virtual Reference Library*, at http://find.galegroup.com.

[6] Yves Congar, *Tradition and Traditions: An Historical and a Theological Essay* (London: Burns and Oates, 1966), 287.

[7] Ibid.

[8] Ibid., 288.

[9] Cyprian Davis, *The History of Black Catholics in the United States* (New York: Crossroad, 1990), 164.

[10] *ACT*, Friday, February 25, 1887.

[11] Joseph H. Lackner, "The *American Catholic Tribune*: No Other Like It," *U.S. Catholic Historian* 25, no. 3 (2007): 23.

[12] For example, see the following articles in the *ACT*: "The Blessed Eucharist," January 17, 1891; and "The Sacrament of Penance," March 7, 1891.

[13] *ACT*, March 11, 1887.

[14] Lackner, "The *American Catholic Tribune*," 8.

[15] M. Shawn Copeland, "Guest Editorial," *Theological Studies* 61, no. 4 (2000): 604.

[16] See "The Pope on Slavery," *ACT*, November 24, 1888, 1.

[17] Congar, *Tradition and Traditions*, 304.

[18] Copeland, "Tradition and Traditions of African American Catholicism," 652.

Chapter 8

Communion Ecclesiology

Implications for Ecclesial and Social
Transformation in the Black Catholic Community

JAMIE T. PHELPS, O.P.

As a theologian whose major research focuses on the mission of the Catholic Church, my theological and spiritual lens always seeks to discern how it is that we individually and collectively continue the will of God as expressed and embodied in the mission of Jesus Christ:

> The spirit of the Lord is upon me, because he has chosen me to bring good news to the poor, he has sent me to proclaim liberty to the captives and recovery of sight to the blind, to set free the oppressed and announce that the time has come when the Lord will save his people. (Lk 4:18–19)

How do we as church continue in contemporary times to embody and do what Jesus embodied and did in his day? As Jesus, fully human, walked the earth his relationships, words, and deeds (healings and exorcisms) manifested the will of God for the men and women of his time. His prophetic life so mediated God's will and way that our ancestors in the faith came to know him as fully God.

As we study the history of black Catholics in our church, we deepen our understanding of how God's will for our salvation was mediated in and through the everyday experiences of the faith-filled lives of the followers of Christ. Our black Catholic ancestors in the faith, responding to the call and power of the Spirit within them, became sacraments of God's love and justice for the community. They struggled so that we could come to the fullness of life intended for all human beings (see Jn 10:10). They struggled so we could live in unity with one another and

115

with all others because of our love of God (see Jn 17:21–23). Our Black
Catholic ancestors in the faith came to know that their call to Christian
discipleship required that they live the "way" of Jesus, embodying for
our times the unconditional love and justice that Jesus embodied in his
time and place in history.

COMMUNION ECCLESIOLOGY

Responding to the prompting of the Holy Spirit, Pope John XXIII convened the Second Vatican Council, which sought to define the nature
and mission of the church in the modern world. The bishops, gathered
in council, acknowledged in the first chapters of *Ad gentes* and *Lumen
gentium* two aspects of the nature of the church.[1] The church is essentially missionary and her primary mission is that of communion, that is,
to be a sacrament of our unity with God and with the whole human race.

> The pilgrim Church is missionary by her very nature, since it is
> from the mission of the Son and the mission of the Holy Spirit that
> she draws her origin, in accordance with the decree of God the
> Father. (*Ad gentes,* no. 1)

> The Church is in Christ like a sacrament or as a sign and instru-
> ment both *of a very closely knit union with God and of the unity of the
> whole human race. (Lumen gentium,* no. 1)

These teachings echo Jesus' declaration of mission in the biblical passages already cited.

Some twenty years after the closing of the Second Vatican Council,
The "Final Report" of the 1985 Roman Catholic Synod of Bishops stated
unequivocally that "the ecclesiology of communion is the central and
fundamental idea of the council's documents. . . . It is the foundation for
order in the church and especially for a correct relationship between
unity and pluriformity in the church." The document explained further
that this communion was essentially a "communion with God through
Jesus Christ in the sacraments" and that "the Eucharist is the source
and culmination of the whole of Christian life."[2] In a later document,
"Letter to the Bishops of the Catholic Church on Some Aspects of the
Church Understood as Communion," the Congregation for the Doctrine
of the Faith elaborated further that communion was a two-dimensional
concept. Communion not only refers to a *vertical* dimension (union with
God) but also to a *horizontal* dimension (communion among members

of the human community). The vertical dimension, one's union with the Father through Christ in the Holy Spirit, is largely invisible but is made visible by "the communion in the teaching of the Apostles, in the sacraments and in the hierarchal order" within the church. Thus the church becomes the visible sacrament of the invisible communion of humankind with God and one another because of God.[3]

The council documents identified multiple metaphors or images of the church, but the church as the people of God was the most frequently referenced image following the council. Its pronounced use as the heading of the second chapter of *Lumen gentium* and its discussion of the unity of the people of God and their mission captured the popular imagination. However, a close examination of the document reveals that while the image of the church as the people of God was explicit, the concept of the church as communion, though implicit, is more pervasive.

As often as the sacrifice of the cross in which Christ our Passover was sacrificed, is celebrated on the altar, the work of our redemption is carried on, and, in the sacrament of the Eucharistic bread, the unity of all believers who form one body in Christ is both expressed and brought about. All men are called to this union with Christ, who is the light of the world, from whom we go forth, through whom we live, and toward whom our whole life strains. (*LG*, no. 3)

The Church, which the Spirit guides in way of all truth and which He unified in communion and in works of ministry, He both equips and directs with hierarchical and charismatic gifts and adorns with His fruits. By the power of the Gospel He makes the Church keep the freshness of youth. Uninterruptedly He renews it and leads it to perfect union with its Spouse. The Spirit and the Bride both say to Jesus, the Lord, "Come!" Thus, the Church has been seen as "a people made one with the unity of the Father, the Son and the Holy Spirit." (*LG*, no. 4)

Christ, the one Mediator, established and continually sustains here on earth His holy Church, the community of faith, hope and charity, as an entity with visible delineation through which He communicated truth and grace to all. (*LG*, no. 8)

So it is that that messianic people, although it does not actually include all men, and at times may look like a small flock, is nonetheless a lasting and sure seed of unity, hope and salvation for the whole human race. Established by Christ as a communion of life, charity and truth, it is also used by Him as an instrument for the redemption of all, and is sent forth into the whole world as the light of the world and the salt of the earth. (*LG*, no. 9)

The Christian image of the church as communion identifies the nature and mission of the church succinctly. The church is a communion of all those who profess belief in Jesus Christ and through the sacraments of baptism, eucharist, and confirmation acknowledge their call to communion with God, with humankind, and with the whole of creation because of a common origin in God. The church, guided by the Holy Spirit "in way of all truth," is a "people made one with the unity of the Father, the Son and the Holy Spirit," who through the eucharist are created and sustained by Christ as one people . . . "sent forth into the world as the light of the world and the salt of the earth" (*LG*, nos. 4, 9).

THE CALL TO COMMUNION

From all of the above, we conclude that the church's mission has a threefold focus or raison d'être. First, the church creates a *community of believers* who grow in union with the triune God through their participation in the sacraments and life of the church. Second, the church is called to be a *transformative agent in a divided community of believers* both Christian and non-Christian. And third, the church is called to be a *transformative agent in a world divided by sin and injustice*. These three parts are integrally related, and one without the others renders the mission of the church incomplete.

The Jesus movement was essentially directed toward the formation of a community of those who were converted by his prophetic preaching of the kingdom of God and who were made whole by his healing and exorcising ministries. As members of the Jesus movement, the apostles and disciples, both male and female, accompanied and assisted Jesus in his ministry of transforming his religious community and the dominant society so it might more closely realize and reflect God's will expressed in Jesus' proclamation of the kingdom (John Paul II, *Mulieris dignitatem*, nos. 13–16). This proclamation essentially aimed to open the minds and hearts of those within the religious community and the dominant society to establish patterns of human and cosmological relationships resonant with those envisioned by God at the dawn of creation and made possible only by God's self-gift of grace.

Jesus' mission, which the church is called to continue, is primarily a mission of enabling all human beings to live in the fullness of their humanity as free and responsible human creatures made in the image and likeness of God. Such a life is only possible in the context of a radical communion, a union with God, with all human beings, and with the universe. Such a radical communion is born of deep contemplative prayer and God's gracious self-gift. God's grace alone enables us to live in right relationships with one another and all creation.

The call to radical communion is vitiated by sinful patterns of racial, gender, and class exclusion in our social and ecclesial institutions as well as the persistent imposition of dominative power by those who exploit or devalue the lives of the poor, of women, and of non-white peoples in expansive imperialism abroad and marginalization of oppressed groups within their own countries.

CHALLENGES TO COMMUNION

As a remnant of the U.S. Roman Catholic Church in mission to and among the black community, we must ask if we been faithful to the mission of Jesus Christ nurtured and sustained by our black Catholic ancestors, whom we acknowledge embodied an uncommon faithfulness to the church and through the church to the God of Jesus Christ. Have we been faithful to God's call to communion, or have we colluded with the patterns of disregard and oppression? Have we replicated oppressive patterns in our relationships with other black people, whether they are African American, continental Africans, or Africans in the Latin American, Caribbean, Asian, and European diaspora? Have we been faithful to God's call to communion with *all people* regardless of race, color, or creed? Are our ways of living and being in mission consistent with God's love and justice toward all women and men, toward all creation?

We black Catholics are challenged by three realities in our current situation as we seek to respond to the call of the gospel and to the invitation of the Second Vatican Council to communion. First, we need to examine and respond constructively to the fragmentation, division, and conflict that obscure the intent of the national black Catholic movements and the mission of parishes in each diocese. Second, we need to explore how we will meet the challenge of the closures of black Catholic parishes and schools. Third, we need to construct bridges of collaboration to overcome the walls of racial and ethnic-cultural divisions constructed and manipulated by the dominative European/Euro-American social, cultural, and political system that benefits those held captive, either consciously or unconsciously, by false notions of white supremacy and black inferiority.[4]

The responsive strategies that we develop must be directed toward realizing the continuance of the mission of Jesus Christ expressed in his vision of liberating oppressed people from debilitating economic and spiritual poverty, mental and physical imprisonment, and moral and intellectual blindness. In all our efforts we must honor the fullness of humanity of all peoples and strive to bring about the unity of the human community with all creation.

FRAGMENTATION AND DIVISION IN THE BLACK CATHOLIC COMMUNITY

Even cursory empirical observations in many parishes reveal that many Catholics, including cross-cultural ministers as well as we black Catholics ministering in the black Catholic community, have immersed ourselves uncritically in the individualism, materialism, and search for power and recognition characteristic of the prevailing U.S. culture. Even though we proclaim that we seek to deepen our relationship with the God of Jesus Christ and participate in the mission of the church, our individual and collective internalization of modern and/or post-modern secular values is reflected in misunderstandings of the meaning of the gospel. As individuals and as local ecclesial communities, we have confused preaching the gospel with self-aggrandizing leadership and posturing in the pulpit, ecclesial meetings, and gatherings. The action and words of some Catholics, including black Catholics, suggest that acquiring money, prestige, and power is far more important than growth in wisdom, age, and grace.

Some ordained and non-ordained ecclesial leaders, both male and female, who experience poor self-esteem and fear meaninglessness, fail to grow in their knowledge and love of Jesus and use their ecclesial roles to preach themselves rather than the God of Jesus Christ. The actions of these persons could be described as "pimping Jesus"! These men and women use their theological education and ministry for self-promotion and personal gain. They cast a shadow on our Catholic ministries and diminish our effective participation in the mission of Jesus.

Instead of proclaiming the gospel and the "way" of Jesus Christ, some of us competitively confuse our way with his way. Instead of building up our local parishes as humble sites of Christian community, we competitively pronounce that our way of being a parish community is the best and only way of being a parish community. The egotistical self-absorption of some masks deep chasms of self-doubt and inferiority. This distracts and inhibits efforts within our dioceses and national black organizations to work collaboratively to address the spiritual and social needs of the black community and the poor. Instead of following our black Catholic tradition of uncommon faithfulness and commitment to the struggle for the freedom and participation of black women and men as free and responsible subjects of the church's evangelizing and social justice ministries, we reject the power of God working in and through us and act with our own personal hubris.

Instead of being authentic disciples of Christ, responsive to the power of God active within us, we fail to be attentive to the needs of those devalued, marginalized, and oppressed in our midst. We fail to address the real spiritual and social needs of our community. We fail to take seriously the call to holiness, the need for ongoing evangelization and spiritual development, and the social justice ministries focused on the poor and the marginalized, the sick and the needy.

The collective efforts of some to be faithful to the mission of Jesus Christ are in danger of being overshadowed and frustrated by those who place themselves instead of Jesus at the center of our ecclesial mission and ministry. Some of us are held captive by our desires for self-importance and for power. Some of us are so blinded by our self-absorption that we fail to recognize and nurture the gifts given to the members of our community for the building up of our community of faith and the implementation of its mission. Such self-absorption consumes the ministerial energy needed to confront the practical challenges that the black Catholic community faces.

BLACK CATHOLIC PARISHES AND SCHOOLS

In recent years we have witnessed the pattern of the closing of schools and parishes in the black community based on the lack of numbers and economic solvency. Some of these schools and parishes *had* lost their effectiveness and vitality and needed to be closed. In fact, in the past two years there have been numerous parish and school closings in New York and Boston, and newspaper accounts report that more than a few dioceses face bankruptcy. Some of these closings result from economic consequences brought on by the pedophilia tragedy that has engulfed the U.S. Catholic community as we recognized the harm to victims of child abuse perpetrated by some of our clergy.

Diocesan "ecclesial welfare" is no longer an option for black Catholic parishes. *We must assume the leadership in designing and implementing a vision and process to harvest an effective presence of the Catholic Church in the black community.* We black Catholics must assume full responsibility for the future of our parishes and schools. We have both the financial resources and skills within our black Catholic community to collaborate creatively with our respective dioceses in devising plans to preserve and develop more effective and vital parishes and schools to mediate the evangelizing and justice ministries of the church.

We need to organize expert educational scholars and practitioners who can research effective methods and identify those black Catholic schools in our communities that exemplify academically and religiously strong curricula and can serve as national models for us.[5] In a similar fashion we need also to bring together lay and ordained church scholars and practitioners who can identify those black Catholic parishes that are Spirit-centered and engaged effectively in evangelizing and social justice ministries within the black community. These parishes and schools and their respective pastoral and academic leaders can be analyzed to ascertain the qualities necessary for effectiveness. These parishes and schools can serve as consultative models for those communities struggling to find their way.

THE CALL TO COLLABORATIVE MINISTRY AND COMMUNION

One of the dynamics that seems to be destroying effective ministry in the black Catholic community is the destructive competitiveness of some of our organizations and programs. Yet such competitiveness was not characteristic of these programs at the time of their initiation. Initially, all the national organizations focused on discovering and developing networks and methods to enrich Catholic presence and action on behalf of justice in the black community.

These national black Catholic organizations, which were found or reborn in the twentieth century, were the fruit of individuals responding to movement of the Spirit in the social and ecclesial realities of the time. The revitalization of these groups must be in response to the movement of the Spirit, which enables us to discern the social and ecclesial realities of the beginning of the twenty-first century. In the past forty years we have experienced profound theological, social, cultural, and economic shifts that require equally profound ecclesial shifts.

One aspect of these cultural or social shifts is the presence of a competitive rather than collaborative spirit among organizations and programs. Jesus' redemptive life, death, and resurrection make possible our liberation from both the personal and the social sin that alienates us from one another and militates against our embracing the call to communion. His gift should not be frustrated by our refusal to overcome cultural, racial, and gender divisions within the church and our national organizations and programs.

Another significant shift is the expansion of the U.S. black community through the recent immigration of continental African priests, sisters, and laity. Along with the continued migration of black Caribbean and Latin American peoples to the United States, these are both gifts and challenges. The principle of communion obliges us to find ways to engage one another in effective dialogue and collaboration.

Embracing the wisdom of the call to communion rooted in the ecclesial vision of the Second Vatican Council, we must move toward unity in diversity through the empowering grace of the Holy Spirit, whose transforming power can enable us to become more inclusive than we think desirable or possible. Somehow our national black Catholic initiatives (including Knights and Ladies of St. Peter Claver, National Black Catholic Clergy Caucus, National Black Sisters' Conference, Secretariat for African American Catholics of the United States Conference of Catholic Bishops, National Black Catholic Seminarians' Association, Institute for Black Catholic Studies, National Black Catholic Congress, National Association of Black Catholic Administrators, African Women Religious Conference, African Catholic Clergy Association, and National Haitian Apostolate) must find ways of working collaboratively to determine the ongoing and distinctive needs of our black communities and synchronize and co-sponsor programs that unify, promote, and nourish us as Pan Africans who constitute the U.S. black Catholic community in the twenty-first century.

We black Catholics as persons made in the image and likeness of God must find a way to image the radical and unity and diversity of the triune God as we respond to God's call to communion. The invisible unity created and maintained by our shared participation in the creative, redemptive, and sanctifying grace of God must become a visible sacrament of unity in a divided world. Personal and institutional conversion rooted in deep contemplative prayer and discernment is the only path to such radical unity.

WOMEN IN MINISTRY

Another tension within our ministerial community is the gender divide. This division must be replaced by male-female collaboration or partnership in ministry in the black Catholic community. While some examples of successful collaboration are evident, in too many places black men, ordained and non-ordained, seem threatened by the presence of black females in ministry. Male patriarchal and/or misogynist attitudes still perpetuate tensions as women seek to discern and exercise their God-given call to participate in the theological and pastoral ministries of the church.

Even though the participation of women in ministry is rooted in gospel precedents and affirmed by recent papal teaching, little attention is accorded to the potential of women for ecclesial ministry. The numbers of black women, religious and lay, engaged in church-related ministries have increased significantly since the Second Vatican Council. Black women use their skills as mothers, evangelists, catechists, directors of religious education, principals of Catholic elementary and secondary schools, teachers and professors, pastoral associates, theologians, and administrators in diocesan offices for black Catholic or multicultural ministry, offices for social or racial justice, and so forth. In this they follow the earliest traditions, which record women as heads of house churches and companions of Jesus during his ministerial journeys.

In the history of the Church, even from earliest times, there were side-by-side with men *a number of women,* for whom the response of the Bride to the Bridegroom's redemptive love acquired full expressive force. First we see those women who had personally encountered Christ and followed him. After his departure, together with the Apostles, they "devoted themselves to prayer" in the Upper Room in Jerusalem until the day of Pentecost. On that day the Holy Spirit spoke through "the sons and daughters" of the People of God, thus fulfilling the words of the prophet Joel (cf. Acts 2:17). These women, and others afterwards, played an active and important role in the life of the early Church, in building up from its foundations the first Christian community—and subsequent communities—through their own charisms and their varied service. The apostolic writings note their names, such as Phoebe, "a deaconess of the Church at Cenchreae" (cf. Rom 16:1), Prisca with her husband Aquila (cf. 2 Tim 4:19), Euodia and Syntyche (cf. Phil 4:2), Mary, Tryphaena, Persis, and Tryphosa (cf. Rom 16:6, 12). Saint Paul speaks of their "hard work" for Christ, and this hard work indicates the various fields of the Church's apostolic service, beginning with the "domestic Church." For in the latter, "sincere faith" passes from the mother to her children and grandchildren, as was the case in the house of Timothy (cf. 2 Tim 1:5). (*MD*, no. 27)

Effective Catholic ministry in the black community in the twenty-first century is the responsibility of all members of the church. All baptized men and women must discern their role in the mission of the church. Those men called to the ordained ministry as priests and deacons must identify and collaborate with those men and women who have been called to exercise the "priesthood of the faithful." The ordained must facilitate the collaboration of ministries exercised by brothers and sisters who have been called to the non-ordained ecclesial vocations designated as women and men religious or consecrated virgins, lay ecclesial ministers, and the lay volunteers who exercise ministries within the church and society. The call to new evangelization requires the participation of all baptized Christians as a community.

EVANGELIZATION

The church has repeatedly focused on the evangelizing and social justice aspects of the mission of Jesus Christ and calls us to embrace these as the primary focus of our ministries in contemporary society. Key church documents articulate the foundational insights and understanding of what these ministries entail. The call to a new evangelization and to communion in some recent teachings in our church is a call to conversion. In *Evangelii nuntiandi* Pope Paul VI wrote that "evangelizing means bringing the Good News into all the strata of humanity, and through its influence transforming humanity from within and making it new" (no. 18). Evangelization involves conversion solely through the divine power of the words it proclaims, a conversion of the individual and collective conscience of people, their behavior and their concrete situation by bringing them into conformity with the gospel. Often this transformation entails "upsetting through the power of the Gospel, mankind's criteria of judgment, determining values, points of interest, lines of thought, sources of inspiration and models of life, which are in contrast with the Word of God and the plan of salvation" (no. 19).

This call to ongoing evangelization invites black Catholic organizations and individuals to engage in self-critique. We must examine our operative values and criteria of judgment in order to ascertain the extent to which we are living and acting in accord with the values embodied in the life and teachings of Jesus. In a similar way we must examine our patterns of relationship to ascertain whether or not we are walking in accord with the gospel.

BUILDING INCLUSIVE COMMUNITIES

Changes in our attitudes regarding race, gender, and class are key areas where U.S. Catholic Christians need to examine their conformity to the ways of Jesus. Some years ago the pastoral letter *Brothers and Sisters to Us* identified racism as "a sin . . . [and] radical evil that divides the human family and denies the new creation of a redeemed world." The letter asserted that racial division must be healed by "an equally radical transformation in our minds and hearts as well as in the structure of our society." Ongoing "dialogue throughout the Catholic community and the nation at large" constitutes the first step of this conversion. Further, these dialogues best take place within the context of programs addressing family ministry, parish renewal, evangelization, and so on.[6]

In the twenty-seven years since the publication of *Brothers and Sisters to Us*, many dioceses have promulgated letters against racism and established programs and processes to assist their membership to address both personal and institutional racism within the church.[7] Fr. Clarence Williams has developed a program for anti-racism training.[8] In addition, two programs for institutional change implemented by Crossroads Ministry and the People's Institute are reported to be helpful for anti-racism work.[9] Once again, it is clear that the Roman Catholic Church in the United States has the available resources to make significant progress in healing interpersonal and institutional relationships distorted by racism, but we must make such efforts a personal and collective priority. Seeking ways for parishes to collaborate in developing racially inclusive communities of worship and social service is a constructive response to the challenge to radical transformation or conversion of our racial attitudes and patterns of exclusion that characterize both ecclesial and social institutions.

Our attentiveness to the social injustice of racism in church and society should not overshadow the attentiveness we must give to the to the teachings of the church relative to the inclusion of women and the poor in our communities and in our ministries. Just as Jesus included women as followers and co-workers in his ministry (Gal 3:28–29), the black Catholic community must commit itself to the inclusion of both black men and women within the ministries of our church. Just as Jesus set the poor at the center of his ministry (Lk 4:16), the black Catholic community must set the poor at the center of its ministry.

CONCLUSION

As we reflect on the many challenges and opportunities that lie before us as a black Catholic community, we must recall the uncommon
faithfulness that allowed our enslaved and colonized African ancestors
to endure the denial of their full humanity, the appropriation of their
lands and wealth, and the exploitation of their cultural gifts. Despite
oppressive conditions they were able to maintain and exercise their full
humanity. They were empowered by the Spirit to create new alternative
institutions, cultural traditions, and thinking by selecting and weaving
together past customs, beliefs, and understandings with those found in
their new situations as colonized divided peoples on the continents that
would become the Americas.

Just as our ancestors remained faithful to a religious world view in
the most daunting and life-threatening situations, let us persist in our
abiding faith in the power of the God of Jesus Christ. Let us animate
God's will by saying yes to the risen Christ and the Holy Spirit who
dwell within each of us and empower and sustain us as a community of
faith. Let us embody the "way" of Jesus as we continue in contemplative
prayer to discern what we should say and do as faithful followers of Christ
called to engage in evangelizing and social justice ministries as we combat
the struggles and patterns of power, racism, sexism, classism, and cultural imperialism that challenge us in our contemporary situations.

This is a *kairos* moment in the journey of black Catholics in the U.S.
Catholic Church. The current social and ecclesial realities place African
American, continental African, African Latina/o, and African Caribbean Catholics at the crossroads. God is placing before us the choice of
life and death. We must choose life—life in communion with God and
all others because of God.

NOTES

[1] The bishops were assisted by theological *periti* (or consultants) and others
who participated in the formal and informal sessions of the council.

[2] Synods of Bishops, "The Final Report," *Origins* 15 (December 15, 1985).

[3] Congregation for the Doctrine of the Faith, "Letter to the Bishops of the
Catholic Church on Some Aspects of the Church Understood as Communion,"
Origins 22 (1992–93): 3–4. Also available online.

[4] Charles Mill, *The Racial Contract* (Ithaca, NY: Cornell University Press,
1997): "All whites are beneficiaries of the [racial contract] though some are not
signatories of it" (11).

[5] Two insightful books about successful education for black children are Abigail and Stephen Therstrom, *No Excuses* (New York: Simon and Schuster, 2003), which documents successful schools all over the nation including the Knowledge Is Power schools in Washington DC; and Miles Corwin, *And Still We Rise: The Trials and Triumphs of Twelve Gifted Inner-City Students* (New York: Perennial Publishers, 2001).

[6] U.S. Catholic Bishops, *Brothers and Sisters to Us* (Washington DC: USCCB, 1979), 3.

[7] See, for example, Cardinal Francis George, *Dwell in Our Love: A Pastoral Letter on Racism* (Chicago: Archdiocese of Chicago, 2001). Available on the archdiocesechgo.org website.

[8] Many Catholics, especially blacks, Latinos/as, and whites, are familiar with this program. More information about this training program and publication may be obtained by contacting Fr. Williams through the Black Catholic Ministries Office for the Archdiocese of Detroit. See the aodonline.org website.

[9] See the crossroadsministry.org and pisab.org websites.

Chapter 9

Faith of Our Mothers

Catholic Womanist God-Talk

DIANA L. HAYES

> She is clothed with strength and dignity,
>   and she laughs at the days to come.
> She opens her mouth in wisdom,
>   and on her tongue is kindly counsel.
>   (Prv 31:25–26)

It can be argued that I am using these verses somewhat out of context, for they are taken from a section of Proverbs that describes the ideal wife! But my purpose is not to consider the qualities of the "ideal wife" but to consider how for centuries, especially in the United States, women of color, and especially African American women, whether Protestant or Catholic, were seen as "ideal" only as models for slavery, sexual abuse, racial discrimination, and any and all other forms of degradation and dehumanization. Yet somehow they remained women "clothed with strength and dignity" who, through their shared wisdom and that of their ancestors, were instrumental not only in preserving themselves but in building up and preserving the black community as a whole— women, men, and children.

The daughters of Africa who now make their home in the United States have had almost five hundred years in which to be perfected as women of God. They came nameless and unknown, identified only as "Negro woman, age about six or twelve or twenty-two." They may have come with family and/or friends, caught up in the sudden invasion of their village life and the daily round of farming or grazing, cooking and weaving, or they came alone, sharing little but fear of the unknown with those captured and traded with them.

129

New relationships were forged as they were thrown, often unclothed, always defenseless, into the holds of countless ships with names like *Jesus* or *Blessed Redeemer,* but which they saw and experienced as floating hells, places of licentiousness and terror, as they were raped, fed slops, and often, at the first sign of "bloody flux," thrown overboard alive, food for the always accompanying sharks.

When they landed, offloaded from the "big canoe" that had taken them over the "river without banks," they found their situations had not improved but worsened. They were separated from family and friends, from those who understood their language or shared their culture, and sold to men with lust in their eyes, to serve as breeders, field hands, wet nurses, and maids of all work. Cuffed and shackled, they were taken to distant farms and plantations and quickly realized that this was to be their fate in life: to work from "can't see to can't see"; to be treated as farm animals, mere beasts of labor; to be bred to strangers, to give birth only to see their offspring sold from them over and over again. In other words, they lived and died as property. Not for them was the protected pedestal of "true womanhood." They were not seen as "ideal" women or wives, even for their fellow slaves. This myth, used to protect but also confine white women, "stressed piety, purity, submissiveness, and domesticity for women as well as innocence and modesty."[1] African American women, however, were not included in this understanding, as they were required to work in the same fields as their men. At the same time, purity and innocence were unattainable because of the uses to which they were put by greedy men and unscrupulous women.

The social and legal institution of slavery that assigned ownership of slave women's bodies to their owners officially denied slave women the right to reject any sexual overtures and, by extension, also denied the presumption of virtue to black women (free or slave), who often had to deal with the sexual advances of white men.[2]

Yet they did not despair, nor did they turn away from all hope. They had not come empty-handed to this new world but had brought with them a deep and abiding faith in a God of creation, a God of justice and honor—however God was named in their particular communities. They were survivors, not in the silly sense of today's so-called reality shows, but in the deepest sense of those who survived experiences conducive to death. It is Hagar, the slave woman and concubine of Abraham, who exemplifies black women's experience of survival. For Hagar experienced what Delores Williams calls the "wilderness experience," an experience that all African Americans have shared in slavery and afterward. Her experience revealed the wilderness not as something to be overcome or conquered but as a place of refuge. In her first wilderness experience, Hagar

> meets *her* God for the first time. Her experience with this God could be regarded as positive by African Americans because God promises survival, freedom and nationhood for Hagar's progeny. The African American community has, all of its life, struggled for survival, freedom, and nationhood.[3]

But Hagar's experience, like that of most slave women, does not end here. She is forced to return to the wilderness as a free woman with her child but without resources of any kind, just as the slaves experienced a "freedom" in name only at Reconstruction's end as they had nothing but themselves.

> Like African American people, Hagar and her child are alone without resources for survival. Hagar must try to make a living in the wide, wide world for herself and her child. This was also the task of many African American women and the entire community of black freed people when emancipation came.[4]

Williams continues:

> The post-bellum notion of wilderness (with Hagar and child as its content) emphasized black women's and the black community's negative economic experience of poverty and social displacement. ... This post-bellum African American symbolic sense of wilderness, with Hagar at its center, makes the female figure symbolic of the entire black community's history of brutalization during slavery; of fierce survival struggle and servitude after liberation; of children being cheated out of their inheritance by oppressors; of threat to the life and well-being of the family; of the continuing search for a positive, productive quality of life for women and men under God's care.[5]

It is not known how many of the millions of Africans who endured the middle passage to the Americas were Catholic Christians (converted and baptized by the Portuguese from the fifteenth century on), Muslims, or followers of the traditional African religions. What is known is that they brought with them a shared world view that, when later syncretized with the Christian faith of their captors, enabled them to persevere, sustained by their belief in a "wonderworking" God who would, in God's own time, free them from the unmerited captivity in which they passed their weary existence.

Brought from the western lands of Africa, people of many tribes, cultures, and languages shared a world view that enabled them to survive four hundred plus years of slavery, segregation, discrimination, and second-class citizenship. This world view was sacred, resisting the dualistic separation of the sacred and secular domains that their captors/enslavers sought to instill in them. African women and men "knew" God intimately as active, either as Godself or through intermediaries, in their everyday lives, and that knowledge nurtured and sustained them. Religion was seen as all-pervasive, surrounding them on all sides. The holy was a constant presence in their lives and all of life was sacred, from womb to tomb, before and beyond, weaving a web of connections that encompassed both the living and the dead. This religious understanding helped them to create community, for individualism was not a part of their self-understanding. Rather, the "I" of the individual was seen to exist and persist only in the "we" of family and friends—blood and fictive kin who played substantial roles in their lives and the lives of their descendants. They took this understanding and wove it into their reception of the God of Jesus Christ who, they believed, had suffered like them and shared in their pain. This God, who had himself been whipped and lynched, had freed others wrongly enslaved, and despite the insistence of their owners that God had willed their captive status, they knew that God would in time free them as well.

THOSE WHO WERE BEFORE US

Black women are a critical part of this understanding for they are the "bearers of culture," those who passed on the stories, the songs, prayers, and memories of the people. They were able to form a connection that, rather than being broken, was strengthened and expanded in the Americas to encompass all who were enslaved.

[Women] were the heads of their communities, the keepers of the tradition. The lives of these women were defined by their culture, the needs of the community and the people they served. Their lives are available to us today because they accepted responsibility when the opportunity was offered—when they were chosen. There is the element of transformation in all of their work. Building communities within societies that enslaved Africans, they and their

people had to exist in, at least, dual realities. These women, however, became central to evolving the structures for resolving areas
of conflict and maintaining, sometimes creating, an identity that
was independent of a society organized to exploit natural resources,
people, and land.[6]

These structures remain to this day as symbols of the strength, courage,
and steadfast faith of these nameless and unknown African women who
laid the foundation for the millions who followed them.

The majority of black Catholics came speaking Spanish or French as
well as their native languages except for those, fewer in number and
later in their arrival, who came with the English Catholic settlers to
the colony of Maryland. Most came long before others from Africa,
beginning as early as the sixteenth century, and were both free and
slave.

> The first Africans to arrive in what is now the continental United
> States were Spanish-speaking and Roman Catholic. The Spanish
> government introduced in 1565 the colony of St. Augustine in north-
> ern Florida. . . . The baptismal registers, which began with the
> colony and are the oldest ecclesiastical documents in American his-
> tory, witness to the presence of Blacks among the first inhabitants
> of St. Augustine. In these registers, Blacks and mulattos are clearly
> designated as such, along with the indication of whether the indi-
> vidual was slave or free.[7]

Today we are just beginning to uncover and explore the histories and
the stories of the women of this and other Catholic colonies. They are
our mothers, our "sheroes," women who somehow, despite all of the
forces arrayed against them, were able not simply to preserve a culture
but to pass it on to those coming after them. We know very little about
black Catholic women, free or slave, except for the names found in old
baptismal and marriage records. But, as Fr. Cyprian Davis has indicated,
these clearly noted who was black or mulatto, quadroon, or some other
mix of Africa with the native peoples of this "new world" to which they
had been brought as well as the blood of their captors and oppressors,
the Europeans, whether French, Spanish, or English speaking. We know
they were co-founders of cities but we also know them as women who
worked long hours and seemingly impossible jobs in order to keep their
families intact, their children baptized and catechized, and their faith
strong in the face of opposition from so many within their own church
as well as society.

Their full story is not yet written, partly because the stories of all women, regardless of race or ethnicity, have historically been ignored for centuries. In the case of black Catholic women, however, it is also because there were so few able to recover or interested in recovering these histories. It is only in the aftermath of the Second Vatican Council that we began to see, as a result of increasing numbers of black Catholic women entering into theological programs of study, efforts to uncover, recover, and proclaim these and other critical stories. It is vital that we do so, for they are the foundation for the black Catholic community today: women who worked side by side with black Catholic men, but who also had the courage and foresight to come together as women in the church today to struggle for change.

They were lay and religious, slave and free, women like Henriette De Lille and Elizabeth Lange, founders of religious orders who chose to live lives of obedience to God rather than as concubines or servants, whose stories have finally been written and published. They also include women like Coincoin, a former slave and successful plantation owner who, after receiving her freedom and that of one of her ten children, spent the rest of her life purchasing the freedom of the remainder as well as all of her grandchildren. We also call forth the names of Ellen Terry, who established Catholic settlement houses in the East and Midwest; and Dr. Lena Edwards, the first board-certified African American female obstetrician and gynecologist. We can say that they all had a dream, a dream of a time when Catholics of African descent would not only be welcomed in their church as full and equal participants in God's mission but would also be leaders, honored for their contributions to the life of the church at every level. Through their perseverance in faith, these women, the "bearers of culture," as all women are, gave birth to a people and a world that persist to this day. As Fr. Cyprian Davis affirms, speaking of black Catholic religious women:

> In an era when black people were accorded little or no respect or esteem, in a time when black women were degraded by slaveholders or abused by white employers, in a society where black women were considered to be weak in morality, black sisters were a counter sign and a proof that the black Catholic community was rooted in faith and devotion, for vocations arise from a faith-filled people. Lest it be forgotten, the two black sisterhoods were not European transplants; they were very much American in origin.[8]

These women were mothers in the fullest sense of the word, one not limited by biological or blood ties. They were mothers to an entire people, seeking through the work that they did to enable them to survive and thrive. As Fr. Davis states: "The African American religious sisterhoods helped lay the faith foundation of the black Catholic community. . . . As pioneers, they often worked without encouragement or support and too often in the face of indifference and antipathy. Without them, the black Catholic community would not be what it is today."[9]

But the sisters were not entirely alone in their struggle. They were joined and supported by black Catholic mothers who, within their families, the domestic church, not only planted the seeds of faith but nurtured them until they bloomed into black Catholic men and women determined to carve out a niche for themselves and their people, not only in the Catholic Church but in the United States as well. It is the lives of faith of these women that serve as the source from which Catholic womanist theology springs forth.

THE BIRTH OF WOMANIST THEOLOGY

Womanist theologians use the "stuff" of women's lives to spin a narrative of their persistent effort to rise above and beyond those persons and situations that attempt to hold them down. Their sources are social, political, anthropological, and especially, literary.[10]

Womanist theology, a theology of, by, and for black Christian women acting to build (and rebuild) community, emerged at a critical time in the history of Christianity and the world, a time of revolutionary change in which "the least among us" began to take charge of their own lives and, as a result, of how their stories were told and their faith life presented. It is a theology that seeks to give women of African descent in the United States a voice by enabling them to speak the truth of their historical and contemporary experiences as black and Catholic women, a truth both bitter and sweet, a truth that relates how they were able to "make it through." The term *womanist* comes, of course, from the poet and author Alice Walker, who sought a descriptive term for "audacious, courageous, bold and daring" black women that neither restricted them with definitions already developed and concretized by others who had not shared their experiences, nor required them to place a "color" before their names to distinguish them from normative society. To be womanist is to be black; to be black is to be womanist, at least, as the term has been developed and deepened by black female Christian theologians such as Delores S. Williams, Jacqueline Grant, and Kelly Brown Douglas, among others. As a critical response to the absent voice of women of color in both feminist (normatively white) and black (normatively male) liberation theologies, womanist theology seeks to bring the presence and activity of black women to the forefront, rather than the background, of the church's awareness and dialogue.

Both Protestant and Catholic theologians have helped to deepen our understanding of this term, in keeping with the ongoing endeavor in which all theologians are ostensibly engaged—the effort of "faith seeking understanding" in such a way that the faith can be explicated for others. It is an exercise in "doing" theology, praxis rather than merely "thinking," without putting the results of that reflection into action. It is an exercise that engages heart, mind, and spirit in the effort to correlate the historical experience of all black folk, man, woman, or child, with the gospel. Thus, womanist theology is also a theology of liberation, one that both liberates those *doing* that theology, turning them from the objects they have been made into by others into subjects of their own histories, as well as liberating theology from the rigid, top-down stranglehold of abstraction and objectivity that, for centuries, has held it in captivity. This approach enables theology to speak on behalf of those unjustly wronged and dehumanized as Jesus himself did.

Womanist theology starts with black women, women of African descent, in their own particular situations. It engages their historical experience and seeks to reorient reality through the eyes of a black woman. Womanist theologians, Protestant and Catholic, seek to speak a new language, a God-talk that is born out of a centuries' long struggle to be free women, seen and affirmed as being created in the image and likeness of God. Womanist God-talk, thus, springs from centuries of denigration and dehumanization, from the denial of our female persons and the right to control our own bodies, minds, and spirits. It is a struggle that continues into the present day, to articulate what it means to be a black woman and, more particularly for me, to be a black Catholic woman in the world and in the church today. It is also a theology that seeks to confront not just race or class or gender or sexuality or any other forms of oppression that continue to flourish into the twenty-first century but to confront all of these at the same time and to eliminate the dualistic separation of various forms of oppression that have kept people who share in oppression apart from one another instead of in solidarity against the status quo. Black women have experienced and continue to experience all of these oppressions in their own bodies and lives, in their families and communities. Oppression cannot be dealt with singly; it must be attacked like the virus it is, one that simply mutates and changes form as it moves from one place and one people to another. It can be eradicated only when it is attacked from an angle that addresses all of its venomous reality.

THE CHALLENGES WOMANIST THEOLOGY RAISES

As women of African descent, we look first to Africa as the cradle of our history, culture, and traditions, seeking to tap into the river of spirituality that flowed through our ancestors and enabled them to survive the middle passage, Jim Crow, segregated pews and segregated sacraments, and still speak a word of life and hope to those coming after them.

There is a "generational continuity" (the passing on of cultural values and personal history), traditionally the domain of women, that can be seen to continue today as black women writers, for example, focus "on Africa not only as historical ancestor, political ally, and basis for ideological stance but as part of a continuum in which Black women, before the slave trade and since, have recorded cultural history and values through their stories."[11]

A "cultural continuity" also exists in the perpetuation of African values and customs in the Americas. "The cultural mores and values systems are passed down through the female members of the society, especially through and to the children."[12] Continuing this tradition, African American communities have attempted historically, through their women, to retrieve, regather, and repair the often scattered and torn-apart roots of their African culture and reshape them in ways that are renewing and reviving for their people today. This is the wellspring out of which womanism pours forth. It reveals a critically different understanding of values and individual and communal responsibility.

Catholic womanist theologians seek to explore the intersection of race, class, gender, sexuality, and religion in an effort to reveal the role the Christian religion, especially Roman Catholicism, has played in affirming, exploiting, perpetuating, and upholding understandings of social constructs that have served to provide not only a language but a pervasive, hegemonic ethos of subordination and oppression of women and persons of color. Grounded in the neo-platonic dualistic separation of the sacred and secular worlds, such an understanding has enabled the spread of a race-based hierarchical/patriarchal system that supported the enslavement not just of other human beings but of other Christians, the dehumanization of women and persons of color, and a stance that supports rather than challenges the oppression of so many.[13]

The challenge today is to look at these social constructs, including religion itself, as they have come to be constituted in the United States, through eyes that have been opened by the recognition of the "other-createdness" from which they emerged. Dualistic systems allow for the emergence of an "either/or" understanding of life, knowledge, morality,

and society. Dualism enables the differentiation of human beings into
"us and them," into "human and nonhuman," into those we recognize
as friend and "others" by whom we feel threatened. It speaks a coldly
sterile language of negativity, dualism, separation, subordination, and
alienation.

Three examples can serve to demonstrate how a womanist critical
lens can take a story we have heard countless times and see it and its
significance very differently. We can begin with the models of womanhood and femininity that have historically been such a significant part
of our church's teachings on women. Mary, the mother of God, is contrasted eternally with either Eve, the alleged cause of humanity's fall
into sin, or Mary Magdalene, the repentant sinner. Are these women as
strikingly different from each other as they have been portrayed? First,
a disclaimer: I am not a scripture scholar; you might say that I am simply
attempting to recover the rest of the story. And when we read Genesis 2
and Luke with a critical womanist eye, we do begin to see something
quite different from the story to which we are accustomed.

Beginning appropriately with the text of Genesis and the second Creation story, a careful reading finds no mention in that story that Eve
committed a sin (her son Cain, the first murderer, is the first sinner),
nor is she cursed by God (the serpent is), nor can it be said the she
seduced or in any other way forced Adam to eat of the fruit of the tree in
the garden's center. She is, ironically, the first person in the Bible to
serve someone food, something women have been doing from then on.
But she and Adam are expelled from the garden because they have acquired knowledge, that is, they have become thinking, aware human
beings. It could be said that they have become fully human.

Yet many if not most interpretations of this story place fault solely
with Eve, the gateway, as she and all women have been called, of hell, a
woman guilty—if of anything—only of seeking greater knowledge than
was deemed good for her. From a womanist perspective, as the descendant of a people forbidden to learn how to read and write at pain of
death but also, ironically, stigmatized as incapable of learning, being only
at best "bright monkeys," Eve's story for black women is not one of sin
but of courage and boldness, of persistence in the pursuit of knowledge,
a persistence rewarded by an increase of pain—whether in childbirth or
in struggling to learn under almost impossible conditions after a day of
backbreaking labor—but a pain deemed worthy of repeating over and
over again (as women do by bearing more than one child, and as the
slaves and freed slaves did when persisting in their efforts to gain an
education despite whippings, beatings, and being burned out of their

homes and schools). The pain is overcome by the reward, greater knowledge, a goal historically deemed worthy of pursuit only by men, and white men at that.

Mary Magdalene has also been maligned down through the ages. For centuries venerated as the Great Apostle and the Apostle to the Apostles because of her unique role in being present at the resurrection as well as being commissioned by Jesus himself, the resurrected Christ, to spread the good news, the gospel, to others, she was unceremoniously demoted and commingled with other unnamed women in the New Testament as a prostitute and repentant sinner. This is a stigma that remains to the present day despite the church's *sotto voce* reversal of that commingling. This appears in a footnote in the *Roman Missal* and in John Paul II's acknowledgment of her, once again, as the Great Apostle. From a womanist perspective, the Magdalene speaks for and to countless unnamed black women, slave and free, who were condemned for their allegedly "sluttish" behavior, a lie put forth by the very men, Christian for the most part, who used their positions of power to rape them and even profit from the offspring produced as a result of that rape. Black women today must still live down the slander of being "Jezebels," women with uncontrollable sexual appetites, as well as "sapphires" or "sistas with attitude," in the newest permutation of the same aspersion, that is, women who are willing to stand on their faith in themselves and their God in order to speak words of truth to their people, and anyone else who needs to hear, words that may seem harsh and at times unloving but that are spoken out of love and the effort to give life, as Mary Magdalene did.

Finally, there is the Virgin Mary. For two millennia we have been taught as women to revere and model ourselves after a Mary, meek and mild, who humbly bowed her head and submitted unquestioningly to the will of God. Feminist theologian Elizabeth Johnson notes in her recent book about Mary the words of author Mary Gordon:

> Mary was a stick to beat smart girls with. Her example was held up constantly: an example of silence, of subordination, of the pleasure of taking the back seat. . . . For women like me, it was necessary to reject the image of Mary in order to hold onto the fragile hope of intellectual achievement, independence of identity, sexual fulfillment.[14]

For Gordon and many like her, Johnson notes that "the Marian tradition is accused of distorting women's reality, of promoting a restrictive

ideal of human fulfillment, of constricting women's social roles, of block-
ing their access to God's blessing in the fullness of their lives. It has
presided over the evil of sexism rather than challenged it."[15]

Once again, let us look at this story from a womanist perspective. In
today's understanding, Mary is still a child, barely if at all into her teens.
She is betrothed to a much older man, as was the custom of the day. She
is approached by the angel Gabriel, who speaks words to her that are
both mysterious and frightening. She does not simply accept what the
angel has said to her; she questions him for she is understandably
"troubled" by his words. She is then told that, having found favor with
God, she will conceive and bear a son whom she will call Jesus. Like
many slave women, Mary is basically being told what her life will be.
Yet she again, probably to the angel's amazement, questions him. As yet
she has not been very meek or submissive; she wants to know *how* this is
possible, *how* it will come about. Gabriel's response is intended to resolve her fears and confusion once and for all, but at the same time to
remind her of the power of God. To further convince her, he tells her
that her cousin Elizabeth, whom Mary knows is not only barren but also
beyond her child-bearing years, has also conceived and is in her sixth
month of pregnancy. Only then does Mary agree to the miracle about to
unfold within her.

What is the significance of all of this? First, like Hagar, Mary is being
spoken to directly rather than through a man such as her husband, father, or uncle. At the same time, she has not sought and does not seek
permission from a man for her response, her "let it be done." Remember
now, Mary, though betrothed, is still quite young and a virgin. But she
knows the customs of her people and the harsh consequences for being
found pregnant prior to having been wed. She would be taken outside of
her village and stoned to death. She knows that what she is being asked
to agree to (and she *is* being asked, because Gabriel, as we saw, has to
convince her that all that he has said is possible) could cost her her life
and would certainly derail her engagement to Joseph, who, as we later
read, does intend to break off the engagement once he discovers that she
is pregnant.

We read the annunciation story in just a few minutes, but for Mary it
surely took more time to make such a momentous decision. God does
not force anyone; we, as humans, freely acquiesce to God's will, but we
do so, not blindly, but knowing that saying a yes to God will irrevocably
change our lives. There will certainly be consequences. And, indeed, the
life of this young woman is changed forever, as is all of history.

It can also be argued that, still unsure and even perhaps a bit disbe-
lieving of all that has taken place, she quickly goes to visit Elizabeth to

see for herself evidence of God's word. It is only when she encounters a heavily pregnant Elizabeth that she proclaims her faith in God in a magnificent song that stands to this day as a proclamation not of passivity or humility but of revolution, of a reversal of the status quo and the breaking forth of God's righteous justice into the world in the form of her son. Mary's song, like other songs by women in sacred scripture, is not a song of pious submission but one of righteous judgment and vindication for all who, like Mary and her son, are born poor and oppressed and unjustly victimized. She is prophesying the coming kin-dom of God, a time and place where those who are poor will receive God's bounty and those who are hungry will be fed while the rich and arrogant, those who are unjust, will be cast away. Is it any wonder that her son Jesus makes an almost identical prophetic statement in his first sermon? (Lk 4:16–30).

By saying yes to God, Mary breaks open human history and subverts it, turning all of reality upside down, for she affirms and acknowledges that the miraculous work of God brought about through the Holy Spirit will result in a new reality for all of humanity. She stands, therefore, as a symbol of hope and courage for so many women, poor and invisible, who, by their actions throughout history, by their willingness to stand up and walk out on faith, like so many black Catholic women have done, can bring about a new and better world for all of humanity. They and their children serve as catalysts for change in the world and for hope beyond it. Mary, therefore, is a sign of contradiction, and a model not of passivity or voicelessness but a bold, daring, audacious, and courageous model for black Catholic women. She is a source of hope for young pregnant girls of today, children giving birth to children, for in her coming to voice through the intervention of her God, they can see the possibilities that exist in what would otherwise for so many seem a hopeless situation.

> Existentially, Mary's response carries with it fundamental definition of personhood. Facing a critical choice, she sums herself up "in one of those great self-constituting decisions that give shape to a human life. . . . This young woman's decision is not a passive, timid reaction but a free and autonomous act [that] encourages and endorses women's efforts to take responsibility for their own lives. The courage of her decision vis-à-vis the Holy One is at the same time an assent to the totality of herself.[16]

These three women—Eve, Mary of Magdala, and Mary the Mother of God—are only a few of the women in sacred scripture who speak words of womanist wisdom and dare to become other than what they have been told they should be. Seen holistically rather than dualistically, seen through the dark eyes of their black Catholic sisters who have borne the burden of rape, forced sterilization, children sold away or taken away by the state, loss of name, history, husband, family—all that makes up a human life—and denied their very humanity, yet these women told God it would be all right if he changed their names. For to be a woman named by God was to be a woman who changed the world. They are sisters in solidarity rather than opposition who speak words of black wisdom and live lives of black hope, courage, and faith in a world that saw them as nothing.

Catholic womanist God-talk is rooted in the cycle of life and death rather than in death alone. It seeks always to bring forth life from that which was seen as lifeless, inhuman, or despised. It is the effort constantly to speak truth to life, knowing, as poet Audre Lorde knew, that "we were not meant to survive."[17]

In so many ways these women, along with Hagar, Deborah the judge, Dinah the daughter of Jacob, and many others named and unnamed down through the ages, were not meant to survive. At least their stories, as they would have them told, were not meant to survive in their original form but would be rewritten, too often by others with a different agenda who knew nothing and probably cared even less of their pain and fears, their hopes and dreams. Theirs are stories that must be retrieved and retold "in memory of them" and countless other women, whose spirits dwell among us still.

THE CHALLENGES BLACK WOMEN FACE

For Catholic womanist theologians the ongoing challenge is to recover and reclaim these and the lives of so many black Catholic women, and men as well, whose stories cry out to be told. We must proclaim their lives boldly so that others may learn of and follow them. The task is not an easy one, for there are many other challenges that confront us as well. One of these, a critical one, is gaining the right to speak out in academia and the church from within our particular context, that is, specifically as black Catholic women. Patricia Hill Collins speaks of black women, especially those now in professional fields, as "outsiders-within."[18] Our positions as women with degrees at the master's or doctoral level, especially in institutions of higher learning, provide us with an "insider's" status, enabling us to participate to a certain degree in academic discourse and have an impact on others in those institutions. At the same time, however, because of our personal situations as black women, we are also "outsiders" whose views are not always welcomed and whose input is often trivialized. We find ourselves straddling two worlds, that of academia or other professions, and that of the black community with its own perspective. In order to belong truly to one or the other, it is assumed that we must give up our existence in the other, as they are not complementary. These assumptions, however, are cynically grounded too often in issues of power, control, and manipulation, yet again, of the black woman's reality.

The exclusion of black women's ideas from mainstream academic discourse and the curious placement of African American women intellectuals in both feminist and black social and political thought have meant that black women intellectuals have remained outsiders within all three communities. The assumptions on which full group membership are based—whiteness for feminist thought, maleness for black social and political thought, and the combination for mainstream scholarship— all negate a black female reality. Prevented from becoming full insiders in any of these areas of inquiry, black women remain outsiders within, individuals whose marginality provides a distinctive angle of vision on the theories put forth by such intellectual communities.[19]

Attempting to survive in these often contradictory worlds is a constant and often enervating challenge that often leaves us feeling as if we are being torn in several directions, required to make choices that have severe consequences not only for self-identity but also for the work that we are trying to do.

As womanist theologians we seek to remove the masks that cover up the inherent illegitimacy of the existing forms of society and their use of language to exclude and restrict.[20] We do this by revealing other more holistic world views that serve to bring about unity rather than division, harmony rather than discord. As black women we have come to realize that in order to authenticate ourselves and legitimate the work that we do, we must also remove the masks that have covered the many worlds in which we find ourselves. Only in so doing can we then reveal these masks to public view and develop a unified challenge to them and to those worlds with which they appear to conflict. The words *appear to conflict* are used deliberately, for the reality is that they do not necessarily conflict but are made to appear so by those who are in some way threatened by them.

This means claiming the legitimacy of our being as black female professionals and working to develop a critical understanding of both past and present in order to participate in building a more holistic future, one in which persons will no longer be required to deny the totality of their being in order to "belong," but can embrace and be embraced for what they bring to intellectual and personal discourse in both the public and private arenas. In so doing, in company with my sister womanists, I seek to speak in ways that are understandable to these communities but with a preference toward the black and other marginalized communities, recognizing that as a result I may be accused of being too *popular,* a term often used to denigrate the language of persons of color, women, and those lacking a string of letters after their name. As Patricia Hill Collins has noted:

> My choice of language . . . typifies my efforts to theorize differently. A choice of language is inherently a political choice. Writing . . . in a language that appears too "simple" might give grounds for criticism to those individuals who think that the complex ideas of social theory [and theology] must be abstract, difficult, and inaccessible. Populist ideas become devalued exactly because they are popular. This position reflects a growing disdain for anything deemed "public" and for the general public itself.[21]

Black women, as their community's bearers of culture, have, historically, been the forgers of new ways of being and speaking in the world. They recognize with Collins that "privatizing and hoarding ideas upholds inequality. Sharing ideas through translation and teaching supports democracy."[22] It is our task today as Catholic womanists to speak life into the future, a future inclusive and representative of all. We do so by working to redefine what it means to be male and female in language that complements the actual experiences of those engaged in living out maleness and femaleness, in ways inclusive of both heterosexual and homosexual understandings. In our stories, songs, prayers, and God-talk (theologizing), black women speak life into being, not a stunted growth unable to flourish and condemned to premature death, not one confined to dry, dusty tomes read and understood by only a privileged few, but a life that is fruitful and representative of a diversity created, not by human hands, but by divine ones.

Black women have, historically, worked to make community, a desire deeply rooted in their African ancestry and made even more important by their experiences in the United States.

> "Making community" means the processes of creating religious, educational, health-care, philanthropic, political, and familial institutions and professional organizations that enabled our people to survive. In the early eighteenth and nineteenth centuries, Black

women . . . made Community . . . through the building and shaping of slave culture. Later the process of "making community" was repeated in post-emancipation agricultural areas and then in urban industrial societies. . . . It was through "making community" that Black women were able to redefine themselves, project sexual respectability, reshape morality, and define a new aesthetic. . . . Black women came to subjecthood and acquired agency through the creation of community.[23]

Today we who name ourselves womanists do so not in opposition but in creation, seeking to "make community" wherever we find ourselves. We define ourselves not over against but in solidarity with, affirming that new ways of self-definition must emerge, not as hand-me-downs or cast-offs or shaped by others' self-understanding, but created out of the fabric of our own lives. In so doing we are creating a new language of liberation that is open to any and all who are willing to speak plainly without assuming their language will give them power and/or authority over another. As womanists, we see as our challenge the gathering of the myriad threads of the richly diverse black community and breathing into them renewed life that can serve as a model of life for our world. That model is centered on the co-createdness by God of all, regardless of efforts to separate by the arbitrary use of divisive language and beliefs that restrict rather than encourage the fullness of life and its possibilities.

All who are oppressed share in solidarity with each other, a solidarity that should not be laid aside for individual desires or "battles." The struggle is communal, not individual, and can be won only if experiences are shared, stories are told, songs are sung, histories are reclaimed and restored, and a new language emerges that speaks words of peace and unity, that unites, that recalls both the pain and the joy of our different heritages and leads us into a brand-new day.

NOTES

[1] Darlene Clark Hine, ed., *Encyclopedia of Black Women in America* (Bloomington: Indiana University Press, 1994), 457.

[2] Ibid., 459–60.

[3] Delores S. Williams, *Sisters in the Wilderness: The Challenge of Womanist God-Talk* (Maryknoll, NY: Orbis Books, 1993), 118.

[4] Ibid.

[5] Ibid., 119.

[6] Bernice J. Reagon, "African Diaspora Women: The Making of Cultural Workers," in *Women in Africa and the African Diaspora*, ed. Rosalyn Terborg-Penn,

Sharon Harley, and Andrea Benton Rushing (Washington DC: Howard University Press, 1987), 169.

[7] Cyprian Davis, "God of Our Weary Years," in *Taking Down Our Harps: Black Catholics in the United States*, ed. Diana L. Hayes and Cyprian Davis, O.S.B. (Maryknoll, NY: Orbis Books, 1999), 20.

[8] Ibid, 30.

[9] Cyprian Davis, O.S.B., *The History of Black Catholics in the United States* (New York: Crossroad, 1990), 115.

[10] Diana Hayes, "And When We Speak," in Hayes and Davis, *Taking Down Our Harps*, 106.

[11] Gay Wilentz, *Binding Cultures: Black Women Writers in Africa and the Diaspora* (Bloomington: Indiana University Press, 1992), xii.

[12] Ibid., xv–xvi.

[13] See Kelly Brown Douglas, *Sexuality and the Black Church: A Womanist Perspective* (Maryknoll, NY: Orbis Books, 1999), 25–29; and Hayes, "And When We Speak," 102–19.

[14] Mary Gordon, cited in Elizabeth A. Johnson, *Truly Our Sister: A Theology of Mary in the Communion of Saints* (New York: Continuum, 2004), 10–11.

[15] Ibid., 11.

[16] Johnson, *Truly Our Sister*, 257.

[17] Audre Lorde, "A Litany for Survival," in *The Collected Poems of Audre Lorde* (New York: W. W. Norton, 1997), 255–56.

[18] Patricia Hill Collins, *Black Feminist Thought: Knowledge, Consciousness, and the Politics of Empowerment*. Perspectives on Gender, vol. 2 (New York: Routledge, 1990), 11–13.

[19] Ibid., 12.

[20] In 2008, for example, we are confronted by an administration that claims to be acting on behalf of peace by instigating war, to be helping the poor and unemployed by providing tax cuts and write-offs for the rich, and to be helping students by requiring standardized tests for children as young as three and cutting back on loans and grants for higher education. The language is cast in words familiar and soothing, but the effect of the actions behind them is oppressive and life-threatening to many.

[21] Collins, *Black Feminist Thought*, xxi.

[22] Ibid., xxiii.

[23] Darlene Clark Hine, *Black Women and the Re-Construction of American History* (Bloomington: Indiana University Press, 1994), xxii.

Chapter 10

HIV/AIDS and the Bodies of Black Peoples

The Spirituals and Resurrection Faith

BRYAN N. MASSINGALE

It is difficult to approach this topic with fresh eyes and new enthusiasm. In this, the third decade of the pandemic of HIV/AIDS, what can be said that has not already been said? The basic facts are well known, perhaps numbingly so: the stark disparities of the disease's course and impact upon persons of color in general and African Americans in particular; the effects of lack of access to health care and needed medical resources; the pervasive stigma and discrimination thrust upon and endured by those living with HIV infection; the "compassion fatigue" and widespread indifference that mark the responses of many to the horror that unfolds around us; all these have been voluminously documented and detailed. Indeed, in a presentation at the meeting of the Catholic Theological Society of America in 2000, I examined all of these realities and more. I argued then that "an American public theology cannot be 'attentive, intelligent, reasonable, and responsible' without coming to grips with the ominous threat that HIV/AIDS poses to the survival of communities of color."[1] Depressingly, much of that previous work could be repeated now, only with exclamation points!

Yet today, this volume on the uncommon faithfulness of black Catholics demands a fresh approach to what many rightly contend is "the most serious crisis facing descendants of Africa since the slave trade."[2] For if black Catholic theologians—and especially black Catholic ethicists—do not constantly call attention to the dire threat that is upon us, engaging it with the best energies of our intelligence and faith, then we become accomplices in our people's destruction. Thus, I intend to examine the realities of the third decade of the AIDS pandemic in the light of the

147

Christian conviction of the resurrection of the body and of the black body in particular. I will note the signs of the time, or the current context of ethical reflection on the impact of HIV/AIDS on black communities in the United States, highlighting new developments, currents, and directions. Then I will examine the belief in the resurrection, as that belief is expressed in a unique cultural product, the African American spirituals composed by unknown persons enslaved as chattel. This cultural world view is chosen because slavery is a common foundational experience affecting all persons of African descent. And, as I will demonstrate, the spirituals also possess a transcultural resonance, making the faith mediated by them accessible to the guild of Catholic theologians who are predominately white and European. This form of indigenous faith reflection will then be brought to bear upon the present situation for the moral wisdom and ethical direction it can provide for living in a catastrophic pandemic that threatens to depopulate communities of color throughout the world.

THE CONTEMPORARY CONTEXT

HIV/AIDS: The Portrait of a Demographic Collapse

Writing in 1994, gay author and activist Randy Shilts made an observation that has proven to be prescient, if not prophetic:

> By the end of the century, AIDS will overwhelmingly be a disease of poor people. This creates a huge political problem. Our society didn't grapple with AIDS in the '80s because it was the disease of gay men. But in the '90s we are going to have a greater problem with the disease because it's not just affecting gays but blacks and Hispanics too.[3]

Yet, as valuable as this observation was in foretelling the apathy or indifference that marks current public interest in this epidemic, Shilts failed to acknowledge that *from the beginning* HIV/AIDS has had a grossly disparate impact upon people of color in general, and African Americans in particular. In 1982, African Americans, being only 11 percent of the population, represented 23 percent of the new diagnoses. This disparity has only increased with the passage of time. Now, more African Americans are reported with HIV/AIDS than any other racial/ethnic group. Though only little more than 12 percent of the U.S. population, African Americans represent more than half (54 percent) of the new diagnoses of HIV infection in the United States[4] and 42 percent of Americans diagnosed with AIDS.[5]

The severe racial imbalance of the disease's impact is further evidenced by the following realities:

- One in 50 Black men is HIV-positive [which is eight times the rate for white men]. One in 160 Black women is HIV-positive [almost twenty times the rate for white women].

- In 1998 African American women constituted 64 percent of new female AIDS cases.

- Black senior citizens represent more than 50 percent of HIV cases among people over age 55.

- Black children represent almost two-thirds (62 percent) of all reported pediatric AIDS cases.

- Although only 15 percent of the adolescent population in the United States is Black, over 60 percent of AIDS cases reported in 1999 among 13–19 year olds were among Blacks.

- AIDS is the number one cause of death for Black adults aged 25 to 44, before heart disease, cancer, and homicide.[6]

As sobering as these as these grim figures are, they achieve even greater significance when examined against the wider national and global picture. Though this essay focuses on the impact of the disease upon African Americans, we should also keep in mind the global disparity of HIV's impact. Though non-white Hispanics are only 15 percent of the U.S. population, they account for about 20 percent of new diagnoses. Together, blacks and Hispanics account for 55 percent of the total number living with HIV/AIDS in the United States, and over two-thirds of those newly diagnosed with this condition. Moreover, the vast majority of those living with HIV/AIDS—95 percent of the total—live in the developing world. Sub-Saharan Africa bears the brunt of this disease, with over 76 percent of the world's cases (though only 10 percent of the global population).[7] Hence, both nationally and globally, HIV/AIDS is a disease borne chiefly by the poor and persons of color.

Such grim realities move one advocacy group to conclude the obvious: "No matter how you slice the numbers—young or old, male or female, gay or straight—this epidemic is attacking Black people most aggressively."[8] What makes these realities even more troubling is that

new HIV and AIDS cases are increasing in the African American community, although they are leveling off or falling for other groups in the
country.[9]

The reasons advanced to account for this differential impact are many
and complex. It would seem that no single factor alone suffices, but that
several factors, acting in concert, underlie this tragic state of affairs.
Activists and health officials list realities such as racism, apathy, poverty, poor access to health care, ignorance, and recklessness.[10] Of these
factors, I would like to highlight three: poor access to health care, cultural stigma, and widespread ignorance about the disease.

LACK OF ACCESS TO HEALTH CARE

The lack of access to health care that afflicts the impoverished and
working poor in this country—who are disproportionately people of
color—contributes to the severe disparity in the impact of HIV/AIDS
upon racial and ethnic groups. For example, the reduction in AIDS-related deaths achieved by the use of new antiviral medications (such as
protease inhibitors and drug "cocktails") evidences a racial imbalance,[11]
for these drugs cannot benefit those who lack the means to pay for them.
As Emilie Townes observes,

> People with private insurance may be able to afford this treatment,
> but for those on Medicaid, there is a monthly cap on drug expenses.
> Many HMOs restrict drug benefits. . . . Drug companies provide
> free drugs to some, but the demand far outstrips the availability of
> such programs.[12]

Dependency upon public health insurance, specifically Medicaid, is
directly relevant to the racial disparity observed in the course of the
disease and deaths from AIDS-related complications. African Americans
are more dependent than whites upon publicly financed health care, with
almost two-thirds of African Americans in treatment for HIV infection
relying on public health insurance. Yet these programs are now in danger of collapse; forty-nine of the fifty states have planned or have already
implemented measures to cut or contain Medicaid costs by cutting health
services to the poor.[13]

In addition, the uninsured are served by a patchwork of community
health centers, public health clinics, and public hospitals ill-equipped
to provide the comprehensive health-care services and counseling that
HIV-infected persons need. Townes points out, "There still is no systematic, structural, and effective antidrug program in communities of

the dispossessed in this nation."[14] This is especially troubling, given that injection drug use is the second most frequent cause of HIV exposure for both African Americans and U.S. Hispanics.[15]

The conclusion is obvious and inescapable: racially based inequities of medical access and treatment greatly contribute to the grossly disparate impact of HIV/AIDS upon communities of color.[16]

CULTURAL STIGMA

My colleague, Shawnee Daniels-Sykes, developed this understanding of *stigma* in a doctoral seminar paper:

> [*Stigma*] . . . is a powerful discrediting and tainting social label that devalues individuals who display attributes that violate acceptable standards in a society. It connotes something unusual and wrong about the moral status of the person affected. . . . The presence of a stigmatized condition evokes disgust or fear or discomfort in the members of the non-stigmatized group. . . . It arouses deep human responses such as avoidance, reticence, denial, and scapegoating.

Because of the stigma associated with behaviors that transmit the HIV virus—especially same-sex sexual relations, sexual promiscuity, and injection drug use—living with HIV has become a public "brand" of moral failure and disgrace. (Hence the still-continuing discourse distinguishing the so-called innocent victims of AIDS—such as children and unsuspecting spouses—from those who become exposed through their own fault and thus presumably "deserve" their fate.)

The effects of the HIV/AIDS stigma among African Americans are at least twofold. First, blacks living with HIV/AIDS are often ostracized by their community because they appear to confirm some of the worst images in white minds about black people, namely, that they are illegal drug users and sexually irresponsible. Thus HIV-positive African Americans are a source of communal shame and embarrassment. Not only have they transgressed moral taboos, but they have betrayed the community by becoming visible embodiments of white prejudices concerning black social deviance and black sexuality.[17]

Second, culturally specific stigmas associated with homosexual activity inhibit recognition and discussion about HIV/AIDS in the African American community. Given a pervasive homophobia in the black community, the equation of homosexuality with sin and immorality in the dominant African American religious sensibility, the early and enduring misidentification of AIDS as a "gay" disease, and a belief that homosexuality is not indigenous to black peoples but rather is an "imported" threat to the black family and black manhood—the community's silence, denial, and castigation of those who bear this stigma become almost inevitable and inexorable.[18] This stance is further abetted by a not uncommon belief among many black clergy that AIDS is divine punishment for sin.[19]

I want to emphasize that my point is not that African Americans are more homophobic than their white counterparts.[20] Many of these cultural stigmas also are present among white Americans. The point is that there are unique factors that shape anti-gay bias and HIV-stigma in the black community, and these play a significant role in retarding effective responses to HIV/AIDS among African Americans.

PERVASIVE IGNORANCE

One of the positive developments occurring in the pandemic's third decade is the increasing number of activist groups within the black community that are breaking the walls of silence and denial surrounding this disease. They are developing and implementing innovative and culturally appropriate ways of speaking about the disease and the measures that African Americans must take to stem the tide of the epidemic's advance. But as they do so, they also are documenting the tragic effects of the corporate denial that has characterized this community's response to the pandemic; among these is a widespread ignorance about the disease and the means of prevention.

In Seattle, the Brother-to-Brother project works in a network of black barbershops. According to Derrick Myricks-Harris, executive director of Brother-to-Brother, the goal of the project is "to provide factual and scientific information in Seattle's black community, and correct misinformation around the existing movements in HIV vaccine research."[21]

Because of the legacy of denial that has been—and continues to be—pervasive, many African Americans lack the information that would lead them to take effective preventative measures against this disease. This contributes to the stark disparities that plague black Americans in the face of HIV/AIDS.

NEW THEOLOGICAL AND PASTORAL ATTITUDES

One of the heartening recent developments in the struggle against HIV/AIDS in African and pan-African communities is an increasing awareness on the part of faith communities of both their complicity and culpability with regard to the community's denial and their need to develop active pastoral responses and changed attitudes in the wake of the pandemic's destruction. I highlight two examples.

The first is a text written by an ecumenical gathering sponsored by the World Council of Churches in Nairobi in 2001. This gathering of African church leaders is significant for its forthright confession that the attitudes, practices, ethics, and theology of the Christian church have contributed to the continent's dire misery. This remarkably candid statement deserves extensive citation:

> As the pandemic has unfolded, it has exposed fault lines that reach to the heart of our theology, our ethics, our liturgy, and our practice of ministry. Today, churches are being obliged to acknowledge that we have—however unwittingly—contributed both actively and passively to the spread of the virus. Our difficulty in addressing issues of sex and sexuality has often made it painful for us to engage, in any honest and realistic way, with issues of sex education and HIV prevention. Our tendency to exclude others, our interpretation of the scriptures, and our theology of sin have all combined to promote the stigmatization, exclusion, and suffering of people with HIV or AIDS. This has undermined the effectiveness of care, education, and prevention efforts and inflicted additional suffering on those already affected by the HIV.[22]

Especially significant is the detailed acknowledgment of the church's complicity, the specificity about how the community's theology and ethics have failed in the face of the crisis before it, and the realization that new approaches and sensitivities are necessary. In short, these church leaders see the need for a profound conversion not only in the church's practices but even in its beliefs: "Given the urgency of the situation and the conviction that the churches do have a distinctive role to play in response to the pandemic, what is needed is a rethinking of our mission, and the transformation of our structures and ways of working."[23]

More modest in its claims, but no less significant, is another statement by a group of black and African religious leaders. What is noteworthy is that this is not only a statement by a pan-African group of religious leaders from all parts of the African diaspora, but also a joint declaration of Christian and Muslim religious authorities. While less detailed in its confession of doctrinal shortcomings, this group was no less explicit in accepting its share of responsibility for the spread of the virus and disease:

The very real issues raised by HIV/AIDS—especially where human sexuality, responsibility, vulnerability and mortality are
concerned—confront and challenge all of us in deeply personal
ways. Catholics, Protestants, and Muslims struggle with these most
human of issues and they differ, sometimes heatedly, in their theological understanding of the nature of sin, sickness and death, and
the fundamental challenges posed by HIV/AIDS. However, the interpretation of scriptural principles for specific problems tends to
be contentious. *As a result, our theological differences and religious
divisions have sometimes contributed, however unwittingly, to the
spread of the virus itself.* Today, there is a great urgency and conviction among faith communities in Africa to join together in the fight
against HIV/AIDS.[24]

One should not make too much of these statements, for they are not
representative of the dominant or principal tendencies in the thinking
and practices of black religious leaders. Nor, however, should we dis-
miss them. They demonstrate the beginnings of a dawning awareness in
the black religious community of the magnitude of the current crisis; a
willingness to move beyond denial and break the silence; and the need
to rethink traditional practices, beliefs and theology in order to rise to
the challenge of the present situation.[25] They also reveal the pivotal and
unique role that the Christian church can and must play in helping black
communities overcome the stigmatization and discrimination that fuel
the spread of this disease within this vulnerable population. To provide
a deeper theological foundation and support for this dawning shift of
consciousness, I now examine an "indigenous" understanding of the
resurrection, one rooted in the African American spirituals, to mine its
wisdom and ethical guidance.

THE BODILY RESURRECTION
IN BLACK SLAVE SPIRITUALS

WHY THE SPIRITUALS?

I begin with a consideration of the reasons for turning to the faith
expression of the spirituals or "sorrow songs," as W. E. B. Du Bois calls
them.[26] I offer two. First, slave religion—its patterns of worship, music,
and aesthetics—expresses the "baseline religious consciousness" of African American Christianity.[27] Chattel slavery is a foundational experience

affecting all persons of African descent. While not normative, the religious faith of the enslaved is an authoritative understanding of the black experience and black religious consciousness.

It is no longer *normative*, for persons of African descent in the United States no longer live in the social and cultural condition of chattel slavery that marked the seventeenth, eighteenth, and nineteenth centuries. Yet the religious expressions of slave religion, and the moral consciousness that springs from them, remain *authoritative* carriers of the black experience; that is to say, they speak with authority and command respectful attention even today. The most important reason for the authoritative status of the enslaved ethical consciousness is that this constellation of sensibility, beliefs, and practices enabled black people to survive the most harrowing and horrific period of their experience in America. Examining the ethical consciousness of the enslaved gives a window into questions such as:

- What enabled this people to survive an environment in which everything in society—politics, law, culture, custom, and even religion—conspired to deny, assault, and vilify their humanity?

- What enabled them to see through the lies that their masters and ministers conspired to teach them?

- What kept their bodies, minds, and spirits together through acts of unspeakable brutality?

- From what reservoir came those springs of endurance that enabled them not only to survive but to create culture: family, beauty, poetry, and song?

To put the matter directly and succinctly, the ethical beliefs and moral sensibilities of the enslaved made it possible for us—the descendants of the African diaspora—to be here now. If for no other reason, then, the ethical consciousness of the enslaved speaks with enduring authority as a privileged carrier of the black religious experience. It is not the only carrier or embodiment of the black experience. But it is a foundational embodiment that any examination of ethics from an African American perspective must respect with privileged attention. The ethical wisdom of the enslaved African, then, offers authoritative guidance even today.

In short, the black slave religious experience and moral consciousness is a primal expression of the black experience. Thus it is an essential

dialogue partner for U.S. Catholic moral theology. One cannot understand the experience of African Americans without a sustained encounter
with the reality and legacy of black enslavement.

This leads to the second reason for focusing on the moral universe of
the enslaved Africans in the United States, namely, the cultural products produced by this community are "classics" and thus are accessible
and instructive for those who do not belong to this cultural heritage. I
use *classic* in David Tracy's sense, that a classic "is assumed to be any
text that always has the power to transform the horizon of the inter-
preter and thereby disclose new meanings and experiential possibilities."[28]
In other words, classics are texts, events, or persons that are rooted in a
particular culture yet also have the power to speak beyond their origi-
nating culture to something universal in the human experience. Thus
they have a timeless and transcultural significance.

I argue that the cultural products of the enslaved Africans are such
classics. One does not need, for example, to have experienced the horrors of slavery to be moved and inspired by Frederick Douglass's
autobiographical account of his journey from bondage to freedom.[29] Similarly, the haunting and plaintive cries of the Negro spiritual—songs such
as "Oh Freedom," "Sometimes I Feel like a Motherless Child," and "Let
My People Go"—continue to reverberate within contemporary human
spirits that yearn for freedom from oppression, exploitation, and injustice.[30] Precisely because these texts—forged in the crucible of
slavery—possess transcultural resonance, they can make the moral universe of the enslaved blacks accessible to the community of U.S. Catholic
moralists (the vast majority of whom are not members of the African
American culture). This opens the possibility for a fruitful dialogue between Catholic moral theology and the black experience.

JESUS' PASSION IN THE SPIRITUALS

Space does not permit an in-depth treatment of the spirituals' moral
insights; the observations I offer are more of a suggestive overview than
a detailed analysis. That being said, it is apparent that the enslaved
African's belief in the resurrection was expressed only in the context of
reflecting on the entire paschal mystery. To put this another way, it is
impossible to isolate the enslaved community's belief in the resurrection
from its meditation upon Christ's suffering and passion. There are three
characteristics of this reflection upon the passion that I want to highlight.

First, there is an emphasis upon Jesus' *silence*. There are but a few
spirituals that narrate words spoken by Jesus from the cross, and even

these do not focus on the traditional "Seven Words" highlighted in white Christian piety.[31] One of the most famous passion spirituals has the haunting refrain: "He never said a mumblin' word/Not a word, not a word, not a word."

> They crucified my Lord, . . .
> They pierced Him in the side, . . .
> The blood came tricklin' down, . . .
> He bowed his head an' died, and He never said a
>   mumblin' word;
> Not a word, not a word, not a word.[32]

This is a Savior who bore his tortures with silent agony, dignity, and protest. He does not speak—or perhaps he is rendered mute—throughout his humiliations, whippings, and unjust judgment. Bruno Chenu observes: "While the Western church emphasized the last words of Jesus, the black church insisted on his silence."[33]

Second, the spirituals are marked by *an immediacy of feeling and pathos*, as the enslaved blacks poignantly identified their trials with those endured by Jesus. Jesus, like them, was a victim of intentional violence and brutality. This is conveyed by the detailed depictions of the physical sufferings inflicted upon the body of the Savior: "An' dey whipped Him up the hill/An' de blood came tricklin' down/An' he nevah said a mumblin' word." Or again, the enslaved bards sang: "Dey whipp'd Him up and dey whipp'd Him down/Dey whipp'd dat man all over town."[34] Thus, Jesus' passion is never disembodied or spiritualized. Nor are his sufferings depicted in voyeuristic excess (as in Mel Gibson's film *The Passion of the Christ*). Rather, the enslaved musician speaks out of the authority of the community's daily experience; this is a Christ who, like the slaves themselves, bore the brunt of the whip and the lash.

Third, in perhaps the most famous of the passion spirituals *we find ethical judgment and indictment* as the enslaved community poses the piercing question, "Were you there when they crucified my Lord?" The haunting cadence of this powerful song causes us to "grimace with shame and grow in responsibility" as we contemplate, on deeper and deeper levels, what it was that Jesus endured.[35]

> Were you there when the blood came a-twinkling
>   down?
> Ooooo-oooh, sometimes it causes me to tremble,
>   tremble, tremble,
> Were you there when they crucified my Lord?[36]

The ethical import of this spiritual is not better expressed than in the words of John Lovell, who notes:

> The setting, the phrasing, the powerful momentum of this poem surely make it one of the great poems of all time. Every great wrong, it says, is committed under the eyes of frightened or uncaring people. For the wrongs of humankind, the finger points at us all. We are all guilty. *We are guilty not so much because of what we do, as what we allow to happen.* And without a doubt, the slave singer was including the slavery of human flesh in the bill of indictment.[37]

Surely, it is not difficult to see the relevance of the enslaveds' reflection upon the passion to the pervasive indifference and cultural stigma that mark the dominant religious and social responses to the scourge of HIV/AIDS that ravages the bodies of black peoples. African peoples afflicted with HIV/AIDS are, like Christ, too often the muted and silenced bearers of a suffering to which too often we are the culpable bystanders.

RESURRECTION FAITH AND THE SPIRITUALS

Yet Christ's passion was not last word. It is the occasion for showing the amazing wonder of the enslaved believers' conviction about the resurrection, despite the daily cruelty that encompassed them. Later versions of "Were You There?" have one of two additional verses appended: "Were you there when he rose up from dead?" And "Were you there when they rolled the stone away?" The faith of the enslaved community could not rest content with evoking the passion; its faith was founded upon the hope of Christ's triumph over death and cruel oppression.[38] I note three characteristics of the slaves' resurrection faith.

First, *Easter triumph shatters the silence of the passion, cross, and grave.* Note the emphasis upon sound and hearing in this spiritual:

> Chillun, did you *hear* when Jesus rose?
> Did you *hear* when Jesus rose?
> Chillun, did you *hear* when Jesus rose?
> He rose an' ascended on high!
> Mary set her table
> In spite of all her foes;
> King Jesus sat at the center place,
> An' cups did overflow.[39]

God's decisive intervention not only breaks the silence of suffering, but it also empowers the enslaved community to announce the good news and join in shattering the silence imposed by unjust humiliation and social forces. Jesus' resurrection loosens the enslaveds' tongues, compelling the community to be proclaimers of new life and freedom. This is conveyed in the following spiritual, "Jesus Is Risen from the Dead," with its repeated injunction to "go, tell":

> In-a this-a band we have sweet music:
> Jesus is risen from the dead.
>
> Go, tell Mary and Martha,
> "Yes, Jesus is risen from the dead."
> Go, tell John an' Peter . . . .
> Go, tell doubting Thomas . . . .
> Go, tell Paul and Silas . . . .
> Go, tell all th' Apostles . . . .
>
> Go, tell everybody:
> "Yes, Jesus is risen from the dead."[40]

Second, just as the enslaved endured the suffering of Christ's passion, *their resurrection faith expressed the conviction that they share in his Easter triumph.* Christ's resurrection grounds the enslaveds' belief in their own salvation and deliverance. Because of Jesus' triumph over unjust suffering and death, the enslaved community could sing of its assurance of "going home"—that is, to heaven, a true "home" unlike this earthly one, a place of rest and comfort, free from the burdens and sorrows of this world. In "He Arose" the community sings:

> He 'rose from the dead,
> And the Lord shall bear my spirit [or His
>   children] home.
>
> They crucified my Savior and nailed him to the
>   cross,
> And the Lord will bear my spirit home.
>
> The cold grave could not hold Him nor death's
>   cold iron band,
> And the Lord will bear my spirit home.

> An angel came from heaven and rolled the stone
> > away,
> And the Lord will bear my spirit home.
>
> The angel said He is not here. He's gone to
> > Galilee,
> and the Lord will bear my spirit home.[41]

The enslaved community, having shared intimately in the sufferings of Christ, can now confidently partake in the assurance of his triumph as well.

Finally, just as reflection upon Christ's passion led to an ethical judgment upon present cruelty and injustice, *the enslaved believers' resurrection faith also grounds a moral indictment against their present condition of bondage.* In "Heaven, Heaven" (also known as "I've Got Shoes"), the enslaved believers sang of their belief in a future that sharply contrasted with their present misery:

> I got a robe, you've got a robe,
> All God's chillun got a robe;
> When I get to Heav'n, goin' to put on my robe,
> Goin' to shout all over God's Heav'n.
> Heav'n, Heav'n.
> Ev'rybody talking 'bout heav'n ain't going there,
> Heav'n, Heav'n,
> Goin' to shout all over God's Heav'n.[42]

In this future state they would have shoes, a crown, a robe, and the leisure to enjoy a harp—that is, the blessings intended for "all God's children" denied in their present condition. But note that this future reversal means that those who kept such things from them in this life—often in the name of a false and idolatrous faith—won't enjoy such future beatitude: "Ev'rybody talking 'bout heav'n ain't going there."

More pointedly, resurrection faith leads to a stance of apocalyptic judgment. *Christ's resurrection from the dead also marks the inevitable end of crushing misery and oppression.* The Lord who triumphed over death will return as judge to bring an end to an unjust world. This cosmic upheaval of ethical scrutiny, judgment, and deliverance is wonderfully expressed in the familiar spiritual "In That Great Gittin' Up Mornin'." Here the enslaved community sings of the "better day a-comin'" that will be heralded by the angel's trumpet blast. But the blast will not be so loud as to "alarm my people" as they come to judgment. And as the sinners (for example, the slave masters and mistresses, buyers and sellers) will have to say "Amen to yo' damnation," the righteous will share in final resurrection destiny:

In dat great gitin' up mornin',
Fare you well, Fare you well.

Sayin' Amen to yo' damnation . . .
No mercy for po' sinner . . .
Hear de rumblin' of de thunder . . .
Earth shall reel an' totter . . .

Den you'll see de Christian risin' . . .
Den you'll see de righteous marchin' . . .
See dem marchin' home to Heab'n . . .
Den you'll see my Jesus comin' . . .

Wid all His holy angel . . .
Take de righteous home to glory . . .
Dere they live wid God forever . . .
On de right side of my Savior . . .[43]

Resurrection faith thus marks a reversal of the enslaved community's participation in the sufferings of Christ's passion. Moreover, just as reflection upon Christ's passion leads to an ethical rebuke and judgment upon the present, so too does contemplation of the resurrection. Resurrection faith is not simply a tale of personal deliverance; it is also a narrative of social judgment and transformation. Faith in the resurrection was the basis for the enslaveds' conviction that injustice cannot and will not be ultimately triumphant. Such an assurance was not only the basis for future hope. This conviction also inspired present action for justice—such as escapes, revolts, and other acts of non-cooperation—in the light of resurrection destiny.[44]

HIV/AIDS AND THE LEGACY OF THE SPIRITUALS

I offer the following observations of the implications of the spirituals' moral wisdom for the pandemic of HIV/AIDS and its impact upon black peoples.

First, resurrection faith, as mediated in the foundational expression of black religion, is a harsh condemnation of attitudes of indifference in the face of massive suffering. Black Christianity's own cultural heritage demands that black religious leadership move to the forefront of efforts on behalf of life. Faith in the resurrection also vehemently indicts the "compassion fatigue" and moral callousness of the privileged—both black and white—for whom the disease's perils seem more remote and distant.

Second, resurrection faith impels pan-African religious leadership to break the silence imposed upon those who suffer the ravages of HIV/AIDS. In our preaching and catechesis we are called to advocate and speak out on behalf of those whose unjustly inflicted stigmas render them mute before the forces of indifference, scapegoating, and self-righteous condemnation. Can we hear the sounds of resurrection and, like the enslaved, form a choir of witnesses who announce new possibilities and proclaim an alternative vision beyond exclusion, discrimination, and stigmatization? Can we dare revise not only our pastoral practices, but even our current teachings on sexuality, in light of the limitless horizons opened by the resurrection? Can we dare *not* to?

Third, it is important to note that the enslaved bards and preachers were neither biblical literalists nor dogmatic fundamentalists. Rather, they subjected the Christian faith and its scriptures to an overriding hermeneutical question: what is consistent with the survival of my people? In light of this concern, they rejected Christian catechesis that encouraged passivity and docility toward slave masters and interpretations of biblical passages that justified the social evil of slavery as God's will. We saw in the World Council of Churches' statement above how some ecclesial officials are coming to a sobering realization: "Our tendency to exclude others, our interpretation of the scriptures, and our theology of sin have all combined to promote the stigmatization, exclusion, and suffering of people with HIV or AIDS." Contemporary church leaders and preachers need to be as creative and courageous as our enslaved ancestors in our appropriation of the Christian tradition. Specifically, the crisis of the HIV/AIDS pandemic demands that Christian leaders and ministers challenge inadequate understandings of Christian faith—that is, interpretations of Christianity that compromise the community's well-being and survival—and especially the blasphemous use of God's name to justify the exclusion, neglect, and demeaning of human beings.

Finally, resurrection faith demands that we listen to the accounts of hope present in the midst of the travails of the present. It was in the crucible of suffering that the unknown black bards of old composed and sang their noble songs. What testimonies of hope might we, the privileged, not be hearing now in the community of those infected and living with AIDS, what voices call us beyond paralyzing despair, summoning us not only to hope but to engage in courageous advocacy for the sake of those who now bear the lash of AIDS upon their crucified dark and dusky bodies? At the least, the faith mediated by the African American spirituals summons us to a stance of solidarity with those whose sufferings mirror those of our Lord.

I conclude with this statement from Andrew Young, the noted civil rights activist and close associate of the Reverend Martin Luther King, Jr. He relates the authoritative relevance of the faith of our enslaved forebears and how their music continues to inspire action to advance the well-being of threatened communities of color:

> Somehow, through the music, a great secret was discovered: that black people, otherwise cowed, discouraged, and faced with innumerable and insuperable obstacles, could transcend all those difficulties and forge a new determination, a new faith and strength. . . . Music was the gift of the people to themselves, a bottomless reservoir of spiritual power.[45]

NOTES

[1] Bryan N. Massingale, "A Public Theology, Black and Catholic: HIV/AIDS in U.S. Communities of Color" (unpublished paper). A summary of this paper appears in "Black Catholic Theology," *The Proceedings of the Catholic Theological Society of America* 55 (2000): 161–62.

[2] Ronald Jeffrey Weatherford and Carole Boston Weatherford, *Somebody's Knocking at Your Door: AIDS and the African-American Church* (Binghamton, NY: The Haworth Pastoral Press, 1999), 105.

[3] Randy Shilts (untitled essay), *Newsweek* (January 3, 1994), 54. Note, however, the implicit disjunction between "gays" and "blacks and Hispanics," that is, the assumption that gay = white. This dualism exists within the black community as well, abetting its collective denial of being afflicted by AIDS, as evidenced in the pervasive belief that this is a disease of gay—that is, white—men.

[4] Balm in Gilead, "HIV/AIDS Facts—African American Women," citing the CDC HIV/AIDS update of February 2002. Available on the balmingilead.org website.

[5] Kai Wright, *The Time Is Now! The State of AIDS in Black America* (Los Angeles: Black AIDS Institute, 2005), 6.

[6] These statistics are taken from Balm in Gilead, "HIV/AIDS Facts." Available on the balmingilead.org website.

[7] See www.cdc.gov/hiv/hispanics/index.htm. See also "AIDS Epidemic Update: December 2007," available on the UNAIDS.org website. For an assessment

of the impact of AIDS on African society, see Jeffrey Bartholet, "The Plague Years," *Newsweek* (January 17, 2000), 32–49.

[8] Kai Wright, "The Time Is Now! The State of AIDS in Black America," February 7, 2005. Available on the blackaids.org website.

[9] "AIDS Grows Up as Black Victims Increase." Available on the journeytowellness.com website.

[10] Ibid.

[11] Peter A. Clark, "A Legacy of Mistrust: African-Americans, the Medical Profession, and AIDS," *Linacre Quarterly* 65 (February 1998): 66–88.

[12] Emilie M. Townes, *Breaking the Fine Rain of Death: African American Health Issues and a Womanist Ethic of Care* (New York: Continuum Press, 1998), 134.

[13] Wright, "The Time Is Now!"

[14] Townes, *Breaking the Fine Rain of Death*, 132.

[15] Centers for Disease Control and Prevention (CDC), "HIV/AIDS among African Americans," rev. August 2008. Available on the cdc.gov website.

[16] Townes, *Breaking the Fine Rain of Death*, 132: "African Americans as a group receive lower levels of routine and preventive health services than other racial-ethnic groups. When poverty is added to this mix, it becomes even more lethal. [For] poor folks have higher levels of HIV infection than middle-class and wealthy folks . . . and are the least able to bear this health burden." Also relevant to the discussion of HIV, health care, and African Americans is many black people's suspicion of the medical profession. This mistrust, rooted in events such as the infamous Tuskegee syphilis experiments on black men (1932–72), and the forced sterilizations of poor black women in the 1960s and 1970s, feeds deep-seated fears that AIDS is an act of genocide against the black community. The legacy of racism in the medical community and the mistrust of the health-care system this engenders are further barriers to effective responses to this pandemic. Townes discusses this distrust, its roots, and its implications in *Breaking the Fine Rain of Death*, 125–28. See also Peter Clark, "A Legacy of Mistrust." Clark traces the genesis of this mistrust to medical "treatments" provided to slaves.

[17] The impact of white racism upon black sexuality—and the effect this racist discourse has had upon the African American community's (retarded) response to HIV/AIDS—is treated by Kelly Brown Douglas, *Sexuality and the Black Church: A Womanist Perspective* (Maryknoll, NY: Orbis Books, 1999); Emilie M. Townes, *Breaking the Fine Rain of Death*, 121–44; and Cornel West, "Black Sexuality: The Taboo Subject," in *Race Matters* (Boston: Beacon Press, 2001), 119–31.

[18] These factors are discussed in depth in Douglas, *Sexuality and the Black Church*, 87–108.

[19] Mindy Thompson Fullilove and Robert E. Fullilove, III, "Stigma as an Obstacle to AIDS Action: The Case of the African American Community," *American Behavioral Scientist* 42 (April 1999), 1117–29.

[20] For an extended discussion of this point, see Keith Boykin, *One More River to Cross: Black and Gay in America* (New York: Anchor Books, 1996).

[21] Seattle Treatment Education Project, "Brother-to-Brother Receives Funds to Raise Awareness about HIV Vaccine Research in Hard-to-Reach Populations," *STEP Ezine* 1, no. 56 (March 26, 2004). Available on the thebody.com website.

[22] World Council of Churches, "Plan of Action: The Ecumenical Response to HIV/AIDS in Africa," Global Consultation on the Ecumenical Response to the Challenge of HIV/AIDS, Nairobi, Kenya, November 25–28, 2001, cited in Donald E. Messer, *Breaking the Conspiracy of Silence: Christian Churches and the Global AIDS Crisis* (Minneapolis: Augsburg Fortress, 2004), 52–53.

[23] Messer, *Breaking the Conspiracy of Silence*, 24.

[24] "A Theological Call to Action," A Statement by the International HIV/AIDS Faith Advisory Board of the Balm in Gilead (2004). Available on the balmingilead.org website.

[25] Similarly, one can point to the 2001 efforts of the Interdenominational Theological Center (Atlanta) and the 2004 declaration of a "state of emergency" by the Progressive National Baptist Convention as additional signs of this nascent awareness by black religious leaders, as cited in "AIDS Grows Up."

[26] W. E. B. Du Bois, "Of the Sorrow Songs," in *The Souls of Black Folk* (New York: Barnes and Noble Classics, 2005).

[27] M. Shawn Copeland, "Foundations for Catholic Theology in an African American Context," in *Black and Catholic: The Challenge and Gift of Black Folk—Contributions of African American Experience and Thought to Catholic Theology*, ed. Jamie T. Phelps (Milwaukee: Marquette University Press, 1997), 114, 136. I am indebted to this essay for the formulation of "authoritative, yet not normative," though I use it to different ends than Copeland.

[28] David Tracy, *On Naming the Present* (Maryknoll, NY: Orbis Books, 1994), 15. See also his discussion in *The Analogical Imagination* (New York: Crossroad, 1986), 12–14.

[29] Frederick Douglass, *Narrative of the Life of Frederick Douglass, an American Slave, written by himself* (1845; New York: Fine Creative Media, 2003).

[30] So avows the noted African American soloist, Barbara Hendricks, who writes: "The Negro Spiritual is the music of all past and present victims of human rights abuse and refugees everywhere; the universality of the emotion they express places them among the songs of humanity" (*Give Me Jesus/Spirituals*, liner notes, EMI Records, 1998). Insightful studies and/or collections of the spirituals are John Lovell, Jr., *Black Song: The Forge and the Flame—The Story of How the Afro-American Spiritual Was Hammered Out* (New York: Paragon House, 1972); Arthur C. Jones, *Wade in the Water: The Wisdom of the Spirituals* (Maryknoll, NY: Orbis Books, 1993); Cheryl A. Kirk-Duggan, *Exorcizing Evil: A Womanist Perspective on the Spirituals* (Maryknoll, NY: Orbis Books, 1997); Richard Newman, *Go Down, Moses: A Celebration of the African-American Spiritual* (New York: Clarkson Potter Publishers, 1998); and Bruno Chenu, *The Trouble I've Seen: The Big Book of Negro Spirituals* (Valley Forge, PA: Judson Press, 2000, 2003).

[31] For example, one spiritual has Jesus speak from the cross, telling the Beloved Disciple to "take my mother home" so that she would not have to witness

the cruel torture and agony he endures: "I think I heard Him say/When he was strugglin' up the hill/I think I heard him say/'Take my mother home'//I think I heard him say/When dey was spittin in his face/'Then I'll die easy/Take my mother home'" (cited in Bruno Chenu, *The Trouble I've Seen*, 188).

[32] Cited in John Lovell, Jr., *Black Song*, 321.

[33] Chenu, *The Trouble I've Seen*, 187.

[34] Ibid.

[35] So avows James Weldon Johnson, as cited by Chenu, *The Trouble I've Seen*, 190.

[36] Lovell, *Black Song*, 304.

[37] Ibid., emphasis added.

[38] Chenu, *The Trouble I've Seen*, 191, 282.

[39] Ibid., 235–36, emphasis added.

[40] Ibid., 193.

[41] Ibid., 248. One should note that *heaven* in the spirituals does not only refer to a state of beatitude beyond mortal life. It also functions as a code word for an earthly existence free from the bondage of slavery. Thus *heaven* or *home* often refers to the North or Canada. Salvation and deliverance, for the enslaved, were not only conditions of the world to come but also a blessedness to be striven for in this. See James Cone, *The Spirituals and the Blues: An Interpretation* (1972; Maryknoll, NY: Orbis Books, 1991); and John Lovell, *Black Song*, among others, on the meaning of *heaven* in the spirituals.

[42] Lovell, *Black Song*, 284.

[43] Chenu, *The Trouble I've Seen*, 221–22, 256–57.

[44] The use of the spirituals for grounding active struggle against social injustice, both in the time of slavery and the present, is wonderfully discussed by Cheryl Kirk-Duggan in *Exorcising Evil*.

[45] Andrew Young, cited in Chenu, *The Trouble I've Seen*, 229.

PART III

PASTORAL CONCERNS

Chapter 11

Uncommon Faithfulness

The Witness of African American Catholics

ARCHBISHOP WILTON D. GREGORY

Glory to God, Glory, All Praise Him, Alleluia,
Glory to God, Glory, All Praise the Name of
the Lord.[1]

I begin this presentation with a glance back at black Catholic history for two very fundamental reasons. First, history offers a mirror in which we may see our humanity. It tells us not only what we have done, but also provides a reflection of who we are and what we can do. Second, an examination of the past often reveals possibilities for the future. These turning points indicate that the future is in motion.

Recall our black experience of Catholic worship. Those of us who are fifty years of age and beyond remember how our hearts delighted when we first heard the melodies, which so resonated with our African American spirituality, composed by Father Clarence Joseph Rivers, a pioneer of inculturation in worship within the African American community in the Catholic Church in North America.

Recall our black experience of Catholic education. It is not surprising but disappointing nonetheless that the early decades of our nation's history lacked any model of a black Catholic school. No one had institutionalized the educational processes for black Catholic children. Parents habitually saw their children being overlooked by an educational system that not only ignored their presence but too frequently demeaned it. In 1828, the Oblate Sisters of Providence opened the School for Colored Girls, later known as St. Frances Academy. The Sisters provided the children with the needed role models and an atmosphere of faith and hope.[2]

Recall that it was not so very long ago that we African Americans struggled with issues associated with our own identity and place within the Catholic Church. What did it mean to be black and Catholic? The work of the National Black Catholic Congresses, which was primarily the work of lay Catholics in response to the lack of an ordained clergy, tackled issues that included articulating and expressing "being black and Catholic," leadership, pastoral ministry, education, and outreach in the community. At the same time the church's leadership was called upon to live up to our church's teaching on racial justice, to practice what was being preached.

In the relatively recent past African American Catholics began to realize what an essential role we black American bishops must play in our efforts to become self-determining. On January 28, 1973, although many bishops imposed hands on the head of then bishop-elect Joseph L. Howze, a remarkable moment came when Bishop Harold R. Perry of New Orleans placed his hands on the head of the bishop-elect. In this act we glimpsed the possibility of black bishops being ordained in more than mere token numbers.[3]

Past events not only point toward but also ensure the future. Scripture reminds us, "Surely there is a future and your hope shall not be cut off" (Prv 23:18). With respect to the church, however, and the black community, in particular, historical perspective illuminates the story: it tells us where black Catholics have been and, to some extent, where we seem to remain, as an enigma within Catholicism.

Nevertheless, if at times black Catholics have been an unnoticed group within Catholicism, we have nonetheless grown steadily and continue to remain faithful and valuable to the church. Despite the overwhelming majority of Protestants and a rapidly growing population of Muslims within the black community, black Catholics stand as a solid witness to the essential "catholicity" of the church in a society still divided by racial differences.[4]

Future research by black Catholic scholars, students, and pastoral ministers must highlight national data and trends that significantly influence the cultural and demographic configurations of parishes and agencies that serve the black Catholic community. *Plenty Good Room: The Spirit and Truth of African American Catholic Worship* provides some useful data that may be used in analysis of strategic issues and trends that may have special impact on the future of black Catholic ministry.[5]

Population: Americans of African ancestry constitute now the second largest identifiable group within the United States. Without the benefit of a formal census, we project African American Catholics represent at least 4 percent of the total U.S. Catholic population of sixty-two million (that is, 2.4 million African American Catholics). Even that number is uncertain due to the increase of many brothers and sisters who are from South and Central America and who have been welcomed within black parishes because of their race, yet who could be counted among the Hispanic communities because their primary language is Spanish. Added to this number is the growing number of African sisters and brothers now living in America.

Priests and Seminarians: There are approximately 250 African American priests. While there was a slight increase among theologate students, up from 2 percent in 1993 to 4 percent in 1999, it is believed that the slight increase in black theologate seminarians may be due to a trend of recruiting more black seminarians from Africa. In 2003 three African Americans were ordained to the priesthood.

Sisters and Deacons: There are five hundred black Catholic sisters and four hundred black Catholic deacons. Black deacons represent 3 percent of the permanent deacons. While these numbers show that African Americans are close to being proportionately represented, we are substantially under-represented among lay ministers.

Laity: African Americans represent only 1.29 percent of lay ministers and 3 percent of students in lay ecclesial ministry formation. Presently there are over thirty-five thousand students enrolled in lay ministry formation programs.

Education and Catholic Schools: Although minorities in Catholic elementary and secondary schools have more than doubled since 1970, black enrollment has diminished somewhat since 1989 and is currently under 8 percent in Catholic schools. There is a significant under-representation of minorities among Catholic school faculty.[6]

These are some statistics that represent challenges to the Catholic identity we so desire. This list is not exhaustive, but rather suggests areas of concern for mutual understanding, discussion, planning, and a vehicle for evangelization. Added to this list of challenges are three overarching concerns that I want to touch upon briefly—leadership, youth and young adults, and racism.

LEADERSHIP

When we review examples of black Catholic leadership, we discover many models of excellence. However, in considering black Catholic participation in the church, we tend to center attention on the numbers of black people who hold offices in their parishes. We consider the extent to which blacks hold institutional roles as religious, deacons, priests, and bishops. Leadership in the church, whether ordained or lay, must be understood as rooted in and derived from our baptismal calling and obligation.

On the other hand, our membership in the Catholic Church has not always been an easy one. The data provided by *Plenty Good Room* pertaining to leadership suggest that many black Catholics tend to agree that diocesan efforts to encourage black people to assume important leadership positions are, at best, inconsistent. Although by no means overwhelming, most respondents agree that their dioceses values the presence of black Catholics. But fewer black Catholics than we would hope agree that the diocese values the input of black Catholics. A majority of respondents to the survey do not believe that their diocese is losing blacks in large numbers.[7] As the hymn goes, "We've had some good days, we've had some bad days, but all of our bad days have become good days and we ought to thank God for our good days."

When we consider black Catholic leadership, some would say it is a leadership that does not "fit" the style of the Catholic Church. A few would say that it has not been a good "fit" to have reinvigorated the Black Catholic Congress Movement; after all, it had been one hundred years since the last Congress.[8] Some would say that it wasn't a good "fit" to start a national Black Catholic Collection for black cultural development; after all, aren't we *all* Catholic? But we have a God of great reversals. And these reversals have become proof positive that God has a way to make all things unfit, fit!

Nothing about our black Catholic journey so far has been easy. Daniel Rudd, a man of great vision, rallied and organized a group of black folks to talk about membership in the church. Mother Elizabeth Lange, a free woman of color from Belize, never turned back when the city and municipalities refused her assistance in aiding poor children, widows, and orphans to live decently. Mother Henriette Delille ignored the authorities in her day when they refused to assist the sick and infirm with medicines and home care.

Some perhaps might now question if it was a good fit to have had an African American president of the U.S. Bishops' Conference at such a critical moment in the history of the church in the United States; after all, black people form such a small number in our church. But God has a way to make all things deemed unfit by some individuals become an excellent fit.

The vision that the first wave of European immigrant pastors drew upon in their development of parish ministry was designed to establish a system based on their ethnic and cultural values and practices. This system focused on membership and on increasing the number of

Catholics from disparate communities. But what were the consequences of such leadership? The church grew, education was accorded a high priority so schools were built, and the growth and development of the parish was the almost exclusive responsibility of the European and European American staff.

All of this changed in the 1980s when many women and men left religious life and the priesthood. In hindsight, as their numbers dwindled, more training should have been provided for the next generation of leaders. Perhaps no one anticipated that these ministers would not be replaced. We presumed that others would follow them and that the parish would continue following time-tested and proven policies and procedures.

There was a sense of ownership of the parish by the parishioners in relation to fiscal matters, the St. Vincent de Paul Society, and the Sodality, but this was not so in the case of the administration of the parish. Unfortunately, this model frequently fostered a sense of dependency, a position of fragility, and even a relationship with the diocese that might be characterized as immature. This dependent relationship is still operative in the minds of some of our people today. This type of connection might be described as preparing us to take on a job but not to become an entrepreneur. We black bishops alluded to this reality in 1984 in the pastoral letter *What We Have Seen and Heard*. We set out an unequivocal demand: "the time has come" for us to take charge of our destiny. The time had come for us to become evangelizers unto ourselves. "Now is the time for those of us who are Black Americans and Black Catholics to reclaim our roots and to shoulder the responsibilities of being both Black and Catholics."[9]

What We Have Seen and Heard was written nearly twenty-five years ago, and the mature fruits of its effort have yet to be fully realized. We may be adults, but we still have some adolescent attitudes regarding our parishes. We have too frequently turned over the future of our parishes and our growth in the faith to pastoral agents from outside of our communities. Moreover, in developing a catechetical experience, one that adequately communicates our black values and spirituality to those whom we have evangelized and those who are lifelong Catholics, we have *not* come of age, as *What We Have Seen and Heard* so proudly stated. We still have not taken full responsibility for our membership in the parish. Our dioceses are strong only when our parishes are vibrant.

Education is an area in which we black Catholics excel, yet, regrettably, no diocese in the United States employs an African American superintendent of schools. Do we not have educators who could serve in this capacity? How can we be "fully functioning people of faith" (as

Sister Thea Bowman called us in her challenge to the U.S. bishops in 1989)[10] and not be enrolled in adult-education programs that ready us to assume responsibility for the future of our parishes, schools, and programs? Or are there other reasons that prevent us from assuming responsibility for our pastoral and educational ministries? Why do we not have more African American pastors? Why are many African Americans leaving the church or perhaps not attending church? Are we preparing ourselves for leadership as the numbers of priests and religious who work with us continue to dwindle?

Ministry to black Catholics is still viewed by some dioceses as "special ministry." If we want priests, deacons, and religious from our community for the life of the church, do we encourage our youngsters to aspire to that service? "Whatever a man sows, this he will also reap" (Gal 6:7). We black Catholics already operate and staff programs intended to vitalize our parishes, educate ordained and lay ecclesial ministers, and prepare leadership: the Institute for Black Catholic Studies at Xavier University, the Augustus Tolton Lay Ministry Program in the Archdiocese of Chicago, the Thea Bowman Institute in the Archdiocese of Louisville, and the Nehemiah Ministry, which produces the *Keep on Teaching* resource manual from the Archdiocese of Baltimore. These programs, institutes, and resources deserve our support and participation.

The very nature of the church includes hierarchical leadership. Yet, we bishops by ourselves are not the whole church. What is needed, particularly now, is broad-based collaborative leadership with a common vision. Without a shared vision our parishes and schools will be poorly managed. We will lose membership, especially youth and young adults, and we will be ignorant of many black Catholic community needs.

We must have unity; we must model oneness. After we have identified and prepared our leaders, we must support them and the vision they put forward. We pastoral leaders, scholars, and intellectuals must work together. The head cannot move in one direction, the neck in another, and the torso in still another direction. We must all strive to be of one accord; then, with the guidance of the Holy Spirit, our ideas will bear fruit.

New leaders must be faithful men and women of high moral character. And, finally, there is an urgent need for leadership development across all ministries. In the past the parish system was often shaped by an immature vision wherein the decisions were made exclusively by the principal or pastor. New leadership must take into account how we organize our schools, our parishes, even how we train people to take the role of leadership. It is imperative that all forms of ministry demonstrate healthy models so that young people are mentored early on in what it means to be a member of a parish. These are minimum requirements. This is an era of specialization, and leadership development is needed in every area of ministry. No longer can we be satisfied to have Sunday school teachers; each parish should identify, develop, and support at least one or two master catechists. No longer can we remain content to operate soup kitchens; each parish needs an advocacy group to address political issues, along with HIV and AIDS ministry, self-help programs like NA, AA, and programs that affirm life.

YOUTH AND YOUNG ADULTS

Another area of vital concern involves our youth and young adults. As a community, we must give significant time and consideration to them as the future of our community is directly dependent upon their well-being. Black Catholic youth and young adults contribute to the strength of the community, both in the present and definitely in the future. No discussion on the present or future state of the black Catholic community is complete without paying proper attention to the concerns and vision of our young people.

Youth and young adults form two distinct groups, and I will address each. *Youth* refers to those of ages thirteen to seventeen, and *young adults* to those of ages eighteen to thirty-five. In 2002, 33 percent of all blacks were under eighteen, compared with 23 percent of non-Hispanic whites. Only 8 percent of blacks were sixty-five and older, compared with 14 percent of non-Hispanic whites.[11] Approximately 20 percent of African Americans are between the ages of ten and nineteen, compared with 13 percent of non-Hispanic whites. These are not insignificant numbers and are actually somewhat staggering. They imply that the black population in the United States is a relatively young population. This age group includes those in middle school and high school as well as those who have dropped out of the school system, single teen mothers and fathers, and those in the penal system.

Poverty remains a grave concern when we speak of our young people. According to the U.S. Census Bureau, the poverty rate among African Americans under the age of eighteen ranks at 30 percent. One in three of our young people live in poverty, a rate three times greater than that of the general population.[12] Poverty is vicious, and the poverty that our youth experience is particularly distressing. It threatens their education, health care, and future. Growing up in poverty often causes depression, low self-esteem, a feeling of abandonment, and destroys hope for the future. Poverty affects participation in the parish and the church. This suggests that we absolutely must invest our time and resources in our youth. Attention and mentoring are positively associated with youth and adolescent self-worth.

In our call to evangelize and to mission, we must take action with Catholic and public education systems. A sound education furnishes a key way out of poverty. Do we understand the importance of vouchers as a means of supporting educational choice? Do we challenge African American legislators, who themselves often benefited from Catholic education but are unwilling to help make that same resource available to disadvantaged youngsters in today's poorer communities? Do we speak out and work for improvements in public education? Still, our Catholic schools remain a hopeful sign in many black communities. They often represent one of the few opportunities for urban youth to receive a quality education.

Our young-adult demographic consists of college-age young men and women, young college graduates who have entered into the work force, non-college attendees in the work force, married couples with young families, young men and women in the penal system, professionals, military personnel, political and community leaders. This is a very diverse group with different needs and aspirations, oftentimes a conflicted generation.

Our young adults have goals and dreams and, like other young adults, issues and concerns. These may include debt, home ownership, family concerns, child care, health care, drugs, crime, education, racism, absentee fathers, and the leadership of the country. Two problems are most urgent: First, HIV/AIDS remains one of the top three causes of death of our young men between the ages of twenty-five and forty-four. We must work quickly and definitively to increase awareness of this pandemic, get people tested, support systems for treatment, and reduce the rate of new infections. Second, unemployment in the black community is double the national average. Unemployment, besides the obvious economic impact, affects one's dignity and self-esteem. Unemployment means that many are forced to consider multiple very low-paying jobs. This situation hurts black parish life because the income base for the parish is negatively affected and young people do not have the time to engage in parish activities.

The good news is that young people play a vital role in any society. They are the engines of the collective vision of any community. Young men and women are naturally filled with an unfettered optimism and buoyancy that drives discovery and progress. Black Catholic communities must listen to the vision coming from its young people. We must not discourage or mute the vision. Our role as leaders and elders is to share our wisdom with the young so that they may achieve their visions. Their visions should be ours, and our wisdom should be theirs.

In addition to attentive listening, there are some things that we can do to assist our youth and young adults. First, we too must have a vision as a community for our young people—a vision to help and not hinder, to strengthen and not weaken their natural optimism and hope. Second, we must identify resources and support vigorously the plan of action for youth and young adults approved at the 2002 National Black Catholic Congress.[13]

In his message to young people at World Youth Day 2002 in Toronto, Pope John Paul II said:

It is in the nature of human beings, and especially youth, to seek the Absolute, the meaning and fullness of life. Dear young people, do not be content with anything less than the highest ideals! Do not let yourselves be dispirited by those who are disillusioned with life and have grown deaf to the deepest and most authentic desires of their heart. You are right to be disappointed with hollow entertainment and passing fads, and with aiming at too little in life. If you have an ardent desire for the Lord you will steer clear of mediocrity and conformism so widespread in our society.[14]

RACISM

Racism lingers as a perennial issue. Many black Catholics along with other Catholic women and men of good will have been involved in bridge-building work throughout the last fifty years, and yet racism seems never to go away. The Catholic Church's concern for racial justice stems from the conviction that Christians must confront racism if our claim to preach the gospel is to be credible. Racism tarnishes the gospel. There is no other way to view it.

Much has changed since the time when Daniel Rudd and his comrades of the Black Catholic Congress challenged the Catholic Church to speak out for justice in society and justice in the church for black people.[15] Credit must be given to the National Office for Black Catholics (NOBC) and other early black Catholic pioneers who worked tirelessly to affirm black Catholic culture and to make black Catholic parish life congruent with that culture and its worshiping people.

Since the publication of *Brothers and Sisters to Us*, the twenty-fifth anniversary of which we celebrated a few years ago, some progress has been made in the struggle to overcome the social impact of the sin of racism. African Americans have been elected to public office and raised to leadership positions in the church and in the private sector. The number of African American youth who are attending college is steadily increasing, and the gap between the median income of African Americans and other Americans is slowly shrinking. There are real changes in the growth of a sense of fairness and in levels of attainment by African Americans in general.

But it is by no means paradise. Much work remains to be accomplished. But the days are over when "Mrs. Brown" had to sit in the rafters if she wanted to attend a Catholic Church or when we had to wait in the back of the line to receive communion or when we were not invited to attend activities that were a part of the social life of the church. We remember the sacrifices made so many years ago for parish life and its growth, and we honor the significant progress that has been made toward racial equality in our lifetime.

Where are we today? Much work remains to be accomplished. What can this community of faith, which calls itself anti-racist, do now to carry us all to the next place on this journey? In his apostolic letter *Tertio millennio adveniente*, prepared for the jubilee of the year 2000, Pope John Paul II invites us to aim at "broadening horizons of believers, so that they will see things in the perspective of Christ" (no. 49). This vision gives hope.

A few possibilities that need further reflection and development include:

- Opening wide the door for qualified laity to serve in leadership roles where permitted in church law;

- Improving the leadership and faith focus in our Catholic schools;

- Improving our proclamation of gospel-based teaching on human sexuality;

- Using the great gifts that women bring to the church more creatively;

- Developing and implementing more aggressive vocation programs;

- Working intentionally for racial reconciliation within the broader Catholic community.

Clearly, there are many issues and problems that African American Catholics must tackle, but high on our list of concerns is the fact that we are black Catholics in an institution that too regularly considers us outside the mainstream. This very issue provoked Daniel Rudd to convene the congresses of the nineteenth century. This very issue prompted the formation of a culture and worship department at the NOBC. This very issue led to the development of the National Black Catholic Pastoral Plan.[16]

How are we to achieve a more profound sense of belonging? How are we to overcome our apathy and the fears of others? During Pope John Paul II's 1999 visit to the United States, when he was in St. Louis, he challenged us all to "put an end to every form of racism, a plague which your bishops have called one of the most persistent and destructive evils of the nation."[17]

From our lived experiences we black Catholics know that simply asking people to change rarely succeeds. Any appeal must demonstrate concretely the persistence and pervasiveness of systemic racism. Organizations like Pax Christi and Catholic Charities USA have adopted abolishing racism as organizational goals and are making attempts to sensitize their members to the privileges limited to the dominant class. We must not forget that we all need one another—white, black, yellow, red, and brown—in order to understand how racism destroys us all. African Americans have a contribution to make toward understanding and changing the climate of racial injustice. As committed Catholics who, more than anyone, desire that one day we all may truly be free, we have a responsibility to be in partnership with all honest, committed colleagues and parishioners of every race and language.

CONCLUSION

Being black Catholic pastoral leaders, scholars, and academics is not about being comfortable and self-congratulatory. All too often we are distracted by our own efforts and overlook what God is doing in our midst. Sometimes we get caught up in extraneous things. We need to challenge our leadership skills, to study the demands that we face, and to confront the limitations that surround us. But we must have no fear. God's word encourages us to wait on the Lord and be of good courage: "Prove yourselves doers of the word and not merely hearers" (Jas 1:22). This was the advice given to an earlier group of Christians who faced daunting trials and yet who managed to succeed beyond even their wildest aspirations. So shall it be with us!

NOTES

[1] Refrain from "Closing Hymn, A Thanksgiving Celebration," music from Clarence Joseph Rivers, *Soulfull Worship* (Washington DC: The National Office for Black Catholics, 1974).

[2] Sr. Reginald Gerdes, O.S.P., "Black Catholic Schools of the Oblate Sisters of Providence," *U.S. Catholic Historian* 7, no. 2 (Spring/Summer 1988).

[3] The National Office for Black Catholics, "Afro-American Bishops: The Basis of Authentic Afro-American Catholicism," *Freeing the Spirit* 11, no. 2 (Summer 1973).

[4] See "Rationale for Opening of Secretariat for Black Catholics within the U.S. Bishops' Conference," *Working Document, National Conference of Catholic Bishops* (Washington DC: USCC, 1987).

[5] Bishops' Committee on the Liturgy, Secretariat for Black Catholics, *Plenty Good Room: The Spirit and Truth of African American Catholic Worship* (Washington DC: USCC, 1990).

[6] Ibid.

[7] Ibid.

[8] Cyprian Davis, O.S.B., *The History of Black Catholics in the United States* (New York: Crossroad, 1990).

[9] *What We Have Seen and Heard: A Pastoral Letter on Evangelization from the Black Bishops of the United States* (Cincinnati: St. Anthony Messenger, 1984).

[10] See Thea Bowman, F.S.P.A., "To Be Black and Catholic," *Origins* (July 6, 1989), 114–18, passim.

[11] U. S. Census Bureau, "The Black Population of the United States: March 2003," 2–3.

[12] Ibid.

[13] National Black Catholic Congress IX, *Pastoral Plan of Action*, Chicago, Illinois, 2002.

[14] Pope John Paul II, "Homily, World Youth Day," Toronto, Canada, July 23, 2002.

[15] *Brothers and Sisters to Us: U.S. Bishops' Pastoral Letter on Racism in Our Day* (Washington DC: USCC, 1979).

[16] Secretariat for Black Catholics, *Here I Am, Send Me: A Conference Response to Evangelization of African Americans: National Black Catholic Pastoral Plan* (Edison, NJ: Hunter Publishing, April 1990).

[17] Pope John Paul II, "Homily," St. Louis, January 26, 1999.

Chapter 12

African American Sacred Music in Catholic Worship

Core of African American Survival in America

KEVIN P. JOHNSON

Since Vatican II, African American sacred music and gospel music have transformed the way in which many black and other Catholic believers worship God in the holy mass and in their everyday lives. This music has been at the core of African American survival in America and has for more than fifty years allowed African Americans and others to worship God in a manner befitting their cultural practices in the holy mass. *The Constitution on the Sacred Liturgy* states very clearly that

> there are peoples who have their own musical tradition, and these play a great part in their religious and social life. For this reason due importance is to be attached to their music, and a suitable place is to be given to it, not only in forming their attitude toward religion, but also in adapting worship to their native genius. (*SC,* no. 119)

African Americans have indeed adapted worship to their native genius in the American Catholic Church.

The African American Catholic worship experience has become the catalyst for dynamic church growth and a primary tool for evangelization. In their 1984 pastoral letter *What We Have Seen and Heard*, the African American bishops stated:

> We believe that the liturgy of the Catholic Church can be an even more intense expression of the spiritual vitality of those who are of

African origin, just as it has been for other ethnic and cultural groups. . . .

There is a splendid opportunity for the vast richness of African American culture to be expressed in our liturgy. It is this opportunity, thanks to the norms established in the revised Roman liturgy, which enables our work of evangelization to be filled with such promise for the future.[1]

THE IMPORTANCE OF QUALITY LITURGICAL MUSIC

The future for African American parishes is connected inseparably to the worship experience. Pastors willing to give pastoral vision, leadership, and commitment to liturgy are necessary in churches where authentic, culturally based African American worship is desired. With pastoral commitment to developing meaningful liturgies, communities can be strengthened and new members evangelized. For most African Americans, bringing a potential church member to mass can be likened to bringing someone home for dinner to meet the family. Therefore, worship must be expressed in a manner befitting the cultural norms of the worshiping community or family.

Due to the paucity of African American vocations in the Catholic Church today, white priests often pastor black parishes. In many cases these men are not familiar or comfortable with a culturally based African American style of worship that may challenge their own ideas about the celebration of the mass. While many pastors strive to understand the needs of African American worship, others still endeavor to impose Euro-American worship styles on black congregations. Twenty-first century liturgical reform efforts, such as the revised *General Instruction of the Roman Missal*,[2] have given these same pastors more reasons to impose a Eurocentric model of worship on black churches. But pastors must take care to introduce current liturgical reforms in a manner conducive to the cultural expression of worshiping communities as mandated by Vatican II. African American culturally based worship models are forward looking, progressive, creative, and universal in nature and will never fit into a pre-Vatican II mold. African American worship is expressive, vibrant, and relies largely on the music of its culture to express itself in spirit and in truth. Catholic documents fully indicate the church's commitment to liturgy. The 1967 *Instruction on Music in the Liturgy* mandates:

Liturgical worship is given a more noble form when it is celebrated in song, with the ministers of each degree fulfilling their ministry and the people participating in it. Indeed, through this form, prayer is expressed in a more attractive way, the mystery of the liturgy, with its hierarchical and community nature, is more openly shown, the unity of hearts is more profoundly achieved by the union of voices, minds are more easily raised to heavenly things by the beauty of the sacred rites, and the whole celebration more clearly prefigures that heavenly liturgy which is enacted in the holy city of Jerusalem. Pastors of souls will therefore do all they can to achieve this form of celebration. (no. 5)

Music must be a top priority for pastors seeking to create dynamic African American worship experiences. In his book *Soulfull Worship*, Father Clarence Joseph Rivers, a pioneer in the development of African American music in Catholic worship, points out that

worship is of primary importance for the Church, not only for the sake of the Church, in the narrow sense, but also for the sake of humanity itself. A very necessary ingredient in human progress is what I call a sense of transcendence—a sense of being able to go, to reach, beyond the boundaries and the limitations of the here and now . . . not because God needs our worship, but because we need it.[3]

Liturgy, the core of the church's mission and existence, will remain vital in the twenty-first century when it is performed well by those ministers who know the power of liturgy. Rivers observes:

The church must devote to worship all that it needs to become consistently, as it should be, a moving experience in which the Spirit of God can soften up the hearts of stone and make them hearts of flesh, in which by the breath of God's Spirit we may be new born again.[4]

CHURCH GROWTH

One church that provides proof of the power of meaningful liturgy is the predominately African American Holy Name of Jesus Catholic Church in Los Angeles. As with many churches, the late 1970s marked the end of the guitar mass at Holy Name. But unlike most churches, Holy Name replaced the guitar mass with a contemporary gospel choir complete with a full rhythm section of drums, bass, guitar, and piano.

This change marked a natural evolution of the African American Catholic experience. As the black Catholics in this parish began to embrace their own culture's music in worship, the liturgy began to attract more and more people. Young people—who had been testing the waters at nearby Protestant churches in order to get "fed"—began to come back to the Catholic Church, where they could feel connected in a way they had never felt before. Evangelization efforts began to flourish, and membership grew, with many ministries sprouting up as young people began to experience the excitement of their faith and their church. As the African American liturgical style became better known to the people in the neighborhood and the city, people visited and joined the church in numbers not seen before in this black community. Other churches in Los Angeles, such as St. Brigid's Catholic Church, also experienced remarkable growth as gospel music was integrated into the worship service.

The growing faith communities that have blossomed in dying African American Catholic parishes evidence the reality that quality African American worship increases church attendance and membership. Churches that were once nearly empty and on the verge of financial collapse and eminent closure have become bustling centers of spiritual connectedness and financial solvency. Church memberships have doubled, tripled, and even quadrupled in some parishes where African American sacred music is done well in Catholic worship. In *The Emergence of a Black Catholic Community* Morris J. MacGregor writes:

> Music has played an essential role in the history of St. Augustine's [an African American Catholic parish in Washington DC]. Across the decades scores of talented parishioners have raised their voices in praise to God, fully conscious that their art served other causes as well. From the first the quality of sacred music in the church not only enhanced the meaning of the liturgy, but also attracted a large audience of visitors, black and white, Catholic and non-Catholic.[5]

Leon Roberts, a noted composer of African American sacred music for Catholic worship, argues that

> the growing popularity of the liturgy at 12:30 mass revived St. Augustine's. As for developments during the time I was there, only God could have achieved something like that. It was not the gospel choir itself that deserved the praise, rather it was the spirit of the people and the power of God working through the people.[6]

UNIVERSAL APPEAL

The power of God at work through music in African American Catholic worship has consistently proven its universal appeal. Worshipers of all races are attracted to the powerful sincerity and witness of this music when performed appropriately. As MacGregor notes, "Martin Luther King Jr.'s observation that Sunday mornings were the most segregated time in America did not apply to St. Augustine's, whose congregation at Sunday masses and vespers was fully integrated during the long reign of Jim Crow in Washington."[7] African American music and worship break down the walls of race, gender, and class and promote the unity of minds. These black churches that were once neighborhood churches remain in communities where demographic shifts have occurred. Now the Sunday morning worshipers may drive fifty miles to come be a part of this black Catholic worshiping community.

Despite the length, the comments of Father John Adamski, pastor of Our Lady of Lourdes Catholic Church in Atlanta, are worth quoting:

African American music seems to have a quality of engaging people in ways different from much of Catholic Church music today. Perhaps it's the rhythmic difference that contributes to making the music feel accessible. Whatever the musical uniqueness, people seem to respond with more than a simply vocal or intellectual reaction. Somehow, the heart and, indeed, the whole self, or soul, seems touched or moved. Thus, many Lourdes' members appear to be engaged and responsive in a manner that is different than in most American, Euro-centric parishes. The appeal of music in the African American idiom is not limited to African Americans, but is also attractive for white people. This may include some sense of participating in something that feels new and different, something out of the ordinary experience of the average white Catholic, but it also appears to touch common human experience. For African Americans, there seems to be a sense that some part of their cultural tradition is being incorporated into Catholic worship, so the whole worship experience isn't simply a "white" experience. Since part of Catholic identity is a celebration of diversity, this musical style functions as an easy way for people who are from different backgrounds to feel connected to each other and, thus, a positive element in building a church community today.[8]

WHAT IS AFRICAN AMERICAN SACRED MUSIC?

African American sacred music, which has its roots in Africa, has played an important role in the evolution of the African American experience in the United States. The rhythm of the drum is a key factor in identifying what can be considered characteristic music of the African American cultural experience. The rhythmic incisiveness of African American music is the hallmark of its authenticity. While not all African Americans have an innate ability to internalize rhythm, sacred music composed by African Americans is culturally connected to Mother Africa. In *The Music of African Americans* Eileen Southern states:

> Despite the interaction of African and European cultural patterns in black communities, with the resultant emergence of new, Afro-American patterns, there persists among black folk musicians a predilection for certain performance practices, certain habits, certain musical instruments, and certain ways of shaping music to meet their needs in the new environment that had its roots in the African experience.[9]

The singing tradition of African Americans also played a role in the development of this idiom. Whether singing Negro spirituals on the plantation or in the concert hall, or singing gospel songs about the victory in Jesus throughout cities in America and the world, African Americans have always been able to find a connection to God. African Americans have always used song to express their life stories, struggles, joys, hopes, and dreams, and their life stories are rooted in the ability of God's spirit to get us through the most difficult and trying moments of our lives. In "The Gift of African American Sacred Song" Sister Thea Bowman writes: "Black sacred song has been at once a source and an expression of Black faith, spirituality and devotion. By song, our people have called the Spirit into our hearts, home, churches and communities."[10] Black people have found their center, their source, through singing about a God and to a God who is more powerful than their most difficult problems.

Whoever wants to understand African American sacred music must realize that it is a music firmly rooted in the stories of black Christians' lives as they have come to believe them to be, that is, life totally and completely dependent on an all-powerful God. Appropriate performance practice of this genre requires that a singer tell his or her own story through the music. It is not enough for the performer to sing the notes correctly, having impeccable intonation, diction, breath support, and posture. No, the performer must be willing to share his or her life story with listeners. The words of the songs must become a testimony of the performer's own life, exposing not only the person's musical abilities but also his or her joys, pains, hopes, and aspirations.

African American sacred music such as Negro spirituals and gospel music served as the primary source material for other musical genres in American music. Musical styles such as jazz, rhythm and blues, rock and roll, and hip-hop are all the beneficiaries of African American sacred music, which had its roots in Mother Africa. In African American churches a variety of styles frequently have been allowed to co-exist; the result has been originality—coming from an interplay of different styles.[11] The combining of these musical styles will undoubtedly lead to the creation of other styles in the twenty-first century.

THE HISTORY OF AFRICAN AMERICAN SACRED MUSIC IN CATHOLIC WORSHIP

The late 1970s and 1980s marked a period of discovery for black Catholic musicians. In the twentieth century Catholic musicians were able to create, within the context of this new black Catholic genre, a type of universal music that was both black and Catholic. National workshops and conferences offered musicians an opportunity to learn and share their excitement and work in Catholic worship taught by the best and the brightest musicians the church had to offer. Black composers such as Clarence Rivers, Leon Roberts, Grayson Brown, Robert Ray, Rawn Harbor, Kenneth Louis, and others contributed to the black Catholic choral repertoire through self-publication, mainstream Catholic publishers such as GIA Publications and Oregon Catholic Press, and of course, the *Lead Me, Guide Me* hymnal. Over the years black composers have contributed a wealth of service music that has helped define African American sacred music written specifically for Catholic worship.

During this period many responsorial psalms were composed, such as Leon Roberts's soulful "Let Us Go Rejoicing" and Rawn Harbor's forward-looking "All the Ends of the Earth." These compositions are both uniquely African American and Catholic. Service music abounded as early as Clarence Rivers's "Mass Dedicated to the Brotherhood of Man," and included Leon Roberts's "Mass of St. Augustine," and Grayson Brown's "Cast Your Bread upon the Water," among others. Avon Gillespie, Rawn Harbor, Roger Holliman, Roderick Bell, Kenneth Lewis, Kevin Johnson, Ray East, Timothy Gibson, and many others contributed African American sacred music for Catholic worship to the repertoire. This period also inspired black composers to write African American sacred music for the concert stage, such as Robert Ray's "Gospel Mass."

WHERE DO WE GO FROM HERE?

The survival of the black Catholic Church of the twenty-first century is highly dependent on the development of its music ministries. The church must engage itself in seeking ways to enhance and, in many cases, create music ministries that will allow for the soulful worship of its people. If the church does not do this, young Catholic men and women will be drawn to other worshiping communities in America where their songs are being sung and stories are being told. The church experience must remain relevant and inspiring to a new generation of believers. The church must begin to address the multi-generational musical needs of its membership. A church that will attract young people, motivate the "old school" generation, and satisfy its elders will continue to minister the music that speaks to the entire worshiping community. This is no easy task for the church today. In this new century many black churches, both Protestant and Catholic, face the grim reality that there are not enough talented musicians seeking church employment.

PROTESTANT MUSICIANS

Many black Catholic churches are forced to recruit musicians from Protestant churches because no Catholic musicians can be found. These Protestant musicians are in such high demand that they often serve both Protestant and Catholic churches each Sunday morning, having to leave the Catholic church before the end of communion in order to make it in time for their "home" church service. These musicians often bring with them the styles of their particular Protestant church traditions and attempt to fit those same musical ideals in the Catholic liturgy. Because of the range of their training, they are often unaware of and unable to draw upon the variety of musical possibilities of the African American Catholic experience.

Music ministers who have grown up in Protestant churches must be careful not to impose the traditions of those churches, with their markedly distinctive traditions and requirements, on Catholic worship. For example, black Catholics are often not as familiar with well-known hymns of the black Protestant church. The music minister would have more success playing a well-known European Catholic hymn with attention given to African American performance practice. In addition, some songs created in Protestant churches are not conducive to the universal expectation of the Catholic worship experience and have religious connotations that do not translate well into the Catholic experience. Songs such as "Get Right Church and Let's Go Home," which is often used in Protestant services, does not fit the context of Catholic worship because the textual meaning is contrary to Catholic theology.

If Catholic pastors are going to hire non-Catholic musicians, they should find a way to train these musicians for ministry in the black Catholic Church. Being black and skilled in black music is not enough for the African American Catholic Church musician. In order to have a profound effect on liturgy, the musician must approach Catholic worship differently from Protestant worship. Musicians who select music for the liturgy must understand how the mass is designed. While the flow of the liturgy is highly dependent upon the celebrant, it is equally dependent upon the music minister's ability to select appropriate music. Catholic and non-Catholic musicians must be taught about the elements of the liturgy and then required to participate in liturgy meetings and other opportunities to get feedback from the community they serve.

In their frantic searches for musicians, some churches fail to consider the available musician's experience or understanding of Catholic worship. Churches often hire musicians who demonstrate the ability to perform a particular style of music. The fundamental misconception that search committees often have when seeking to hire music ministers in the black Catholic church is that any person experienced in the gospel-music idiom will be able to lead a contemporary African American Catholic worshiping community. This is far from the truth. Gospel music or any music used in liturgy must be carefully thought out with a sensitivity to the content and flow of Catholic worship. One who understands the importance of music in an African American Catholic community will take the necessary steps to ensure that the music ministry presents the worshiping community with that which is authentically black and authentically Catholic.

Authentically Black and Catholic (Universal) Music

The goal for the musician in an African American Catholic Church must be to create a musically balanced worship environment that is authentically black and authentically Catholic. As Clarence Rivers posits in *Soulfull Worship*:

> Musically liberated Catholics—like our forefathers who combined African and white protestant music to help produce the rich musics of black America—must be free to use traditional Catholic

musics, and allow them free interplay with our Afro-American musics. The results will be a still greater enrichment of the Afro-American styles, further originality. The Afro-American tradition in music is a tradition of freedom and creativity. There are not, therefore, any absolute limits on what is "black," as long as black men themselves freely choose it because they find it to be of value.[12]

Today we find a church where rap music is considered the preference of the young hip-hop generation of church-goers, gospel music the prefer-ence of old-school Christians, and the hymns of the church and Negro spirituals the choice of the church elders. As black Catholics, some of us still prefer the European Catholic model of worship to the African Ameri-can model. With this in mind, the musician must have a commitment to creating a universal music not limited by categories or stylistic short-sightedness. "Be careful," Rivers warns, "therefore, not to imagine that blackness should be stereotyped into any given mold or definition. Such rigid dogmatism is more akin to European Scholasticism than it is to the Afro-American tradition."[13]

The African American musical experience in Catholic worship con-sists of a synthesizing of traditional music of Mother Africa, often utilizing drums and African texts, Euro-American hymns, Negro spirituals, a variety of gospel music, jazz, pop, rap music, and European Catholic music. This universal palette of musical experiences is consistent with the universal church. This explains the broad appeal of the African American Catholic worship experience. Rivers writes: "The fullest free-dom for Black Catholics, musically speaking, will come not merely after we have learned what there is to learn from our black musical heritage, but only after we have come to imagine our yet unrealized musical pos-sibilities. To cease to dream and to create is to become enslaved.[14]

MUSICAL COMPOSITION

The evolution of African American Catholic worship will depend greatly on black Catholic musicians' ability to compose quality music for the church. The Catholic Church has always encouraged composers who are led by the Spirit of God to compose music for the liturgy and worship. *Sacrosanctum concilium (The Constitution on the Sacred Liturgy)* urges that

composers, animated by the Christian spirit, should accept that it pertains to their vocation to cultivate sacred music and increase its stores of treasures. Let them produce compositions which have the qualities proper to the genuine sacred music, and which can be sung not only by large choirs but also by smaller choirs, and which make possible the active participation of the whole congregation. The texts intended to be sung must always be in conformity with Catholic doctrine. Indeed, they should be drawn chiefly from the sacred scripture and from liturgical sources. (*SC,* no. 32)

However, the progress made by black composers of Catholic church music in the last half of the twentieth century will not be enough to sustain the African American Catholic worshiping community in the twenty-first century. The *Lead Me, Guide Me* hymnal is a wonderful resource, but it does not contain compositions written after the late 1980s. It provides superb documentation of the beginnings of the African American Catholic musical landscape, just as the *African American Heritage Hymnal* has done with Protestant church music.[15] As African American Catholics, we must define our role in the American Catholic Church and in the lives of the hip-hop generation. New music must continue to be disseminated in black Catholic churches throughout America, for this music will continue to refine and define the manner in which worship is carried out. Failure to do so will cause musicians in the black Catholic Church to overuse the music in hymnals such as *Lead Me, Guide Me* or result in the inappropriate use of popular gospel music in the mass or in an environment of worship that is staid and outdated. Black Catholics have not built up the stores of musical repertoire that define our worship as have many other believers and cultures. Despite the ability of the black musician in the Catholic Church to draw from a variety of musical sources, music composed by and for African American Catholics can more completely capture the manner in which it seeks to worship in song.

PROFESSIONAL MUSIC MINISTRY

Churches must find ways to offer a living wage to music ministers. The lack of understanding or inability to provide musicians with a just wage presents a crucial problem for the quality of music in African American Catholic worship. The churches must be able to attract and retain competent musicians familiar with liturgy and with an appreciation for the unique treasure of the African American Catholic worship experience. Rivers is blunt on this issue:

A parish music program is not a part time job, when viewed both from the perspective of the musical needs of the parish, and from the perspective of the musicians' need to constantly keep their skills in readiness by rehearsing and drilling themselves in those skills:

and also from the perspective of the musicians' need to constantly enlarge their skills so that they may become more professionally catholic and thereby become more capable of serving a community that must be catholic, i.e., universal, open to all men of all cultural preferences. As long as the parish musician is thought of as a part time employee and paid accordingly, we will have great difficulty in convincing potential Church musicians to consider this field for their life's work. And we will always have the problem every few years of trying to find a new director because these musicians will soon move on to greener pastures; and their stopover in Church work will merely be a temporary expedient.[16]

Pastors who understand the role of music in African American Catholic churches do not pastor dead and dying churches. They understand the priority of worship and put in place music ministry that continually grows congregations and church memberships. Every successful mainstream black church with growing congregations has a well-paid music staff. Moreover, in this hip-hop era, if the Catholic Church is to attract and keep its young people, pastors must hire music ministers who are intent on building a music ministry. Once black Catholic churches find a way to hire professionally trained musicians to lead their music ministries, they can begin to train black Catholic youth to be church musicians.

OPPORTUNITIES FOR TRAINING

Black Catholic churches must train their own musicians. In order to grow the next generation of Catholic musicians, young people need to be mentored by well-trained music ministers. Many Protestant churches have adopted a music-institute model that serves as an ongoing musical training program for youth housed within the church and directed by the music ministers. For example, when the Archdiocese of Atlanta closed Our Lady of Lourdes Catholic School, Our Lady of Lourdes Catholic Church dedicated the entire third floor of the former school building to the Drexel Institute for the Arts. Named for St. Katherine Drexel, the founder of the school, the institute not only provides a model of leadership in the arts in Atlanta, but also trains the young people in the parish in liturgical music. Further, the institute serves the adult population of the parish through ongoing private musical instruction and music-minister training. This program was born out of a school closing that devastated the parish community. But African Americans have always been able to overcome adversity to create something out of nothing. Programs like this one can happen when a parish community—pastor and members—understands the role and significance of music not only in liturgy but also in African American daily life.

The black Catholic Church of the twenty-first century must actively encourage music ministries to create and/or to participate in diocesan and national conferences, mass choirs, and projects that expose regional musicians to outstanding examples of music ministry. Workshops on a national level that draw upon and engage the best practices of African American Catholic ministries should be funded and conducted on an annual or semiannual basis. Pastors must make dollars available and encourage or require their musicians to attend these conferences. A new standard of excellence in music ministry is required if we are to fill the void left by the passing of some of our brightest black Catholic musical leaders.

CONCLUSION

The black Catholic Church of the twenty-first century is very different from the church of Clarence Rivers, Thea Bowman, Leon Roberts, and other black Catholic musical pioneers. Their work provided the leadership and vision necessary to define the parameters and possibilities for African American music in the Catholic Church. Cyprian Davis comments in his essay "Speaking the Truth":

> African Americans have profoundly changed liturgical music. On the other hand, African American Catholic musicians have also added to the scope and breadth of African American sacred music. Far too often Black Catholics found themselves singing the songs of Zion in a foreign land. With hesitation and with effort did we take down our harps to sing a new song. And then we realized that it was no longer a foreign land and no longer a strange song. The former things had passed away.[17]

While the musical groundwork has been laid for the musicians of this new millennium, much is still left to do. The work of creating African American Catholic sacred music is not complete. We must continue to add to the stores of African American sacred music written for Catholic worship. Black composers must continue to compose music for use in the liturgy that meets the challenge of the new millennium to serve diverse congregations. Publications such as *The Lead Me, Guide Me* hymnal will continue to be written as a testament to the progress and evolution of African American Catholics.

African American liturgy has touched the hearts of many worshipers, both black and white, and African American parishes have benefited from the universal appeal of its music and worship style. Yet, the quality and authenticity of black Catholic liturgical music must never be compromised in order to serve multicultural and/or majority non-black congregations. As the church becomes more universal, African American Catholic liturgy must emerge as a soulful combination of traditional African American and Catholic liturgical musics. This can only be accomplished by renewed efforts to train young musicians in the ways of black Catholic worship and pastoral commitment to hire qualified professionals to lead music ministries.

NOTES

[1] *What We Have Seen and Heard: Pastoral Letter on Evangelization* (Cincinnati: St. Anthony Messenger Press, 1984), 30, 31.

[2] Congregation for Divine Worship and the Discipline of the Sacraments, *General Instruction on the Roman Missal* (Washington DC: USCC, 2003).

[3] Clarence Joseph Rivers, *Soulfull Worship* (Washington DC: National Office for Black Catholics, 1974).

[4] Ibid.

[5] Morris J. MacGregor, *The Emergence of a Black Catholic Community: St. Augustine's in Washington* (Washington DC: Catholic University of America Press, 1999).

[6] Leon Roberts, quoted in ibid., 516.

[7] MacGregor, *The Emergence of a Black Catholic Community,* 487.

[8] John Adamski, letter to author, March 2, 2004.

[9] Eileen Southern, *The Music of Black Americans: A History,* 2nd ed. (New York: W. W. Norton, 1983), 21–22.

[10] Thea Bowman, F.S.P.A., "The Gift of African American Sacred Song," in *Lead Me, Guide Me: The African American Catholic Hymnal* (Chicago: GIA Publications, 1987), x.

[11] See Clarence Joseph Rivers, *The Spirit in Worship* (Cincinnati: Stimuli, 1978).

[12] Rivers, *Soulfull Worship,* 42.

[13] Ibid.

[14] Ibid., 43.

[15] Delores Carpenter and Nolan E. Williams, eds., *The African American Heritage Hymnal: 575 Hymns, Spirituals, and Gospel* (Chicago: GIA Publications, 2001).

[16] Rivers, *Soulfull Worship,* 40.

[17] Cyprian Davis, "Speaking the Truth," in *Taking Down Our Harps: Black Catholics in the United States,* ed. Cyprian Davis and Diana L. Hayes (Maryknoll, NY: Orbis Books, 1998), 284.

Chapter 13

African Catholics in the United States

Gifts and Challenges

PAULINUS I. ODOZOR, C.S.SP.

In this essay I use the term *African Catholics in the United States* to refer to (a) those African members of the Roman Catholic Church who were born in Africa and who came to the United States as practicing Catholics, and (b) the children of such persons, especially those who still consciously identify themselves with a particular ethnic group or country in Africa.

It has not been easy for me to write about African immigrants because they appear to be among the least documented group in this country. No one seems to know for sure who they are or where or how to locate most of them. The situation is distressing because one knows through one's contacts and associations that this group exists and is very vibrant. This invisibility in civil and ecclesiastical records is in some ways a mirror of the situation of Africa as a whole in the psyche of many people in this part of the world. It seems at times that Africa is like the Loch Ness monster, "rumored to exist, of venerable antiquity, actually seen by some, but not of much relevance in the contemporary world."[1] To many political planners and policy-makers in the Western world, Africa remains an irritating appendage to the human community. The same seems true in large part in the official circles of the U.S. Catholic Church—until recently, as in, for instance, the publication of the bishops' pastoral letter on Africa in 2001.[2]

Besides the lack of official statistics and awareness, or rather, in addition to the problems raised by these, there are other issues that complicate undertaking research on African Catholics in the United States. These issues are well illustrated in the following anecdote. Recently, the daughter of a close friend of mine was preparing for confirmation. The parents were asked by their parish to find a sponsor for their daughter. My friends are very devout Catholics from Nigeria. Accordingly, they set down a few criteria for deciding whom to invite to be their daughter's confirmation sponsor. Their criteria were simple, or so they thought initially. And given the large pool of friends and acquaintances they had, they believed they would have no problem finding the right person for this role. The sponsor had to be Nigerian and in good standing with the church. That is to say, this person had to be a practicing Catholic. Initially, they had hoped that this person would be married in the church and still living with his or her spouse. To their shock, they soon discovered that they had set the bar too high, because (1) a good number of the people whom they knew who had migrated to this country as faithful and practicing Catholics in Africa had stopped going to church completely, and, in the case of married couples, only one of them was now practicing; (2) many of those who were still active as Christians had left the Catholic Church and joined a Pentecostal church; and (3) many of the Catholics who came here as married Catholic couples were now divorced and sometimes remarried.

The issues I have isolated from my friend's situation succinctly capture the situation of many African Catholics in the United States and, I dare say, Canada today. I want to address the challenges faced by African Catholics in the United States today, and I also want to to highlight the gifts this group of Christians brings to the church of the United States. Finally, I will offer some reflections on the situation of African Catholics today. By presenting the challenges they face before discussing the gifts they bring, I hope to move directly to the heart of the faith for this group of immigrants to America.

CHALLENGES

The comments and analysis that follow are based on interviews I conducted with a number of African Catholics, practicing and non-practicing, over a period of time. It quickly became obvious to me that many African Catholics are confronted with sociological problems arising from migration away from their familiar, supportive terrain to an alien one that devalues and dislocates the newcomer. In such situations some persons fare better because they have better coping mechanisms and/or other resources. Others fare worse, not only because they have inadequate coping mechanisms, but also because they confront built-in mechanisms that hinder integration into the system. The result is alienation. Many

African Catholics who now live in the United States report that they have had to battle alienation from the church in one way or another.

I want to examine three issues that pertain to this problem. First, most of my interviewees indicate that they have been through a crisis of identity as Catholics since they came to the United States. One of them said to me:

> The first thing that hit me when I walked into a Catholic church in this country was that I was a minority. I had never felt different that way in the church. I really became conscious of my minority status. This feeling was reinforced for a very long time by people's attitude toward my family and me. Few people dared to sit close to us in the church. It was as if we had a wasting disease. Sometimes it seemed difficult for some people to share the kiss of peace with us.

A second cause of alienation for many African Catholics in the United States arises from a feeling that they are merely tolerated as members of some parish communities. A famous Nigerian writer who was educated at convent schools in Nigeria told me of her experience concerning her first encounter with her parish in the university town where she had just been hired. She went to the parish office to inquire about enrollment in the parish. The parish secretary who met her at the door told her right away that they had no aid to give her. She did not ask who she was or why she was there. As soon as she saw her come out of the cold in her winter clothes, the secretary assumed she was there for a handout. Moreover, when the priest came out to see her, he mentioned another parish in town where he thought she would fit in better. Of course, after attending this all-white parish for a while, she knew that she was merely tolerated. Had her faith not been strong, she would have left the Catholic Church.

Another Nigerian literary scholar who had been a deputy vice-chancellor (the equivalent of a provost) in one of Nigeria's elite universities, a very devout and knowledgable Catholic, recounted his experiences in a certain parish. He had been very sick for a while. However, he had willed himself to attend mass on this particular Sunday, since it was Easter. As he got into the church, his parish church, he was stopped at the foyer by an usher who kept on showing people to their seats while he stood there, ignored. Whenever he started to go to a seat, this rather bulky usher stood in his way. Here he was on an Easter Sunday morning receiving totally un-Easterlike treatment. Very upset, he turned and went home. After this incident my correspondent felt he had to change parishes.

Another person I interviewed spoke of a white pastor in his parish who refused to shake hands with him or his wife after mass. This priest always stood at the door of the church to greet parishioners at the end of mass. However, as soon as this black couple came up to him, he would turn away and refuse to extend his hand or even acknowledge them. This went on for a long time until this family decided to move out of the area and into a new parish. These incidents might seem trivial, but they are not. Actions speak louder than words. Moreover, for people under the yoke of other forms of discrimination in the wider society, these slights from a church have a crushing weight and can shake people's faith to the core. Many people who experienced these types of actions left the church. In the case of my interviewees above, the only reaction, thankfully, was that they left their respective parishes and neighborhoods in search of more receptive parish communities.

A second major area of challenge for African Christians is worship. Although the issues here are legion, I will present only a few. First, many African Catholics find the worship in many Roman Catholic churches here uninspiring, lifeless, or starchy at best. Most people I interviewed point to this issue as a major reason many African Catholics end up joining the Pentecostal churches. Some also talk about the homilies as being generally designed to appease the congregation—to make church members feel good rather than to challenge them. One of my interviewees put it this way: "The priests [homilists] tread softly on religious/moral issues instead of calling it as it is." By doing this, this correspondent continues, "they fail to touch us emotionally or challenge us existentially." This is quite an issue, because, for the African, religion must affect a person emotionally, challenge the person existentially, and uplift him or her spiritually.

A third set of challenges for African Catholics in the United States relates to adjusting to a slightly different way of being church. Some Western and African critics lament that African churches are sometimes very hierarchical. This critique rarely mentions that there are avenues the African churches have evolved for lay involvement in the church, especially through the various associations that constitute aspects of this hierarchy. These associations serve four major functions—they help the Christians to pray; they provide avenues for faith-based social action; they involve lay Christians in the governance of the church by providing them a collective visibility and voice; and they provide a platform for interaction and support among the people.

In many parts of Eastern and Central Africa, for example, the small Christian communities are impressive examples of the church as the family of God. In West African societies the age-grade associations or other forms of groupings within the church provide points of insertion into the wider church family for the Christian. In nearly all these places, the lay councils at various levels—community, parish, diocesan, and national—provide both community and voice to most Catholics. Through these channels the lay Christians express their faith and provide concrete input about the running of their church.

Given this situation in their home parishes, one can understand how many African Catholics can be lost when they relocate to the United States or Canada. Some who had been very active members of the church are shocked to find that there is little or no opportunity for them to play any meaningful role. They are frustrated that all that is left for them is to show up for mass on Sundays. Usually when they arrive in this country, they try to make themselves known to their local pastor. The reception they get is usually less than enthusiastic. Even when the pastor and his staff appear to be friendly, these Christians who had had serious leadership roles in their churches back home soon discover that there is nothing for them to do except occasionally show up for a parish fair or such event. This situation is a sad commentary on the American church in a number of ways, and it weakens its evangelizing mission. In fact, in most cases there is no such understanding of the role of the church.

Another weakness is that the church, which abounds in talent and wisdom, does not seem to know how to deploy its many willing members for work, nor has it been able to evolve a happy means of cooperation between the hierarchy and the laity. As Thomas P. Rausch, S.J., puts it, "Though the council rediscovered the dignity of the vocation of the baptized, the Church is still struggling to find ways to fully express the laity's share in the mission of Church."[3] Rausch goes on to lament the sad outcomes of this lack of serious lay involvement in the mission of the church. These include (1) lack of institutional checks and balances that should allow lay people some say in the way authority is exercised at various levels, (2) lack of an avenue for addressing the problem of an incompetent pastor or an authoritarian bishop, (3) lack of avenues for bringing their own concerns and experience to the decision-making process of the universal church, and (4) lack of structures of accountability. The result, Rausch writes, is that many lay persons "feel that the Church is treating them as children."[4] Although Rausch's remarks apply across the board, they apply specifically to the American church to a nearly scandalous extent. Even though African churches are far from ideal on this issue, they are in many very significant ways ahead of the American church.[5] In America the suspicion between the laity and the hierarchy can sometimes run very deep. The result is that too much precious pastoral energy is often wasted on issues that are taken for granted in many other churches, and opportunities for the promotion of the gospel are lost.

Compounding the situation for the African Christian is the economic situation they face in their new country. The distraction of trying to survive economically often combines with all or some of the factors I have already mentioned with deadly consequences.

A fourth area of serious challenge for the African Catholic in America is that of marriage and family life. Marriages of an inordinately high percentage of African Catholics living in America have failed, are failing, or will soon fail. Given that Catholic marriages in most African countries are usually among the most stable, this is an issue of great concern. The crisis in the marital sacrament is precipitated by many economic and social factors that the African immigrant encounters in this country. For example, rearing children is exceptionally strenuous for many African couples. Whereas it took a village to raise a child where they came from, in America they are left alone with no resources or support base such as the ones provided by the network of friends and family back in Africa. Add to this the strain imposed on them by the economic reality they face here as well as the frequent need to provide financial support for relatives in Africa. The situation is so stressful that many of the families quickly become dysfunctional under the multifarious pressures.

In Africa the extended family cushions young families from some of the stresses of combining the responsibilities of holding down jobs, procreating and catering to children, and meeting sundry social demands. Here in the United States the accumulation of these pressures keep most people on edge, and they snap more easily than they would in Africa because the families in Africa generally exercise a beneficent and stabilizing influence on marriages. Before things get out of hand, families have ways of intervening and "dousing" potentially serious problems. Here, those mechanisms are not available to married couples. Africans in the United States try to replace the extended families with various associations, but the impact of these associations on the domestic life of their members is considerably limited.

Given the above realities, many otherwise fervent African couples initially find themselves skipping church and eventually drop out altogether. How can they continue to attend church when Sundays are spent either trying to catch up on sleep and other social obligations or doing an extra shift at work to earn a little more? One disturbing effect of all this is that in time cracks begin to show in the marriages of these people because of these stressors. With little community or ecclesial support, the cracks soon become a gully and the marriage ends in separation or divorce with dire consequences for everyone involved—the couple, their children, and the extended families back in their countries of origin. The situation is not helped by the fact that many African couples have imbibed the ethos of their host countries, where many couples resort to easy divorce rather than find ways to settle their disputes.

GIFTS

I have spoken at some length about the challenges facing African Catholics in America. It must not be assumed by this there is nothing but gloom and doom for these persons or that the American church has nothing positive to offer them. Even more important for our purposes here, it must not be imagined that African Catholics in the United States are simply passive victims and consumers in the American church. Quite the contrary. African Catholics in this country are a very gifted group. They are in turn blessing the American church with their gifts. Perhaps the most obvious gift that African Catholics bring to the American church is their presence. Even though we do not have exact figures of the number of African Catholics in this country, it is safe to say that they number in the hundreds of thousands and counting. These African immigrants generally bring with them a faith that is fresh, a faith that comes from the heart. They are usually very highly educated, and many of them would have been active members of their faith communities in their countries of origin.

There are about five hundred priests of African origin and well over that number of religious women of African origin now working in this country. These are engaged in parish ministries, chaplaincies, teaching in parochial schools, school administration, and so on. During the conference on solidarity with Africa organized in September 2003, some of these groups of sisters and priests were invited to give an account of their work in the United States. As a result of these presentations, it became very clear to many who attended the conference that these religious men and women from Africa are serving a very important missionary purpose here, not just by filling gaps, but especially by bringing in different and fresh perspectives to ministry and to church life.

REFLECTIONS

One of the new realities of life in the United States and Canada is the increasing numbers of new immigrants from Africa. In many parts of the United States the church has not paid sufficient attention to this reality. Whereas one sees serious efforts made to welcome immigrants from Latin America and to cater to their spiritual needs as a people, one rarely sees that much zeal and interest with regard to African peoples. The result is that many Africans who were otherwise regular and active members of the church in their homelands have all but lapsed in the practice of the faith. Sometimes dioceses have allowed for an occasional mass or liturgical rite that might speak to the spiritual needs and interest of some of the African immigrants. The gesture proceeds from a certain sense of goodwill but also reflects a gross underestimation of the diversity of Africans in the Americas. These are mixed groups of people, albeit from the same continent, who have distinct liturgical styles, customs, and languages. African-flavored rites are not an adequate response to the people's needs for culturally competent worship; instead, they are merely an expression of tokenism.

The first problem in what I have described is that of reception. The churches in this country must discover effective ways of reaching out to receive new immigrants from Africa and to minister to their particular spiritual needs. It seems that many people here, having chosen to ignore their own immigrant past, or being of the second, third, fourth, or fifth generations of immigrant families, find it difficult to appreciate the challenges that newcomers face and the giftedness they bring to the American way of life. In recent times the U.S. church has consistently affirmed that not one of Christ's faithful should be lost simply because he or she has relocated to this country in search of opportunities. In earlier times Irish nuns and priests followed their compatriots to this land to minister to their own until they could stand on their own in the American mainstream. The same was true of Germans, Croatians, Hungarians, Poles, and others as well. The African soul deserves a similar investment, and the redemption of the U.S. church is at stake.

The Roman Catholic Church in the United States must take seriously its role as a missionary church. With reference to Africans and other immigrant groups to this country, there must be outreach programs aimed at welcoming newcomers and encouraging them to keep their faith alive by contributing their gifts of faith, culture, and celebration to enrich the American church to the greater glory of God. The genius of African peoples who are recent immigrants to this country must not be wasted through carelessness or neglect. The church must also be prepared to stand in solidarity with those immigrants—Africans and others—who struggle to find the liberty and justice that this great nation promises its own. There are too many for whom fair wages, decent housing, political participation, legal justice, quality education, and access to health care are still an elusive dream.

In summary, the immigrant nature of this country implies continuous change in the tone and texture of life here, including religious life. The result is that the church in this country will always be, in some sense, an immigrant church. Although there are myriad challenges associated with this reality, countless blessings come from this phenomenon as well. For one thing, the American church should never be an old or spent church. Rather it should be a church that, like the proverbial phoenix, renews, drawing from its new immigrants to renew itself constantly. Yesterday, it was the Europeans. Today it is Africans and Asians and Hispanics. Can this church really rise up to the challenge of the moment as it did in previous years and not allow itself to forfeit the grace of the moment through myopia or prejudice? Time waits for no one. This is a moment of grace.

NOTES

[1] See Peter Hebblethwaite, *The Runaway Church: Postconciliar Growth or Decline?* (New York: Seabury Press, 1975), 13.

[2] Even now, and in spite of that laudable text and some laudable follow-up activities by various entities at the University of Notre Dame, the words in *A Call to Solidarity with Africa* remain just that, words. For example, very few U.S. bishops showed up for the conferences either at Notre Dame or in Nigeria. The Bishop of Fort Wayne-South Bend wrote letters to all the bishops of the United States to invite them to the event at Notre Dame. Only four U.S. bishops honored his invitation. Contrast that with over twenty bishops who went to the conference in Nigeria.

[3] Thomas P. Rausch, "The Lay Vocation and Voice of the Faithful," *America* 189 (September 29, 2003), 9.

[4] Ibid.

[5] The system of lay involvement in African churches developed largely from the cultural patterns of sharing authority and out of sheer necessity. In the parts of Africa I am conversant with, no pastor can succeed without active lay involvement in the parish at various levels. It is quite surprising that parish councils in many U.S. parishes are a sham without any real teeth or clout. This is contrary to my experience of parish life in Africa. Lay involvement in parish work started in the missionary era in Africa when there were not enough priests

to go round. The laity were the primary evangelizers, catechists, and teachers. They literally ran the parish in many important ways. That practice has endured in many places in spite of the attempt by some bishops and priests at complete clericalization of the church in recent times. For example, in many parts of Africa the pastor sooner or later becomes aware that he serves at the pleasure of the people. Sometimes a point is reached where due to palpable incompetence or gross indiscipline the laity asks that the priest in question be removed. Any bishop with an iota of common sense or love for the church is bound to listen to such demands or face very dire consequences.

Chapter 14

Pan-Africanism

An Emerging Context for Understanding the Black Catholic Experience

CLARENCE WILLIAMS, C.P.P.S.

This chapter sketches the work of the National Black Catholic Clergy Caucus (NBCCC) as a catalyst in forming and articulating a pan-African perspective for the Roman Catholic Church in the United States. Pan-Africanism may be understood as a perspective or world view, as a philosophy, and as a movement. As a perspective, pan-Africanism emerges from historical, cultural, and sociopolitical experiences shared by peoples of African descent on the continent and in the diaspora. The Atlantic slave trade's reduction and objectification of black peoples was a crucial precipitating factor. However, the moral and spiritual daring of the enslaved Africans to restrain cultural differences and antagonisms enabled them to forge new bonds of solidarity in resistance, giving rise to an incipient pan-African perspective or world view.

As a philosophy, pan-Africanism calls for the transformation of the consciousness of peoples' of African descent, whether on the continent or in the diaspora. Pan-African philosophy holds that transformation of consciousness is a crucial step toward the long-term goal of social transformation, which seeks the liberation of history and the full development of humanity.

As a movement, modern pan-Africanism has its roots in the encounters of the international community of intellectuals of African descent on both sides of the Atlantic since the early twentieth century.[1] These intellectuals envisioned their lives and the history of African people in the Motherland and the diaspora through the lens of common challenge and sought to realize African personality and new cultural and sociopolitical possibilities freed from European and Western hegemony, which extended to the Roman Catholic Church.[2] Thus, pan-African perspective may be found as well in the black American Catholic experience and runs parallel to the issues and strategies that secular pan-Africanism promotes.

At the same time, we cannot forget that the papal bull *Dum Diversas* of Pope Nicolas V in 1452 authorized the Portuguese to enslave Africans who were not Christians. Since most African people practiced other religions, this action hastened the demise of the continent and fueled the slave trade. In 1502, just ten years later, the first enslaved African entered Hispaniola, the contemporary nations of Haiti and the Dominican Republic.[3] Christian supremacy would be the antecedent of European and white supremacy over and against people of African descent for the next five hundred years.

The emerging perspective of pan-African Catholicism presented here considers three factors: the black world, that is, Africa and its diaspora; the hegemony of European and white supremacy over the lives of African peoples; and the Roman Catholic Church. In the remainder of the chapter I review the efforts of the NBCCC to realize a pan-African perspective and highlight some of its achievements in initiating and sustaining this discourse for the past fifteen years, giving particular attention to the formation of the Pan-African Roman Catholic Clergy Conference (PARCCC). PARCCC is a new organization that intentionally engages partners in an ongoing conversation in the United States and abroad to develop a Pan-African Catholic discourse. To this end, PARCCC has sponsored three international conferences in the past twelve years. Key to PARCCC's success is a new method for dialogue that respects and regards ethnic, racial, and cultural differences.

A NEW METHOD, A NEW PARADIGM

In presenting the work of the NBCCC and the PARCCC, I draw upon a method developed for ethnic, interracial, and cross-cultural dialogue. This pluricultural method known as "building bridges" emerged from four national dialogues between African American leaders and Hispanic/ Latino leaders—"Building Bridges in Black and Brown." The method is is characterized by five stages of development: conversation, connections, considerations, construction, and crossing.[4] Each stage is an indication of a more profound development of mutual awareness among the dialogue partners, which, in turn, facilitates peer-to-peer pluricultural education. This method will allow a survey of the motivations, decisions, and conferencing of the NBCCC in collaboration with multiple national and international agencies. Their mutual interaction gives impetus to the emerging context of pan-African Catholicism in the United States, Africa, Latin America, and the Caribbean.

To illustrate this method's capacity to support a pan-African Catholic movement, think of encounters between black priests in the United States and priests recently arrived from the African continent. The conversation stage of this pluricultural method began with the NBCCC's efforts to focus awareness on the phenomenon that more and more priests of African descent were arriving in the United States. The stage of *consideration* was a growing feeling among black American priests of a lack of social interaction, even alienation from African priests because of an absence of conversation. The *connection* stage was the mutual realization that both black U.S. clergy and African clergy were being perceived ambiguously at best and depreciatively at worst by the larger church community, whether lay or clergy. The *construction* stage was the personal engagement of the NBCCC's membership and those African clergy who desired a forum for meeting and relationship building between the groups. The *crossing* stage of the movement was the ability to share a distinct frame of reference from which to continue conversation and networking.

After a fifteen-year effort a pan-African Catholic movement has emerged as a fact of life in the American church. The fruit of this movement is evident in an increasingly active exchange among the various groups, who have found a discourse within which to contextualize their shared experience and to forge a new direction within the experience of today's globalization process, which affects the African world.

A paradigm may be explained as a blueprint that directs the ways in which we think and act. For the most part, a paradigm remains assumed or taken for granted, but when examined, it may facilitate a critical assessment of a context and allow for the conscious choice of new directions. As a movement and as a discourse, pan-African Catholicism requires a new paradigm.

BRIDGE BUILDING

A bridge-building conversation allows us to bring to the foreground of our discourse how Africa has been understood by powerful international political and religious forces as the only place for black people to be. In other words, on the lips of powerful whites in the United States, the slogan "Africa for the African" meant that black Americans should be sent back to Africa and that they and their posterity were to be deprived of the fruits of their labor and toil. This accounts for the creation of the West African country of Liberia. *Liberia,* which is Latin for "liberty," was to be the home of newly freed black people after the Civil War.[5] It was a place where African Americans were to enjoy democracy with their own race. This was the thought of some black Americans and President Abraham Lincoln, who thought that free blacks could not live in peace with whites in an open society. Thus, among advocates of black consciousness, Liberia long has been a paradigm of a longing for a homeland.

Following nearly two centuries of deliberation, finding the best means to realize the obligations of freedom is the work of the pan-African movement throughout the world, whether voiced by W. E. B. Du Bois or Bob Marley, Walter Rodney or C. L. R. James, Marcus Garvey or Franz Fanon. The contemporary conversation on secular pan-Africanism offers well-reasoned voices. From this base I articulate the most recent thinking to draw a parallel for pan-African Catholic thought.

In the bridge-building paradigm, four issues are crucial. Globally, pan-Africanism was a cry of Africa after the First and Second World Wars. On the lips of Africans, the slogan "Africa for the African" signaled the ardent desire and struggle of black people for political and cultural freedom—for conditions on the continent through which black people could be themselves, live in freedom, enjoy their own resources, and seek their own destiny. To pursue the pan-African vision, four issues had to be faced by activists, thinkers, and writers, and would be raised in the efforts of the Pan-African Roman Catholic Clergy Conference. First, there was the need to put an end to "Eurafrica," that is, an Africa that was an extension of Europe's interests and visions for African people and their resources, an Africa that was the invention of Europe.

The second issue of pan-African secular philosophy is throwing off the colonial grip on the new governments of Africa; while country and flag may be African, the "powers that be" are still European or Western. The third issue is the ongoing struggle of the African state to exist independently of forces outside its borders. And the fourth issue that is being proposed, in the light of a twenty-first-century European common market, is how to realize an interdependent Africa wherein each country has its circle of influence, as each concentric circle reinforces the others in economy, security, and political stability.

A pan-African Catholic perspective mirrors quite similar positions in its own development through the PARCCC movement. First, the black Catholic movement grasped itself in the midst of a "Eurafrica" reality. In 1968 the NBCCC issued its manifesto stating that the "Catholic Church was a white, racist institution." With this charge the caucus sought to identify the church as controlling in a self-serving way the life of its black members. Cutting the cord of "white religio-cultural" dependence was an act of black Catholic self-determination and echoed sentiments expressed in pan-African philosophy's critique of Eurafrica. This declaration of self-determination also demonstrated that black Catholic leaders grasped that their Catholic experience was far too European to support the development of a black consciousness. The founding of the National Office for Black Catholics (NOBC) remedied this intellectual and psychological dependence on the white church and gave African American Catholics a sphere of intellectual, psychological, cultural, and, to some extent, fiscal independence.

Second, the phase of the "flag republics" has its parallel in black Catholic life. In the late 1960s and early 1970s most African American Catholic parishes did not have black pastors. Some angry black Catholic leaders referred to these parishes as "plantations" that were administered by white benevolent missionaries. African American Catholics were treated as children, and black pastoral and lay leadership was nonexistence. With the NBCCC's insistence on "authentically black" parishes, the number of black pastors gradually increased throughout the country and black bishops were named in historic precedents. Black leadership was becoming part of the institutional church.

The third aspect of pan-African Catholicism that paralleled secular Pan-Africanism was the cultural independence of black Catholic worship. Black Catholic worship stylizations of music, preaching, and call-and-response participation borrowed freely and astutely from black Protestant religious culture. Black Catholics met these innovations with such enthusiasm and success that they not only were accepted but also expected. The phrase "Black is beautiful" captures not only the flavor of these beginnings, but also their connections to the burgeoning black arts and cultural nationalist movements.

At present, African American Catholics face the same challenge of development as African people around the globe in the twenty-first century: how are we to build bridges between the pluricultural worlds of Catholics of African descent within the United States and those beyond the national borders? The "beyond" aspect of this challenge stems from requests by clerical and episcopal leaders in the Caribbean and Latin America to bond with and share our "black and Catholic" genius with our 124 million brothers and sisters to the south in Latin America and the Caribbean who share our faith. Meeting this challenge does not allow us to ignore efforts to cement ties with the Motherland's 141 million African Catholics (see Table 14–1 below).

Table 14–1
Global Count of Catholics of African Descent: 270 Million*

AFRICA: 140 MILLION		LATIN AMERICA: 106 MILLION	
Country	*Number (in millions)*	*Country*	*Number (in million)*
Angola	8.0	Brazil	65.0
Benin	1.6	Columbia	20.0
Burkina Faso	1.4	Ecuador	1.5
Burundi	4.0	Guatemala	0.2
Cameron	3.9	Honduras	0.2
Cen. Af. Rep.	0.8	Mexico	12.0
Chad	0.8	Panama	2.0
Dem. Rep. of Congo	28.0	Venezuela	5.0
Ethiopia	0.5	**TOTAL**	**105.9**
Gabon	0.8		
Ghana	2.3		
Ivory Coast	2.9	**NORTH AMERICA and THE**	
Kenya	7.5	**CARIBBEAN: 21 MILLION**	
Malawi	2.8	*Country*	*Number (in millions)*
Mozambique	4.2	Cuba	4
Nigeria	34.0	Dominican Republic	8
Rwanda	3.8	Haiti	6
Senegal	0.5	United States	3
South Africa	3.0	**TOTAL**	**21**
Sudan	3.8		
Tanzania	10.0		
Togo	1.3	**U.S. Statistics of Black Catholics**	
Uganda	10.0	1300 Parishes	
Zambia	3.0	250 African American Priests	
Zimbabwe	1.1	300 African American Sisters	
TOTAL	**141.0**	380 African American Deacons	

*The 270 million Catholics of African descent represent 25 percent of the 1.1 billion Roman Catholics throughout the world in more than fifty-nine countries. The count is based on millions and fractions of a million. Countries listed above have at least .2 million count of Catholics of African descent, while other countries not listed have fewer than this number. The racial conventions used to identify "African descent" vary throughout the world. Also not accounted for are the emerging Asian populations of African descent.

The principal resources are *The World Christian Encyclopedia,* edited by D. Barrett; *The 2004 Catholic Almanac,* edited by Matthew Brunson; the African American Secretariat of the U.S. Catholic Bishops' Conference; the Internet; and global in-the-field research. Contact: *CatholicAWN@aol.com*

Building bridges can serve as a helpful paradigm to understand the task before the black Catholic community in the twenty-first century from a North American perspective. In the 1960s and 1970s the task before the black leadership in society and the church was to decry the scourge and sin of racism. Racism was a swollen and turbulent river; many people were plunged into the deep waters of poverty, poor education, inadequate housing, imprisonment, and chronic unemployment. The response of leadership was to march, protest, and parade with picket signs as witnesses to these injustices. In the 1980s black leadership called people to self-determination, insisting that there would not be a change unless they depended upon themselves to fight racism and stay out of its waters. The struggle for political and economic self-determination became the order of the day, and the ritual of Kwanzaa was a way of promoting and celebrating cultural self-actualization and black values. In the 1990s black leadership urged networking in the hope that by reaching out, we could pull our brothers and sisters out of the river. But in the twenty-first century we have moved to the cry of prevention. Thus, we must build a bridge across the river of racism so that people will not drown in racism, poverty, and their vicious effects.

The bridge-building task of the PARCCC has two important dimensions or arenas. The first arena is formed by the activities of the national black Catholic clergy, bishops, religious men, and seminarians who were members of the NBCCC within the United States; the second is building of bridges beyond our borders, especially in Latin America.

THE NATIONAL CONVERSATION

The seed of pan-African Catholic discourse was sown in the 1990 meeting of the NBCCC, during which the membership voted to observe the five hundredth anniversary of evangelization in the Western hemisphere. A planning committee was established consisting of Fathers Martin Carter, S.A.; Victor Cohea; Cyprian Davis, O.S.B.; Rayford Emmons; and Clarence Williams, C.P.P.S. The committee devised a process for a planning conference the following year in Atlanta in order to discern the theme for an international NBCCC-sponsored conference in 1992 under the title "The Pan-African Roman Catholic Clergy Conference" (PARCCC).

In 1992 the first PARCCC convened in New Orleans with the NBCCC. The members of the NBCCC invited priests of African descent to begin the bridge-building work with a conversation on the five hundredth anniversary of the evangelization. Speakers represented East and West

Africa, Brazil, and the Afro-Spanish-speaking experience. Through shared conversation we discovered the parallel histories of African colonialism and African slavery in the Americas as our peoples' initial encounter with the Roman Catholic Church. Of particular note is the paper by Fr. Hipolito Tshimanga, C.I.C.M., "Blacks' Spirituality of Liberation."[6] Fr. Tshimanga reflected on the universal themes of oppression and the challenge of black theology and pastoral action on behalf of the black community. He focused that challenge on "the rescue of self-esteem" in the African personality in the Motherland and in the diaspora.[7] The success of the three-day conference sharpened the awareness of the North American black clergy, religious, and seminarians and invigorated their desire to continue such conversations. This seminal meeting outlined the three themes that would resonate in subsequent conferences: the need and significance of a new black identity in the context of a white supremacy culture,[8] establishing new relationships with one another for collaboration within our communities and our churches, and the articulation of the mission of black consciousness in the church and society as it acted out its newly found awareness and value system.[9]

THE GLOBAL CONVERSATION

That same year the NBCCC was invited to send a delegation of priests to the Afro-Hispanic Continental Congress of Black Catholics in Esmeralda, Ecuador. This would begin a series of recurring invitations to share the developments of black theology, black consciousness, and pastoral ministry with our Caribbean and Latin American counterparts in parallel movements in the hemisphere. From these meetings and exchanges, documents from the Spanish-speaking countries, which include approximately sixty million Catholics of African descent, began to appear capturing the influence of North American "black Catholic consciousness" in the context of the black community of Latin America's need to find its voice.[10] Similar documents were also published in Portuguese for Brazil's approximately forty million Catholics of African descent.[11]

NATIONAL CONSIDERATIONS

In the United States racism remains a chief prism through which much of African American life is viewed. This consideration was the focus of the second PARCCC, convened in Detroit in 1995. The presenters spoke to the issue of racism from the perspective of recovery from racisms that have distorted the African personality wherever it is found and how to enunciate approaches to healing the problem within our church and society. Fr. Felix Mushobozi, C.P.P.S., of Tanzania outlined the similarities and difference between the models of racism discussed in the Western hemisphere in relationship to the nature of racism in the African colonial context. The various speakers from throughout the world related the trauma of white supremacy in the African context of colonialism,[12] in the Latin American context of *mestizaje*,[13] the Brazilian context of "racial democracy,"[14] and the racism/anti-racism discourse of the United States. Though each African nation and cultural community in the diaspora had unique histories, there were common themes in the trauma of their journeys. These common threads of brokenness and healing included the evidence of the horrific reality of genocide and the intergenerational effects that are seen in the distorted self-images, cultural denial of race as an issue of everyday life, and the ongoing struggle to overcome these vestiges after five hundred years.[15]

GLOBAL CONSIDERATIONS

The freedom with which the North American black Catholic community discusses racism is not a shared reality in many other countries and communities of Catholics of African descent. In much of Latin America the African presence is a "forgotten root" in historical and social reality.[16] When the black population is mentioned in church documents, class status displaces race as the rationale for black marginalization.[17] In the various cultures of Latin America and the Caribbean, there is a tradition of not remembering or seeing the African presence as important in the racial mixing of the people. Cultural dynamics conspire to make African presence invisible in the life of these nations. Elisa Larkin Nascimento, an expert on the pan-African movements of Latin America, writes:

> Latin America has built itself a reputation for non-racism, non-discrimination and benevolence towards its African population. . . . This vision is contrasted with the situation of such racist societies as South Africa or the United States, where apparently the Latins [Latin Americans] believe there is no race mixture.[18]

Each conference speaker pointed out the horrors inflicted upon people of African descent in various Latin societies and their projections of black people as subhuman. Sadly, speakers also pointed to the crucial role of the Roman Catholic Church in blessing the social arrangements that support white supremacy in their respective cultures, which reinforce the old master-slave hierarchy. The institutional church's admission of complicity in supporting the psychological, religious, and social trauma of millions came forth in 1988 in the document *The Church and Racism*.[19] And while visiting the West African Republic of Senegal, Pope John Paul II apologized to the people of the African continent for the church's role in the slave trade. His speech was preceded by meditation within the famous Slave Castle, the site of an international museum on the slave trade.[20]

Pan-African Roman Catholic communities, which are finding pride in their blackness, do so in the face of a past that many would like to deny and forget. This is an important consideration when trying to bridge the pain in the encounter of an articulate North American sense of racism with the hidden and silenced realities of race and racism within most Latin American and Caribbean national cultures as well as in the Motherland.[21]

NATIONAL CONNECTIONS

The third conference was focused on how to come to know the African clergy and religious and those from the African diaspora of Latin America and the Caribbean. The third PARCCC was convened in Philadelphia in 2001. The title of the conference was "Who's in the House?" Through presentations by speakers from Africa, the Caribbean, and Latin America, black U.S. clergy and religious came to a better understanding of the reasons why clergy and religious from the continent and the diaspora were coming to the United States. Chief among the reasons put forward were study, ministry, and the opportunity to construct new lives.

These new faces in the black Catholic community represented a sixfold increase of immigrants of African, Caribbean, and Hispanic/Latino descent from the previous twenty years. That many of these immigrants are Catholic demonstrates the impact that their presence has made on the awareness of black Catholics—lay, clerical, and religious.[22]

GLOBAL CONNECTIONS

Black Catholics have taken pilgrimages to Africa in order to discover their connection with the Motherland and the pan-African Catholic experience. Whether these trips have been sponsored by established national black Catholic organizations or local diocesan offices for black

Catholics or lecture tours, these experiences have built bridges and interest in the global experience among black Catholics. The expression of black identity in countries varies. Such variances can be observed on a continuum of celebrating blackness: in Togo, the facade of the cathedral is adorned with angels with dreadlocks, while in Ivory Coast in the Basilica of Our Lady of Peace, the tallest church building in Christianity, no people of African heritage appear in the stained-glass windows except the late President Félix Houphouët-Boigny standing in a crowd scene. Yet, irrespective of geographical location, the need of black peoples to connect with one another globally will depend on the level of consciousness we bring to the complexity of the black experience.

NATIONAL CONSTRUCTION

As the population of African, Caribbean, and Latin immigrant grows in the United States, black American Catholics find themselves reframing and clarifying their identities in society and in the church. Those who are immigrating also are reframing their identities, foreshadowing a new understanding of "Africans in America" as distinct from "African Americans." The reframing of black identities must embrace the reality of the Haitian presence as a distinct reality, especially in Florida and on the East Coast. Will groups such as the Haitians, Belizeans, Panamanians, Afro Latinos (both Portuguese and Spanish speaking), Afro Indonesians, Melanesians, and East Indians find themselves reframed in the church and society in the emerging pan-African dialogue? As each group assumes an "American Catholic" identity in this increasingly pluricultural reality, a sense of public identity in the American church will be crucial to the preservation of their social face and their valued inculturated expressions of faith.

In our national stage of constructing a bridge, a significant moment of growth and pain will center on construction of new identities in the pan-African Catholic experience. The challenge in the United States will be whether we can share our identities in the church or whether we have to identify our differences more so that our likenesses can be valued.

GLOBAL CONSTRUCTION

The interdependence of the pan-African reality is increasingly clear to some leaders both inside and outside the United States. Today, there are religious congregations of men and women who see their future in the formation of African men and women to serve in the black Catholic community in the United States. Such groups are actively constructing a bridge to a shared future. The Josephite Fathers and Brothers and the Sisters, Home Visitors of Mary are representative. Each of these congregations maintains houses of formation in Nigeria for seminarians and vowed women religious. Each supports a ministry dedicated to the evangelization and pastoral care of black Americans. Other religious communities and dioceses are recruiting African men and women for formation and service in the United States. These are viable constructions that will influence how we as a church and a society understand the world in which we "live, move, and have our being."

NATIONAL CROSSING

The paradigm of bridge building culminates in crossing the bridges that have been constructed in a way that continues the conversation, consideration, and connections. The ongoing relationship of various organizations, activities, and collaborations characterizes the "crossing" moment of bridge building. This is a reality in the U.S. context, in which the PARCCC leadership now meets regularly with African Catholic organizations not only to support to them in their journey in their new country, but also to continue learning from them. This crossing moment within our borders led to a proposal at the 2002 PARCCC to begin a training program that would provide an orientation to American culture for immigrating African clergy and seminarians.[23] Crossing moments include the restructuring of programs within the black Catholic offices to reflect and include new populations of Catholics of African descent within archdioceses and dioceses. Msgr. Raymond East, the director of the Office for Black Catholics in the Archdiocese of Washington, notes that in the last thirty years the number of black Catholics in the archdiocese has grown from 70,000 to 100,000, largely due to immigration.

We have [a] longstanding Haitian community at the Shrine of the Sacred Heart; the first Ge'ez Rite parish, Kidane Mehret, for Ethiopian and Eritrean Catholics; a Nigerian Catholic Community, Blessed Tansi Igbo Catholic Mission; and the Notre Dame Reine de Monde Francophone community at St. Camillus and two other gatherings of French-speaking Catholics.[24]

This outreach of inclusiveness is found throughout the country as black Catholic parishes open their doors to new faces, accents, cultures, and needs. In opening their doors and hearts to these new members of the African diaspora, black Catholics receive the gifts that these immigrant brothers and sisters bring to worship, education, and the practice of the faith.

At the national level, black Catholics encountered the globalization process in the 2002 National Black Catholic Congress held in Chicago from August 29 to September 1. This congress was attended by a delegation of black priests and sisters from Brazil headed by Bishop Gilio Felicio of Bage and also by a delegation of black Catholics from London. The keynote speaker was Bishop Charles G. Palmer-Buckle of Koforidua, Ghana. These and other representatives of the global pan-African community gathered, along with roughly three thousand delegates from across the United States, in a crossing moment that was mutually informative, educational, spiritual, and supportive. This truly was a benchmark event for the pan-African reality of all those present.

GLOBAL CROSSING

Crossing moments in the global community of the African diaspora find challenges in the bridge-building process due to finances, breakdowns in cross-cultural communications, the coordination of national conference calendars, and limitations in administrative leadership. Nevertheless, these obstacles have been overcome by the NBCCC's commitment to realizing its mission. The NBCCC has sent delegations to Latin American national conferences to provide an ongoing crossing experience for the United States and the rest of the hemisphere. The first such delegation met with a group of Brazilian bishops, priests, brothers, and seminarians in 1992 in São Paulo at the invitation of the Brazilian Bishops' Conference. This meeting was highlighted by a film, *Rejoice! Featuring Black Catholic Worship,* that documented the Afro-Brazilian church's efforts at inculturation and expressing black identity. This visit also produced a segment on racism in the church of Brazil and an interview with Bishop Dom Marie Pires, Brazil's first self-identified black bishop. A second invitation took NBCCC representatives to the Continental Congress of the Afro-Hispanic Catholic community in Esmeraldas, Ecuador, in 1994. The NBCCC hoped to share deeply the knowledge of U.S. black consciousness in theology, liturgy, and pastoral actions. Various individual members of NBCCC have built on these initial meetings, and subsequently black priests and religious have come to the United States to participate in national conventions of black clergy and religious. The creation of PARCCC was recognized by the Brazilian movement, and an invitation was extended to begin a deeper sharing. In 2003 a planning meeting was held by members of the Afro-Brazil clergy, religious, and laity for a large delegation of black U.S. Catholics to journey to Brazil for a cultural immersion in 2005. Also in the 2003 exchange, two national conferences in São Paulo hosted presentations introducing racial sobriety, a new approach to healing racism that black Catholics in the United States have embraced. The future for crossing moments looks bright. The plan for the U.S. cross-cultural experience will herald a format for increased crossings of the bridges that have been built in this hemisphere.

The fruits that come from crossing the bridge between countries and cultures in the context of faith are countless. However, one example demonstrates the value of this exchange. A ritual event that has brought together various segments of the U.S. black community is the celebration of Kwanzaa. This cultural celebration was established in 1966 in secular circles and entered mainline black Christianity in the 1970s. The first Kwanzaa celebrated publicly in Latin America was in Rio de Janeiro by a Franciscan priest, Frei Athaylton Belo, O.F.M., in 1997. The importation of a black American cultural expression was the result of Frei Belo's 1996 visit to Detroit, where the Office for Black Catholic Ministries celebrated Kwanzaa between Christmas and New Year of 1996. Kwanzaa has been a growing event in the church of Brazil.

Crossing is not only a North to South phenomena in the pan-African vision of bridge building but, like the U.S. national bridging between black Catholics and new immigrant populations, there is work at home to do also.[25] This interdependence in the pan-African reality is present in the Latin American and Caribbean Catholic structure of *Encuentro* every two years. These groups also sponsor conferences and seminars on various pastoral issues and theological concerns for the *communidade negra* in Latin America and the Caribbean.[26] The present vision of crossing envisions the pan-African world of Catholicism as a garden. In our "federated" reality of African people in a pluricultural global experience, we can be distinct and interdependent as "flowers with our roots in many gardens."

CONCLUSION

This exploration has sketched the emerging realities of black Catholicism in the twenty-first century within the U.S. context. A main feature of this faith experience is the acknowledgment that, due to the forces of globalization, Catholics of African descent have become a part of the American church experience. We are challenged to build bridges to and from our new neighbors and potential brothers and sisters in the black Catholic struggle. The emerging conversation in the pan-African world provokes a mutual reframing of identities as we explore the larger reality of the presence of Catholics of African descent in the Roman Catholic Church. For example, a Ghanaian cardinal working in Rome becomes "framed" in the Western media as a "black" cardinal. Or, take the example of the canonization of St. Josephine Bakhita: the first African female raised to sainthood in almost two millennia becomes a cause of celebration both for the African and American black Catholic world. In light of these experiences a pan-African Catholic lens allows an appreciation of the breadth and depth of religious living presented by two hundred million Roman Catholics of African descent. Bridge building provides a paradigm through which to grasp this living richness as a global pan-African Catholic vision emerges.

The initial and providential work of the NBCCC and the present work of PARCCC are key to the development of an interdependent and federated experience of the Catholic faith. As Catholic members of the human race, whatever the hue of our skin, we hold dear the four marks of the church: one, holy, catholic, and apostolic. A pan-African Catholic vision can assist us in realizing the growing strength of the true church in an unprecedented leap forward. As the old hymn insists, "We've Come This Far by Faith."[27] The bridges we build today will have tremendous value for those who are to follow, who will use these twenty-first-century bridges to journey to the next century. Just as we hear today the call for *communio*[28] in the local church, a call for consensus over division, so too the pan-African vision calls for solidarity based on our common struggle, our common faith as Catholics, and our spirituality.[29] Unlike the secular pan-African movement, we black Catholics around the globe are on a spiritual journey. We are drawn together not only by historical and certain social experiences, race, and, to some extent, culture, but also by faith. In the past the Catholic Church, with its collusion in the slave trade, was a source of division in Africa. Through grace, the church has become a profound and mysterious source of unity for people of African descent. If we respond to that grace and if we choose the lens of a pan-African vision, we may well become a sign and provocation for a creative and healing praxis of solidarity among ourselves and all other persons of good will.

NOTES

[1] See Kadiatu Kanneh, *African Identities: Race, Nation and Culture in Ethnography, Pan-Africanism and Black Literatures* (London: Routledge, 1998).

[2] Walter Rodney, *How Europe Underdeveloped Africa* (Washington DC: Howard University Press, 1981).

[3] NBCCC, *Statement on Racism* (New York: NBCCC, 2001).

[4] Building Bridges in Black and Brown. See also United States Catholic Bishops' Committee on African American Catholics, *Reconciled through Christ: On Reconciliation and Greater Collaboration Between Hispanic American Catholics and African American Catholics* (Washington DC: United States Catholic Conference, 2000).

[5] Lerone Bennet, "Did Lincoln Really Free the Slaves?" *Ebony* 55, no. 4 (February 2000): 54–60.

[6] Speakers and their papers included a paper on the Caribbean perspective by the Society of Friends of the West Indian Museum in Panama; a paper on the Panamanian reality by Fr. Dennis A. King, C.M.; a presentation on the Brazilian reality by Fr. David Raimundo Santos, O.F.M.; and a pan-African overview by Fr. Rayford Emmons of the United States.

[7] NBCCC, *The 5th Centenary of Evangelization of the New World* (1992), 51–65.

[8] Ibid., 105–14.

[9] Ibid., 79–94.

[10] Comite del III Encuentro de Pastoral Afroamericano, *III Encuentro de Pastoral Afroamericano* (Portobelo, Republic of Panama: Comite del III Encuentro de Pastoral Afroamericano, 1986).

[11] Antonio Aparecido da Silva, ed., *Existe Un Pensar Teologico Negro?* (São Paulo: Paulinas, 1998).

[12] Hipolito Tshimanga, "Psychology of Racism in French-Speaking Africa," a presentation at the Pan African Roman Catholic Clergy Conference, Detroit, Michigan, 1995.

[13] Bideri Nyagasaza, S.X., "Racism in Colombia, South America," a presentation at the Pan African Roman Catholic Clergy Conference, Detroit, Michigan, 1995.

[14] Athaylton J. M. Belo, O.F.M., "Recovering from Racism in Brazil," a presentation at the Pan African Roman Catholic Clergy Conference, Detroit, Michigan, 1995.

[15] For the U.S. perspective, see Clarence Williams, C.P.P.S., *Recovery from Everyday Racisms* (Detroit: Institute for Recovery from Racisms, 1998).

[16] Ron Walters, "Black Power in Brazil," *The Final Call Newspaper,* December 23, 2003.

[17] Consejo Episcopal Latinoamericano, *Lineas Pastorales Afro-Continentales* (Bogotá: Secretariado de Pastoral Afroamericana-SEPAFRO, 2003).

[18] Elisa Larkin Nascimento, *Pan Africanism and South America* (Buffalo, NY: Afrodiaspora, 1992), 12.

[19] The Vatican Pontifical Commission on Justice and Peace, *The Church and Racism* (Washington DC: The United States Bishops Conference, 1988).

[20] John Paul II, Meeting with the Catholic Community of Gorée Island, February, 22, 1992. Available online.

[21] Tshimanga, "Psychology of Racism in French-Speaking Africa."

[22] Genaro C. Armas, "Black Groups Seek to Close Cultural Divide," *The Michigan Citizen*, May 24, 2003.

[23] Proceedings from the fourth PARCCC, Techny, Illinois, August 27–29, 2002.

[24] Raymond East, "Serving the Diverse and Growing Black Catholic Community," *The Catholic Standard*, January 29, 2004.

[25] This theme is covered well in Nascimento, *Pan Africanism and South America*.

[26] The interchange of national perspectives can be seen in the Latin American Bishops 1986 publication, III *Encuentro de Pastoral Afroamericano*. The *Encuentro* was held in Portobelo, Republic of Panama.

[27] For a treatment of the pan-African Catholic hymnal, see M. Shawn Copeland, "The African American Catholic Hymnal and the African American Spiritual," *U.S. Catholic Historian* 19, no. 2 (2004): 66–82.

[28] Wilton Gregory, "Viewing the Church as a 'Communio': Three Challenges," *Origins* 33, no. 24 (2003): 410–12.

[29] Cyprian Davis, O.S.B., "Black Catholic Theology: A Historical Perspective," *Theological Studies* 61, no. 4 (2000): 656–71.

Contributors

M. Shawn Copeland holds a joint appointment in the Department of Theology and in the Program in African and African Diaspora Studies at Boston College. Her teaching, research, and publications focus on theological anthropology, human suffering, black Catholic theology, political theologies, and theological method.

Cyprian Davis, O.S.B., a monk of St. Meinrad Archabbey in Indiana, professor of church history in the School of Theology, and professor of African American history in the Institute of Black Catholic Studies at Xavier University in Louisiana is the author of several books and articles on black Catholic history, notably *The History of Black Catholics in the United States.*

Archbishop Wilton D. Gregory, the sixth archbishop of the Archdiocese of Atlanta, has played a leading role in the U.S. church as president of the United States Conference of Catholic Bishops. With a doctorate in sacred liturgy, Archbishop Gregory has written extensively on pastoral issues and has published numerous articles on liturgy, particularly in the African American community.

Diana L. Hayes is professor of systematic theology at Georgetown University. She is the author of four books on black and womanist theologies and spirituality, and co-editor of two books on racial/ethnic diversity in the Catholic Church. Her areas of specialization include liberation theologies in the United States, multicultural diversity, and religion and politics.

Kevin P. Johnson is the chairman of the Department of Music at Spelman College. He teaches and conducts music clinics nationally and has worked as a director of music at various parishes for thirty years. He is a choral arranger and composer with works published by Colla Voce, GIA Publications, Treble Clef Press, and Lion & Lamb Publishers.

Bryan N. Massingale, a priest of the Archdiocese of Milwaukee, is associate professor of moral theology at Marquette University. His work focuses upon Catholic social thought, liberation theologies, African American religious ethics, and racial justice. Massingale is president-elect of the Catholic Theological Society of America and convener of the Black Catholic Theological Symposium.

Timothy Matovina is professor of theology and the William and Anna Jean Cushwa Director of the Cushwa Center for the Study of American Catholicism at the University of Notre Dame.

Cecilia A. Moore teaches at the University of Dayton in the Department of Religious Studies and at Xavier University of Louisiana in the Institute of black Catholic Studies. Her area of specialization is U.S. Catholic history. Currently, she is working on history of Black Catholic converts in the twentieth century.

Diane Batts Morrow is associate professor of history and African American studies at the University of Georgia. Her current research continues the story of the Oblate Sisters of Providence into the mid-twentieth century.

LaReine-Marie Mosely, S.N.D., is assistant professor of theology at Loyola University Chicago, where she teaches on the undergraduate and graduate levels. Her areas of specialization include Christology, soteriology, black theology, black Catholic theology, and womanist theology.

Paulinus I. Odozor, C.S.Sp., a Nigerian Spiritan, is an associate professor of Christian ethics at the University of Notre Dame. His major publications include *Moral Theology in an Age of Renewal: A Study of the Catholic Tradition since Vatican II* (2003), and his articles have appeared in journals in Africa, Asia, Europe, and North America. Fr. Odozor is currently working on a book exploring the question of morality and tradition from an African Christian theological perspective.

Jamie T. Phelps, O.P., is director of the Institute for Black Catholic Studies and Katharine Drexel Professor of Systematic Theology at Xavier University of Louisiana, New Orleans. Her areas of teaching, specialization, and publication include church mission, evangelization, inculturation, black and womanist theologies, Christology, and spirituality.

Albert J. Raboteau, the Henry W. Putnam Professor of Religion at Princeton University, is among the foremost authorities on African American religious history. He is the author of four books, including the path-blazing *Slave Religion: The "Invisible Institution" in the Antebellum South*.

Katrina M. Sanders is an associate professor of history at the University of Iowa and teaches courses in the history of American education. The history of black Catholic education is among her research interests. She is the author of *"Intelligent and Effective Direction": The Fisk University Race Relations Institute and the Struggle for Civil Rights, 1944–1969*.

Clarence Williams, C.P.P.S., is senior director for racial equality and diversity initiatives, Catholic Charities, U.S.A. He develops and conducts comprehensive diversity and racial equality training for local agencies and leads national workshops on race relations based on an approach that he calls Racial Sobriety.

Index